COMMUNISM IN GERMANY UNDER THE WEIMAR REPUBLIC

Ben Fowkes

MACMILLAN PRESS
LONDON

First published 1984 by
THE MACMILLAN PRESS LTD
London and Basingstoke
Companies and representatives
throughout the world

Hardcover ISBN 0 333 27270 6
Paperback ISBN 0 333 27271 4

Printed in Hong Kong

Contents

v

List of Illustrations and Maps

ILLUSTRATIONS

MAPS

The first four illustrations are reproduced by courtesy of Dietz Verlag, Berlin, and the fifth by courtesy of Bundesarchiv, Koblenz.

Preface

This book is an account of German communism in its organisational embodiment, the Communist Party of Germany (KPD). Dissident groups of communists (and there were many) are for this reason excluded from the story, except where they achieved a sufficiently powerful impact to affect the way the KPD itself behaved. This kind of interaction occurred rarely, perhaps only once: in the case of the earliest, and proportionately strongest, group of dissidents, who formed themselves into the Communist Workers' Party of Germany (KAPD). Subsequent groups had a minimal impact on the party, once expelled. Even the defection of many leading trade-unionists in 1921 and again in 1928 was insufficient to deflect the party from its chosen course. For most of its history the KPD inhabited a self-sufficient world, which made it immune even to the powerful arguments advanced by the Trotskyist opposition of the early 1930s. When top party leaders fell foul of the Comintern (as they so often did) their departure caused scarcely a ripple among the ordinary members of the party.

The 'communism' I propose to investigate is therefore 'orthodox communism', the communism of the KPD, from its foundation in 1919 to its suppression by the Nazis in 1933. The chronological limits are conveniently determined by the transition from legality to illegality. I have concentrated on the activities and aims of the party's leaders, saying little of the middle cadres, let alone the ordinary members. The party was organised in such a way as to ensure that the political line was taken from the top and that individual initiatives did not take place. Even so, it would have been of interest to build up a picture of the average party member, his or her state of mind, the instinctive hostility to Social Democracy, the faith in the Soviet Union and in the proletarian revolution, to enter the obscure world of the 'communist subculture', to observe the exhausting round of activities and meetings required of a militant. I have not felt equal to this task, so brilliantly performed by Annie Kriegel for the French communists.[1] At the other end of the spectrum one might have looked at the contributions to Marxist theory which emerged from within, or alongside, the KPD. But this would in practice have meant writing part of a history of Marxism in the twentieth century.

The present work has the modest objective of providing a connected account of the party's history, both as a case study in the internal evolution of the communist movement, and for its contribution, which was at times very significant, to the contemporary German political scene. The research pursued for over thirty years by scholars inside and outside Germany has been almost exclusively centred on the 'high politics' of the KPD, as is only natural given the character of the main sources.[2] But even within this broad area different approaches are possible. One may concentrate attention on the party's internal faction fights.[3] One may study day-to-day communist policies and their relationship to the broader political context,[4] and finally one may take the theoretical standpoint and look at the theory and practice of socialist revolution as exemplified in the KPD.[5] All these approaches have their value, the first perhaps more for periods of political stagnation, the second for the occasional moment of revolutionary paroxysm, when the party's decisions could actually change the course of history, the third as a key to understanding the reasons behind the twists and turns of policy at a level deeper than that of power struggles between individuals. I have tried to achieve a harmonious compromise between all three. The book is cast in the form of a chronological history of the KPD, but the final chapter shows that the party was also a living organism, with its own internal laws of development, a micro-society like all communist parties, embedded in the soil of capitalism yet not entirely one with it. The companion volume of documents, *The German Left under the Weimar Republic*, is intended to bring the reader into closer contact with the sources, and in particular to explore the whole problem of the division of the German working-class movement into mutually hostile parties and the consequences following from this.

I should like to thank the Friedrich Ebert Stiftung, Bonn, and the Bundesarchiv, Koblenz, for allowing me access to certain documents.

List of Abbreviations

ADGB	*Allgemeiner Deutscher Gewerkschaftsbund* (General German Trade Union Confederation)
BL	*Bezirksleitung* (District Directorate)
ECCI	Executive Committee of the Communist International
OMS	*Otdel Mezhdunarodnoy Svyazi* (International Relations Section)
PEUVAG	*Papiererzeugungs-und Verwertungs-Aktiengesellschaft* (Paper Production and Utilisation Company)
RF	*Die Rote Fahne* (Berlin)
RFB	*Roter Frontkämpferbund* (League of Red Front Fighters)
RGO	*Revolutionäre Gewerkschaftsopposition* (Revolutionary Trade Union Opposition)
RILU	Red International of Labour Unions
RSB	*Roter Soldatenbund* (League of Red Soldiers)
SPD	*Sozialdemokratische Partei Deutschlands* (Social Democratic Party of Germany)
USPD	*Unabhängige Sozialdemokratische Partei Deutschlands* (Independent Social Democratic Party of Germany)
VKPD	*Vereinigte Kommunistische Partei Deutschlands* (United Communist Party of Germany)
ZA	*Zentralausschuss* (Central Commission)
ZK	*Zentralkomitee* (Central Committee)

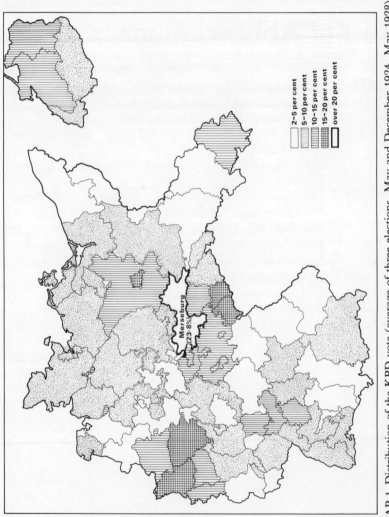

MAP 1 Distribution of the KPD vote (average of three elections, May and December 1924, May 1928)

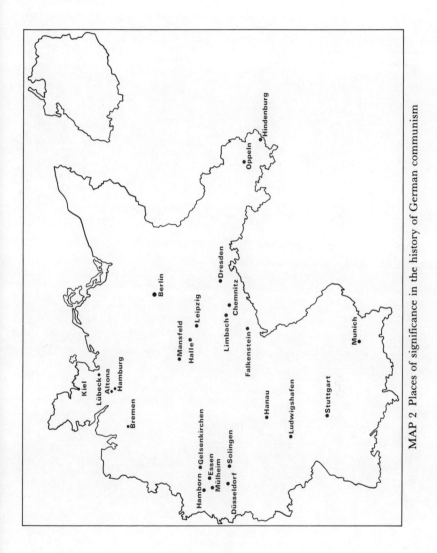

MAP 2 Places of significance in the history of German communism

1 The Prehistory of German Communism

MARXISM AND SOCIAL DEMOCRACY IN THE NINETEENTH CENTURY

Some political movements (such as liberalism) exist in reality before they exist in the mind. Communism on the other hand existed in the mind long before there was a real communist movement. It is no part of the purpose of this book to trace the vicissitudes of the communist idea during the eighteenth and nineteenth centuries. We are concerned rather with communism in its politically organised form. The starting-point is in this sense the year 1847, when Marx and Engels entered the League of the Just, a conspiratorial group of German exiles founded in Paris a decade earlier, and integrated the latter's naive communist faith into a system based on the new science of political economy. To quote Engels, the Communist League, as the League of the Just was renamed in 1847, aimed at 'the overthrow of the bourgeoisie, the rule of the proletariat, the abolition of the old, bourgeois society . . . and the foundation of a new society without classes and without private property'.[1] As a statement of the ultimate communist aim, this continues to suffice. But there were two problems: how was the aim to be achieved – directly or indirectly, by violent putsch or peaceful propaganda – and how was the proletariat to be won over to communism?

In the context of mid-nineteenth-century Germany the answers were clear to Marx and Engels. The proletariat would be won over by peaceful propaganda, a communist putsch was out of the question, and the present task of the League was to push forward the coming democratic, not socialist, revolution, in Central Europe. This is made quite clear by the 'Demands of the

1

Communist Party in Germany' issued in March 1848 as a leaflet, and drawn up by Marx and Engels on behalf of the Central Committee of the Communist League. None of the demands went beyond a radical democratic programme; all of them could be achieved without the overthrow of bourgeois rule. Germany was to be an indivisible republic; it was to be run by a parliament elected by universal suffrage; feudal estates were to be taken over by the state; education was to be universal and free. More radical (but still not communist) demands were for a guaranteed existence for all workers through the establishment of 'national workshops', progressive taxation, railway and canal nationalisation, and 'the arming of the whole people'. The last demand, revolutionary in appearance, was simply an extension of the popular call for a Citizens' Militia, following the tradition of the 1789 French Revolution. The practice of the Communist League in 1848 and 1849 was not at variance with these demands. The League 'stood at the head of the extreme democratic movement' where possible.[2] The newspaper Marx edited, the *Neue Rheinische Zeitung,* concentrated on two tasks in 1848 and 1849: the fight against absolutism and for a democratic German republic, and the defence of the German revolution against Russia.[3] When, towards the end of 1848, it became evident to Marx that the German bourgeoisie was not up to the task of carrying through a bourgeois revolution, a change of tactics seemed to be required. The German proletariat must itself perform this task in cooperation with the petty bourgeois democrats, driving their proposals forward to their logical extreme. This would bring them into conflict with private property.[4]

By the time that these conclusions were being drawn the revolutionary era had come to an end, not to recur in Marx's lifetime. His decision to devote his life to studying the laws of motion of capitalism was an implicit admission of this, although he naturally hoped that the revolution would soon be set off again by an economic crisis. In 1852 the League was dissolved. It was to have no successor until 1875, and then under entirely different conditions. When the Gotha Congress of 1875 decided to found the 'Socialist Workers' Party of Germany', no voice was raised in favour of including the word 'communist' in the title. This was not just a question of terminology. There was no personal continuity between the communism of pre-1848 Germany and the social democracy of the 1870s except as provided by Engels, the new party's *éminence grise*. The Gotha Programme was a combination of doctrines of state socialism inherited from Ferdinand Lassalle's 'General Association of German Workers' with what August Bebel and Wilhelm Liebknecht thought of as Marxism. It was severely criticised by Marx at the time, although the criticisms did not have any impact for fifteen years. Not until the Erfurt Congress of 1891 could German Social Democracy be said to possess a Marxist programme. Even then, reservations were made by Engels, as guardian of the Marxist tradition. He criticised the Erfurt Programme's tendency to suggest that Germany could evolve peacefully towards socialism without the violent overthrow of the imperial constitution and the establishment of the 'one, indivisible German republic'.[5] The task of completing the 'bourgeois revolution', which bulked so large in the earliest communist programme, was ignored, both in theory and practice, by the pre-1914 SPD, like most other Social Democratic parties. The aim of the SPD was not to overthrow the Kaiser's absolutism but to improve the economic and social position of the working class within the framework of capitalism. The democratic revolution was relegated to the far horizon, to be accomplished simultaneously with the final goal, full socialism. The pre-war SPD may have prided itself on its Marxism, but it was in no sense a communist party, even though the first leaders of the KPD were compelled for lack of an alternative to serve their political apprenticeship in it.

The 'revisionist controversy' of the 1890s and 1900s ended in the apparent victory of orthodox Marxism, but the party's practice actually conformed to the recommendations of the revisionists. By 1914 communism was still an idea, not a movement, in Germany. Hence the vital importance of the Bolshevik example. Only in the Russian Empire, and perhaps in Bulgaria, were there Social Democratic parties which could be regarded as embodying the communist ideal, as formulated by Marx and Engels in the 1840s. Of course it is easy to say this in retrospect, but very few people had any inkling at the time of the true meaning of the splits of 1903 in the Russian and Bulgarian working-class movements. Where a Trotsky could lose his way, so could a Rosa Luxemburg. The presence of Martov and

Plekhanov, with their revolutionary credentials, on the Menshevik side, was one source of confusion; another was the polemical harshness and exaggeration Lenin customarily resorted to in order to 'bend the stick in the other direction'. It took the outbreak of the First World War to reveal the true situation, to bring some order into the confused struggle of the Russian émigré factions, and to provide an international basis for the development of communism.

With hindsight we can say that a struggle for communist politics was being waged in the German working-class movement before the war, but not under that form. The radical leftists in the SPD were attempting to recover ground allegedly lost since the days of Engels, when, they imagined, Social Democracy had been a genuinely revolutionary movement. They wanted to rebuild the old house, not construct a new one. This was an objective shared by the 'Marxist centre' of the party. The revisionists, in contrast, wanted to strike out on a new path. But in fact the anti-revisionist movement of the 1890s and 1900s was not homogeneous. A three-way rather than a two-way split was being prepared by events, and it came to fruition after 1920, with the future Spartacists forming the third, or extreme left, faction of Social Democracy.

This was an international phenomenon, affecting the Poles, the Dutch, the Bulgarians, the Russians and the Germans, often in different ways.

LEFT RADICALISM AND THE MARXIST CENTRE BEFORE 1914

In Germany two factors combined after 1910 to produce the phenomenon of 'left radicalism'. First, the change in the SPD leadership. With the rise of a new generation, symbolised by the election of Friedrich Ebert in 1913 as party chairman, the old Marxist centre, which had held the SPD's rival factions together by a combination of revolutionary ideology and day-to-day reformist practice, was replaced by a purely reformist leadership, and this now began to undertake disciplinary measures against a left wing previously tolerated as an ally against the revisionists. Rosa Luxemburg found it impossible to place her articles advocating the mass strike weapon in the party's central press organs. Franz Mehring was eliminated from the editorial board of the theoretical periodical *Die Neue Zeit* in 1912, and Karl Radek was in effect expelled from the SPD in 1913 by being declared no longer eligible for membership.[6]

At the same time, the left radicals began to realise that they could no longer use the machinery of the party. The *Leipziger Volkszeitung* had been an organ of radicalism under Paul Lensch; but in July 1913 he resigned as editor and the radicals were left with no major press outlet. This was why in December 1913 Rosa Luxemburg, Franz Mehring and Julian Marchlewski (Karski) started to issue a news bulletin to propagate left radical views within the party – the *Sozialdemokratische Korrespondenz*.[7]

The main reason for this polarisation of the camps within Social Democracy was not the development of mass struggles and the coming of a revolutionary situation – this did not occur – but the shadow of war. The temporising attitude of the SPD leaders towards the successive international crises between 1905 and 1914 was naturally opposed by the left of the party. Karl Liebknecht in particular was prominent from 1907 onwards in advocating agitation inside the barracks and among young people against militarism, though his views on universal disarmament and understanding between all nations as a solution to the problem were regarded by other left radicals as utopian. From 1913 Rosa Luxemburg increasingly began to add her voice to his, and was sentenced in February 1914 to one year's imprisonment for inciting soldiers to disobey orders. In their joint fight against imperialism and militarism, as these phenomena manifested themselves in their specifically German aspect, Rosa and Karl were unconsciously preparing their lonely stance of opposition during the First World War. As Paul Frölich wrote, 'Rosa gave the struggle its theoretical basis, Karl was undoubtedly the leader in action.'[8] The party leadership tried to muzzle them, partly on the prudential basis that too fierce an agitation against militarism would endanger the SPD's organisations by exposing them to reprisals from the government, partly through fear of alienating fringe middle-class support. Anti-imperialist agitation was a luxury the party could not afford, if it wanted to remain respectable and keep on winning votes at election time. The party executive went very far indeed in accommodating itself to the requirements of the armed forces. The SPD voted for the tax bill of 1913, which provided the financial backing for a further expansion of the German army, and the former 'Marxist centre', or the 'left centrists' as Schorske felicitously describes them, were also driven into opposition and temporary alliance with the left radicals. At the Jena Congress of 1913 both groups made common cause against the tax bill vote.[9] This superficially blurred over the difference between them, but in reality their motives were different. Kautsky thought the pacific tendencies in imperialism would ultimately prevail; crises were interruptions in a general move towards international understanding.[10] For Luxemburg 'the question of militarism and imperialism' formed 'the central axis of political life'. Imperialism was the last throw of capitalism, and the struggle for colonial outlets would inevitably bring war between the imperialist countries.[11]

The left radicals were therefore even before 1914 an identifiable current in party life. Apart from Luxemburg and Liebknecht there were many other prominent personalities associated with left radicalism. Franz Mehring, the historian of Social Democracy, was one of the first to realise the need for a break with the centre (1910); Clara Zetkin, like Mehring a veteran of the period of proscription in the 1880s, was a leader of the socialist women's movement and edited the SPD women's paper *Gleichheit* in a spirit of radicalism for 25 years; Karl Radek, though treated with suspicion by the others because of rumours of a lack of financial probity, was an important journalistic advocate of left radical views in Germany thanks to his Bremen connections (his articles appeared in the *Bremer Bürgerzeitung*, of which his friend Johannes Knief was chief editor); Anton Pannekoek was another regular contributor to the *Bremer Bürgerzeitung*. Dutch by nationality, he lived in Bremen from 1909 onwards, and provided a significant link with the first group in Western Europe to break with official Social Democracy, the Dutch leftists around the journal *De Tribune*, who set up their own political party in 1909. Finally, there was what one might call the 'Polish connection'. Several members of the SDKPL (Social Democracy of the Kingdom of Poland and Lithuania) sought to push the German party to the left at this time. Rosa Luxemburg herself is the foremost example, but one should also mention Radek (a member of the SDKPL until expelled in 1912), Julian Marchlewski (Karski), and Leo Jogiches (Tyszka).

The list of pre-war radical Social Democrats active in Germany is impressive. But as a group they were rather top-heavy. The people we have mentioned were journalists, party luminaries and often, it must be admitted, foreigners, which reduced their chances of implanting themselves securely in the party organisation. There were some exceptions, in particular Fritz Westmeyer, party secretary in Stuttgart, and Fritz Heckert, leader of the Chemnitz Bricklayers' Union. Only in these two areas (Württemberg and the Erzgebirge) did the left radicals enjoy mass backing, and hold positions of genuine power within the party.

In Württemberg this led to a head-on clash between the city organisations of Stuttgart and Göppingen (which were 'radical') and the wider organisation covering the whole state (which was 'revisionist'). The conflict began as a struggle for control of the local party paper, the *Schwäbische Tagwacht*, which was temporarily settled in 1911 by a compromise whereby the 'radicals' were allowed to edit the paper, but ultimate control was to be exercised by the *Land* committee. The Stuttgart organisation was also at loggerheads with its *Reichstag* deputy, the revisionist Karl Hildenbrand. In both cases the influence of the rural and small town organisations, exerted through the *Land* committee, was sufficient eventually to outweigh the party members from industrial Stuttgart. Hildenbrand stayed on in the *Reichstag* until 1918; and by November 1914 the *Land* committee had kicked the 'radicals' off the newspaper, swung it behind the German war effort, and placed Wilhelm Keil, a fiercely patriotic right-winger, in the position of chief editor.[12]

The left radicals of Stuttgart were almost all destined to become communists (the exception being Artur Crispien, later leader of the right in the USPD). An astonishingly large number of future Spartacist leaders cut their political teeth in Württemberg: Clara Zetkin, Jakob Walcher, Edwin Hörnle, Fritz Westmeyer, August Thalheimer and Käthe Duncker were all involved in the fight against Keil and Hildenbrand. And once war broke out the Stuttgart city organisation was the first in Germany to split into anti- and pro-war factions (December 1914).[13] The radicals in Stuttgart ultimately failed because they were unable to influence the rest of Württemberg. The Chemnitz radicals, in contrast, were able to extend their control over much of the surrounding region of the Erzgebirge. Hence the local branch of the party in Chemnitz was the only organisation to go over directly to the Spartacists during the First World War.[14]

THE IMPACT OF WAR

Despite these instances of radical defiance there was no doubt where power lay in the party when the decisive test of the outbreak of war came upon it. Both the SPD executive and the General Commission of the Free Trade Unions were firmly in the hands of reformists, who had long since decided to soft-pedal opposition to militarism in the interests of immediate success. The decision of the SPD parliamentary faction (3 August 1914) and the Free Trade Unions (2 August) to support the war should have been expected by the left radicals. But it still came as a shock. Nothing had been prepared for this eventuality, mainly because it seemed inconceivable that the party leadership would go back on a solemn undertaking, reaffirmed as late as 25 July 1914, that 'no drop of blood of a German soldier' would be 'sacrificed to the power lust of the Austrian ruling group, to the imperialist appetite for profit'.[15] When the catastrophe occurred, each individual was left to react according to his or her conscience. Karl Liebknecht voted against the war credits within the SPD fraction. But when the decision came out in favour of them (by 78 to 14) he bowed to party discipline and joined the rest of the party's deputies in voting in public in the affirmative (4 August). He was, however, the first to realise his mistake (by September 1914).[16] Rosa Luxemburg's reaction to the war was to try to persuade people to sign a manifesto against it. Only seven people came to a meeting she called, and Mehring's was the only prominent name. Only one party organisation came out against the war immediately, Niederbarnim, in Berlin.[17]

It took the left radicals some time to recover from August 1914; it took even longer before the 'Marxist centre' raised its head again. There were good practical reasons for the delay: the party apparatus bent its efforts to ending all discussion, to maintaining 'the *Burgfrieden* within the labour movement'.[18] Where the executive failed, the military authorities stepped in. Meetings were prohibited (21 September, Stuttgart, 4 November, München-Gladbach, 24 November, Leipzig, 29 November, Altona), radical newspapers were prevented from appearing until good behaviour could be guaranteed. *Vorwärts* was suppressed in September, then allowed to reappear after its editors promised not to mention the class struggle (1 October). Rosa Luxemburg underlined the near impossibility of agitation in a letter of 12

October 1914: 'All the central party institutions are dominated by opportunist elements, and all opposition is dashed to pieces as the masses cannot revolt.'[19] The tribune of the *Reichstag* could still be used, and on 3 December Karl Liebknecht voted (alone) against the war credits. In February 1915 he was called up for military service; Rosa Luxemburg was imprisoned for two months. The authorities played a cat-and-mouse game with opponents of the war throughout 1915. Clara Zetkin was arrested and released. Wilhelm Pieck, Ernst Meyer, Hugo Eberlein and Jakob Walcher all underwent a period of imprisonment. Westmeyer was sent to the front (where he lost his life). The situation did not improve in the later stages of the war: for instance Luxemburg and Liebknecht were both arrested and imprisoned in 1916, and they remained in gaol until 1918.

The first really significant achievement of the radical opponents of the war was the production in April 1915 of the first, and until 1919 the only, issue of *Die Internationale*. This journal was edited jointly by Rosa Luxemburg and Franz Mehring, and its contributors included Clara Zetkin, August Thalheimer, Karl Liebknecht, Käthe Duncker, Paul Lange and Heinrich Ströbel. All, apart from Ströbel, would eventually be found in the communist party. *Die Internationale* gave the later Spartacist group its first name – the *Gruppe Internationale*. It was the nucleus around which the later leadership of the KPD crystallised. There were, however, two other groups of revolutionary socialists in Germany with a much greater affinity to Bolshevism in their insistence on immediate separation from the SPD and their perspective of turning the imperialist war into a civil war: the Berlin group around Julian Borchardt's journal *Lichtstrahlen*, and the so-called Bremen Left Radicals, Radek's former comrades, who started to publish the newspaper *Arbeiterpolitik* there in 1916. Finally, one should also mention the activities of Willi Münzenberg in Switzerland. As Secretary of the Swiss Socialist Youth Movement he organised an international conference in the Easter of 1915. This conference voted to break with the Second International and set up a new Youth International. The production and distribution of its journal, *Die Jugend-Internationale* (first issue 1 September 1915) is an early example of cooperation between German Spartacists and Russian Bolsheviks.[20] However, tactical differences hindered any closer links with the Bolsheviks until 1917: Meyer and Thalheimer, representing the *Gruppe Inter-*

nationale, voted with the majority at the Zimmerwald Conference of opponents of the war in September 1915 against Lenin's call to 'overthrow the capitalist governments' as a preliminary to a 'lasting peace'. As Meyer explained, 'No noteworthy part of the German proletariat is yet to be had for such actions as Lenin's manifesto enumerates.'[21]

The former 'left centrists', the later leaders of the USPD, were slower to awaken from the shock of war than the left radicals. During 1915 the future Independents proceeded by easy stages in the wake of Karl Liebknecht and Otto Rühle (the latter voted in March 1915 against the war credits alongside Liebknecht). On 9 June 1915 nearly a thousand SPD party and trade union officials signed a protest against the SPD executive's policy of support for the war.[22] Shortly afterwards, Karl Kautsky, Hugo Haase and Eduard Bernstein issued a public manifesto in the *Leipziger Volkszeitung*, entitled 'What the Present Moment Dictates', in which they asserted that the war, originally one of defence, had become a war of conquest on the part of the German High Command, and called on the SPD to campaign for peace.[23] Finally a group of oppositional *Reichstag* deputies decided to defy the party executive (21 December 1915). Fritz Geyer declared in the name of 17 SPD deputies 'We reject the war credits', and a further 22 left the Chamber rather than vote. Liebknecht and Rühle voted against the credits as a matter of course, and were expelled from the party a month later.[24] The defiance of Fritz Geyer and his comrades opened the way to a split in the SPD *Reichstag* fraction, which was consummated on 24 March 1916 by the expulsion of 18 parliamentary opponents of the war credits from the SPD. They replied by setting up the Social Democratic Working Union (*Sozialdemokratische Arbeitsgemeinschaft*), an association of dissident Social Democrats which aimed to mount a purely parliamentary opposition to the war.

SPARTACUS AND THE USPD

The growth of a Centrist opposition to the war posed a tactical problem for the Spartacists (the name universally applied to this group once the first letter signed 'Spartacus' was distributed, in January 1916). Should they stress the differences? Should they try to work with the Centrists and avoid scoring theoretical points against them? Rosa Luxemburg was strongly in favour of retaining a connection with the mass Social Democratic movement (which the Centrists, unlike the Spartacists, unquestionably represented) although the objective must always be to try to achieve ideological hegemony over the 'Marxist centre' and not be sucked into their morass of muddled thinking and concessions to chauvinism. A conference was held in Liebknecht's flat on 1 January 1916 to decide these issues. Everyone present was agreed that clarity must come first, that a clear dividing-line should be drawn vis-à-vis the Centrists. But only in an ideological sense: no steps should be taken towards an organisational split. Rosa's theses on 'The Tasks of International Social Democracy' (called the Junius Theses because they were printed as an appendix to the 'Junius Pamphlet', *The Crisis in German Social Democracy*, April 1916) were accepted by the January Conference, not as a basis for discussion but as a point of crystallisation for all elements of the extreme left. 'In regard to our platform, I do not think it should be presented like those "radical resolutions" at Party Congresses which are then made into a broth suitable to everybody's taste.' Instead it was to be 'accepted or rejected without alterations. I.e. we stick to it even if the majority vote against, or, for all I care, it is unanimously rejected.'[25]

The Junius Theses are the founding text of Spartacism. They outlined the policy Spartacus was to follow for the rest of the war. Even so, some participants had reservations about them. The Chemnitz group complained about the absence of 'a practical programme of action' to guide their day-to-day work.[26] But this was not the aim of the Theses. They were intended to determine the group's attitude to the grand questions of war and peace, which took precedence over all others at this time. The main divergence between these theses and those of the Bolsheviks was the refusal to draw any organisational consequences from their extreme political position. Nowhere in the document were the Centrists directly attacked, nowhere was the need to form an independent revolutionary party indicated. In this sense, the Spartacists were not the forerunners of communism in Germany. This description should rather be applied to Johann Knief (of the Bremen left) and Rudolf Lindau (of the Hamburg left), who criticised the theses because they did not prepare the inevitable split with the Centrists.[27] Rühle[28] and Borchardt[29] were also in favour of a split. Most of the Spartacists followed Rosa's line, which was to stay in any working-class party that would have her – even the SPD – on one condition: freedom of agitation. On this view the onus of the decision to split the party would be placed on the opponent, the SPD executive. As Ernst Meyer said in January 1917: 'We shall remain in the party as long as we can wage the class struggle in it against the executive.'[30] Since the Centrists were even keener to stay in the old party if possible, the final break was delayed until the SPD executive itself took the initiative and expelled all the oppositionists, centre and left. Thereupon a new party was set up, the Independent Social Democratic Party of Germany (USPD), at the Gotha Conference of April 1917. Ernst Däumig, one of the USPD leaders, described its aims in this way: 'To achieve the highest possible degree of effectiveness in the old Social Democratic spirit', 'to restore the confidence of the working class in democracy and socialism' and 'to serve the cause of peace by restoring German Social Democracy's reputation in the International'.[31]

The Spartacists entered the USPD, for reasons later recalled by Karl Liebknecht: 'We belonged to the USPD in order to drive the most valuable elements in it forward, to squeeze out of it what we could, to radicalise it, to further its disintegration.'[32] To secure these objectives one of the Stuttgart Spartacists, Fritz Rück, demanded 'the greatest possible freedom of action' at Gotha, and the USPD majority conceded the point, as the new party's statutes make clear: 'The . . . application of the organisation statute is . . . a matter for the localities, districts and regions, which are to have far-reaching independence and freedom of action.'[33] Even so, many Spartacists were uneasy, including Fritz Heckert from Chemnitz[34] and Paul Levi, who wrote in the Bremen *Arbeiterpolitik* that a clear break should be made from the Centrists 'if they continue to stand where they are'.[35] The reaction of the left radicals in Bremen and Hamburg to the foundation of the USPD was to proclaim 'the complete political failure, the death of the *Gruppe Internationale*' and to call for the building of a new, international socialist party in Germany.[36] Owing to Radek's opposition the proposal for a new party was dropped, and the Bremen left concentrated purely on propaganda for Bolshevism for the next year and a half.

Even after its entry into the USPD the Spartacus group did not secure mass influence. It tried hard: leaflets were issued, and the

'Spartacus letters' were circulated in 'six thousand copies' in 1917.[37] The real numerical strength of the group at this time is a matter for speculation. An upper limit of 10 000 'in the second half of the war' has been put forward.[38] Karl Liebknecht's stand against the war met with sympathy in broader circles than these, as shown by the Berlin protest strike by 55 000 workers in June 1916 against his imprisonment, but this did not imply identification with his political position. A year later the workers acted again, largely on account of factors of a material, economic character. The severe hardships of the fourth year of war led to the mass strikes of April 1917. The immediate cause was clearly the drastic reduction of the weekly bread ration, although the Spartacists tried to inject a political element. The shooting of the sailors Max Reichpietsch and Alwin Köbis in September 1917, after the naval mutiny of the summer, entered into the martyrology of Spartacism and communism, but had no immediate repercussions. The Bolshevik Revolution of October 1917 was greeted with sympathy, but the workers ignored Spartacist appeals to follow that example. Then, on 28 January 1918, something more serious occurred: a mass political strike. Half a million Berlin workers downed tools to protest against the annexationist demands of their government at the Brest–Litovsk peace negotiations with Bolshevik Russia. They were led by a group of trade unionists who had emerged during the strike of April 1917, called 'the revolutionary *Obleute*' (shop stewards), who were 'for the most part USPD supporters, but not very rigidly so'. The Spartacists had only one member among the *Obleute*,[39] and their attempt to give the strike a more revolutionary character by calling for an uprising was a failure.[40] The Action Committee elected to run the strike comprised members of the USPD and SPD, and on 3 February it called for a return to work; there was no other course to take, since the German government showed no sign of changing its foreign policy, and the solidarity strike in the provinces had already collapsed. There was a certain amount of repression; 84 people, including Wilhelm Dittmann, a prominent USPD leader, were arrested on 2 February, Jogiches was arrested in March, 50 000 Berlin workers were sent to the front, among them Richard Müller, one of the leaders of the *Obleute*. This was nothing in comparison with the blood spilt by the democratic republic in 1919; but it was quite enough to decapitate the movement of January 1918.

After this, the fate of imperial Germany was left to be decided purely on the field of battle. Instead of revolution from below, as the Spartacists and the Bolsheviks had hoped, there was a 'revolution from above', set off by the prospect of certain military defeat. This story has been told many times, and well. Here we shall simply pick out one conclusion from the evidence: the driving force in the 'revolution from above' was the German General Staff. Ludendorff and Hindenburg recognised defeat on 29 September 1918, and insisted on placing power in the hands of the democratic politicians. Only after the 'revolution from above' had been accomplished did the masses re-enter the scene.

The importance of the period of Prince Max von Baden's cabinet (4 October to 9 November 1918) lay in the rapid succession of measures of democratisation, which transformed the old Wilhelmine *Reich* and allowed freedom of agitation and organisation to the advocates of revolution, above all the Spartacists. On 7 October a joint conference of Spartacists and Bremen left radicals worked out a programme for the impending German revolution, including such standard democratic demands as those for amnesty; dismantling of dictatorial wartime measures; abolition of the German principalities; democratisation of the army. War loans were to be confiscated, banks and coalmines to be expropriated, large estates were to be handed over to the peasants and agricultural workers, a minimum wage was to be introduced, food distribution was to be placed under workers' representatives. These were socialist demands, but compatible with the framework of capitalism: 'Proletarians, these are not your goals, . . . but they are a touchstone of the genuineness of the ruling classes' alleged democratisation.'[41] Finally the conference voted 'to start setting up Workers' and Soldiers' Councils immediately, wherever such Councils have not yet entered into activity'.[42] There were no Councils (*Räte*) in Germany either then or three weeks later: a further sign of the powerlessness of Spartacus to affect events even in those closing days of the war. Karl Radek was told on his arrival in Berlin that there were only 50 Spartacists there when the November Revolution started.[43] The position was somewhat better in Bremen and Stuttgart. But Berlin would inevitably be the scene of the decisive acts of the revolution. When Karl Liebknecht was released from prison on 21 October he did his best to spur the Berlin masses into action, and he encouraged the 'revolutionary

Obleute', who had retained their influence on the workers despite the repressions of the earlier part of the year, to organise demonstrations with the aim of forcing the pace of development towards revolution.[44]

The *Obleute* themselves preferred to await the decision of the masses. Emil Barth described Liebknecht's idea of mounting street demonstrations as 'revolutionary gymnastics' on 28 October, and his influence prevailed.[45] Finally, on 2 November, when the collapse of the Central Powers was already an accomplished fact, it was decided to prepare for an uprising on 11 November. Liebknecht's motion for an immediate general strike was rejected by 46 votes to 5. Far from forcing the pace, the *Obleute* were determined to lag behind. Only in one place – Stuttgart – did the Spartacists possess enough influence to call a general strike and set up a Workers' Council (4 November). The Council lasted one day; the police arrested its members, including the leading local Spartacists Thalheimer and Rück.[46]

THE NOVEMBER REVOLUTION AND THE COUNCIL MOVEMENT

Meanwhile the real revolution was in preparation at the other end of the country, with the seizure on 4 November of the town of Kiel by mutinous sailors, and the formation there of a Workers' and Sailors' Council. The movement spread rapidly along the North German coast: on 5 November Lübeck rose, on 6 November it was the turn of Hamburg, Bremen and Cuxhaven. Then it passed to the centre and south of the country: 6 November Düsseldorf and Halle, 7 November Erfurt, Hanau, Brunswick and Munich, 8 November Leipzig and Chemnitz, 9 November Stuttgart again. In most cases the Independents formed the majority of the Workers' and Soldiers' Councils; but in some towns Spartacists gained control. At Hanau there was Fritz Schnellbacher; at Brunswick there was August Merges, 'president of the Brunswick socialist republic';[47] at Chemnitz Fritz Heckert headed a Council including SPD members.[48] Hamburg was under the influence of the left radicals Fritz Wolffheim and Heinrich Laufenberg.[49]

Meanwhile, in Berlin, Liebknecht was continuing to press vainly for immediate action. On 6 November the executive committee of the Berlin *Obleute* confirmed its decision to wait until

11 November. Liebknecht's proposal to start on 8 November was rejected.[50] He now decided, together with Ernst Meyer, to present the Independents with a *fait accompli*: a leaflet was issued by Spartacus calling on the workers and soldiers of Berlin to set up Councils, take over the government, and establish immediate contact with the Russian Soviet Republic.[51] In the meantime, the *Obleute* and some of the more left-leaning USPD leaders also decided to call for action.[52] These calls to action only anticipated events by one day. They may have contributed to what happened on 9 November, but they did not cause it. On 8 November the SPD leaders realised that the workers could be held back no longer. They had their own contacts in the Berlin factories, who informed them that evening that 'they would simply be overwhelmed' if they tried to oppose the movement.[53] The soldiers, on the other hand, could still be relied on. The SPD leaders were aware of this, but 'to avoid useless bloodshed' they ordered them not to fire on the workers when they came out into the streets on the morning of 9 November. Thus the November Revolution was accomplished in Berlin in an orderly fashion. Scheidemann proclaimed the German republic at 2 p.m.; Liebknecht proclaimed the 'Free Socialist Republic of Germany' at 4 p.m. The situation which emerged was something in between. Workers' and Soldiers' Councils were at last set up in Berlin; Prince Max of Baden appointed Ebert Chancellor of the *Reich*, preserving the fiction of constitutional continuity (he had no right to make this appointment: only the Emperor or his Regent could appoint a chancellor, and Max was neither); after negotiations between the SPD and the USPD a body entitled the Council of People's Representatives (*Rat der Volksbeauftragten*) was set up as the new government of Germany, with three SPD and three USPD members. The next day a Full Assembly of Berlin Workers' and Soldiers' Councils met and confirmed the People's Representatives in office. But it also elected an Executive Council (*Vollzugsrat*) composed of 14 workers (seven USPD, seven SPD) and 14 soldiers (largely SPD in political inclination). This was declared to be the 'supreme organ of the revolution' and to have the task of supervising the work of the People's Representatives. The Spartacists played no part in these events since they refused to cooperate with an Executive Council in which the SPD counter-revolutionaries were represented.[54]

The duality of power between the official government and the

Workers' and Soldiers' Councils was reproduced all over Germany, but its significance was lessened by the fact that the SPD usually dominated both government and Councils, bestriding in this way the dualism of the November Revolution. Moreover, the old state apparatus remained intact: the socialist revolution still lay in the future. The German November Revolution was able to secure peace and get rid of the royal houses, but unable to achieve even a genuine democratisation of society, let alone socialism. This presented the German left with two tasks. The USPD took up the first, the Spartacists the second. Neither succeeded.

The reason for the USPD's failure lay in its internal divisions: while the party executive, including the People's Representatives Hugo Haase and Wilhelm Dittman, wanted to cooperate with the SPD in the new government and integrate the Councils into the traditional system of bourgeois parliamentarianism, hoping thereby to secure socialist democracy without dangerous experiments in proletarian dictatorship of a Soviet kind, the left of the party, especially among the Berlin *Obleute*, wanted to move towards full socialism and were strongly influenced by the Bolshevik example, without being communists. They opposed the National Assembly and wanted to make the People's Representatives entirely responsible to the Berlin Executive Council, then give power to a National Congress representing all the German Workers' and Soldiers' Councils, to be convened as soon as possible. They were therefore constantly dragging the USPD executive back from involvement in government. This uncertainty of aims was to have fateful consequences in the demonstrative resignation of the USPD from the government in December and the call to arms in January.[55]

As for the Spartacist objective, we have described it as socialism, and this could not be achieved because despite the apparent dual power situation of November the German proletariat as a whole was by no means ready to fight for the overthrow of bourgeois society. However, in looking at the extreme left in 1918 we have to distinguish between the Spartacist leaders, for whom the ultimate goal lay somewhat in the distance owing to the political immaturity of the German workers, a factor they were fully aware of, and the Bremen left radicals, who on 23 November held a conference with other leftists from Hamburg and Berlin at which they set up a kind of communist party, the

IKD (International Communists of Germany) and boldly proclaimed the end of the period of 'scientific communism' and the coming of 'practical communism'.[56] The founding conference of the Spartacus League (11 November 1918) set itself the more modest aim of winning over the majority of the working class for a programme of extending the revolution in the direction of socialism. It was clear to the Spartacists who met on the evening of 10 November in the editorial offices of the *Berliner Lokalanzeiger*, seized shortly before by over-enthusiastic supporters, that they lacked the strength 'to turn the semi-revolution into a full-scale one . . . and to put the Workers' and Soldiers' Councils into power genuinely'.[57] Hence any direct challenge to the authorities, such as the seizure of the *Berliner Lokalanzeiger* building and the production of *Die Rote Fahne* there (10 November) was unwise, and the Spartacus League abandoned the premises a day later in face of the resistance of its owner, who was backed by the Ebert government.

The founding conference of 11 November elected a thirteen-strong *Zentrale*, or Central Committee. The inner circle of leaders consisted of Karl Liebknecht, Rosa Luxemburg, Leo Jogiches and Franz Mehring. The other members were Willi Budich, Hermann and Käthe Duncker, Hugo Eberlein, Paul Lange, Paul Levi, Ernst Meyer, Wilhelm Pieck and August Thalheimer. Party cards were issued and the first real attempt was made to coordinate Spartacist activities throughout Germany. Yet they stayed in the USPD. 'This was bound to conflict with the unity of that party', as Pieck later recalled.[58]

Spartacus continued to be essentially a propaganda organisation. Preparations were put in hand for the production of a daily newspaper (this took most of the group's energies until 18 November); mass demonstrations were to be organised; agitation among the soldiers was to be conducted by the Red Soldiers' League (RSB), led by Willi Budich.[59] On 18 November *Die Rote Fahne* finally reappeared. Rosa's first leading article was sober in tone: there was no cause for jubilation, she wrote, since the basic aim, the overthrow of capitalism, had not been achieved. Germany was not a socialist republic, the workers were not in power. The first task was to destroy any illusion to this effect.

The situation in November 1918 was confused and transitional. This is how Levi described it in retrospect: 'In November 1918 state power became a "no man's land"; it had slipped out of the hands of the bourgeoisie but the working class had not picked it up.'[60] The tragedy of Luxemburg and Liebknecht, and the Spartacists in general, was that they were not given time to change this. The question of power was posed too early: on 6 December (troops raised by the SPD fire on a peaceful RSB demonstration); 24 December (battle between the People's Marine Division and troops from the front sent in by Ebert to free Otto Wels, who was being held hostage until the sailors received 80 000 marks back pay); 5 January (protest against the sacking of Emil Eichhorn). The Spartacists did not desire these conflicts. They did not want to overthrow the Ebert–Scheidemann government either before or after the USPD representatives had resigned from it (29 December). They were too conscious of their own weakness for that. But their hand was eventually forced by the growing embitterment of a section of the Berlin masses.

THE FOUNDING OF THE COMMUNIST PARTY OF GERMANY (KPD)

The position of the Spartacus League as a peaceful propaganda group within the USPD could not be maintained for long. By staying in a coalition with the SPD, by failing to oppose the decision to call a National Assembly, by refusing to call an emergency congress, the USPD leaders were making it pointless for the Spartacists to delay setting up a communist party. On 20 November Rosa attacked the USPD executive in terms which suggested an immediate break: 'No excuses, no ambiguities – the dice must fall. Yesterday parliamentary cretinism was a weakness, today it is an ambiguity, tomorrow it will be treason to socialism.'[61] The ideal solution would have been to separate the masses from the leaders, of course; it became clearer and clearer that this would not happen. On 14 December the rival positions of Spartacus and the USPD were exposed in their respective newspapers. *Die Rote Fahne* published the Spartacus Programme, 'What does the Spartacus League want?'; *Die Freiheit* published 'A German Tactic for the German Revolution', condemning Bolshevism and Spartacism and describing the summoning of the National Assembly as 'the revolutionary task of the moment'. On 15 December a general meeting of the USPD of Greater Berlin took place: here the Spartacists might expect to do well, since they were working closely with the *Obleute*. But Rosa's resolution calling for opposition to the idea of a Constituent Assembly, the resignation of the USPD from the government, the seizure of power by Workers' and Soldiers' Councils and an emergency congress of the USPD was defeated by 485 votes to 195.[62] There was still a chance that the National Congress of Workers' and Soldiers' Councils, held between 16 and 21 December, might overrule the right-wing socialists and decide to take power, with the USPD carried along by the tide. The opposite happened: it voted to hand over its powers to Ebert. A large majority of the delegates supported the SPD (288); the USPD had 90 delegates, of whom only ten were Spartacists; there were also eleven 'united revolutionaries', i.e. left radicals unattached to the USPD. Karl Liebknecht and Rosa Luxemburg had not been elected delegates (not being factory workers or military personnel) and were not allowed to attend even as guests. Eugen Prager later commented: 'The mass of politically illiterate soldiers' delegates hung round the neck of the Congress like a lead weight.'[63] Its decisions were appropriate to its composition: the National Assembly elections were set for the early date of 19 January; Ernst Däumig's motion that a second National Congress be held before the National Assembly discussed a new constitution was rejected by 344 votes to 98.[64] The Congress of Councils was a political suicide club, Däumig complained.[65] The USPD leaders refused to draw any conclusions from these events. Haase, Dittmann and Barth stayed in the government. This was the last straw for the Spartacists. (The *Obleute* were also angry, but did nothing about it.) On 22 December the *Zentrale* of the Spartacus League decided to call a party congress of its own, though making a last minute attempt to get the USPD executive to convene an emergency congress by sending it a three-day ultimatum. When this was scornfully rejected[66] the only Spartacist who remained unconvinced about the need to found a separate party was Leo Jogiches.[67] Levi later suggested that if Jogiches's advice had been taken, and the Spartacists had stayed in the USPD 'for another three or four months . . . the whole problem of how to divide the revolutionary masses in that party from their opportunist leadership would not exist'.[68] This particular historical avenue was not to be explored: a conference of Spartacists on 29 December decided by an overwhelming majority to found a new party.

At the founding congress of the KPD (S) (i.e. Communist Party of Germany, Spartacus League), held between 30 December and 1 January, 127 delegates from all over Germany were present. 83 represented Spartacus, 29 the IKD, 3 the RSB, and there was one observer from the FSJD (Free Socialist Youth of Germany), which later became the communist youth movement, but was opposed at this stage to a merger with the Communist Party. Finally, there were 11 members of the Spartacist *Zentrale*. Of the 99 delegates whose names are known, 29 remained in the party until 1933, 6 were murdered in the course of 1919; the remainder left the party's ranks in the various splits of subsequent years, or for some other reason.[69]

Many of the participants were utopian radicals, who looked forward to an imminent seizure of power (this applies both to the Spartacists and the International Communists), and their optimistic views were shared by Karl Liebknecht himself. The sway exerted by left radical ideas at the founding congress was shown by the decision not to participate in the National Assembly elections, which was passed by 62 votes to 23.[70] Paul Levi's speech for the opposite point of view was repeatedly interrupted by angry delegates.[71] The extreme left claimed that parliament was a bourgeois institution, rightly suppressed in Soviet Russia, and incompatible with the Council, or Soviet, system, which was the basic institution of the proletarian revolution. Levi later described the decision to boycott bourgeois parliaments as the root of all the difficulties within the party in 1919 and 1920; but Rosa herself was not inclined to take it too tragically, writing to Clara Zetkin that 'the question will be pushed into the background by the tremendous events now taking place'.[72]

When she took the floor to expound the programme her speech was extremely cautious in its conclusions: strikes were, as ever, the main method of combat, power could not simply be seized at the centre, the work must be done from the ground up, 'the process will perhaps be somewhat more long drawn out than one was at first inclined to consider'. Nothing could be prophesied, but 'who cares, as long as it happens within our lifetime'.[73]

Almost all the delegates agreed that the existing trade unions had had their day, Fritz Heckert forming the solitary exception. The IKD submitted a proposal to make it compulsory for all communists to leave the trade unions. This was not directly rejected, but evaded by submitting it to a party commission.

Rosa Luxemburg too, though not entirely satisfied with the slogan 'Out of the trade unions', nevertheless thought the Workers' Councils had made them historically obsolete. 'We are replacing the trade unions by a new system on an entirely new basis', she said, 'Factory Councils and Workers' Councils, and, further up, an entirely new structure.'[74] The IKD's justification for leaving the trade unions was different: they wanted to set up 'unity organisations' instead, and thereby overcome the traditional split between the political and trade union wings of the working-class movement.

The merger between the IKD and the Spartacists at the founding congress of the KPD went relatively smoothly. The left radicals, in the IKD and among rank-and-file Spartacists, did not attempt to take control of the party *Zentrale*, despite their apparent preponderance at the congress. The new *Zentrale* was almost identical to the old. Mehring and Budich were dropped; Frölich was added, the sole representative of the IKD. It was possible to incorporate the left radicals because the organisation of the party was extremely loose, with more affinity to the USPD than to the Bolshevik model. 'We must put an end to the old system of subordination of local organisations to a *Zentrale*', said Hugo Eberlein in the business report. 'Local organisations must act autonomously and not wait for orders from above . . . The task of the *Zentrale* will be to give ideological and political direction.'[75]

One group whose presence in the KPD would have been extremely welcome was the Revolutionary *Obleute*. The events of December, and especially the refusal of the USPD to leave the government until 29 December, had driven the *Obleute* to the left, and there were negotiations during the founding congress between Liebknecht, acting for the Spartacists, and the *Obleute*, with the aim of merging the two groups. It is sometimes said that the decision of the KPD congress not to participate in the elections frightened off the *Obleute* and thus nipped in the bud a promising *entrée* for Spartacus into the ranks of the organised Berlin proletariat. In fact, this was not the main reason for the breakdown of negotiations. The *Obleute* set a number of tough conditions, prompted by their jealousy and suspicion of the Spartacists, including equal representation on the programme commission, predominant influence on the communist press, a right of veto on street demonstrations, and the striking out of the words 'Spartacus League' from the KPD's official title.[76] This was not a promising basis for agreement, and Liebknecht could do nothing more in view of the hostile attitude of most of the KPD congress to the whole idea. The contact broken off early in 1919 was only resumed a year and a half later, when most of the *Obleute* who remained politically active pronounced in favour of entry into the communist party. By then, of course, the situation had changed beyond recognition.

2   From Radical Sect to Mass Party, 1919 to 1920

THE PROTEST ACTION OF JANUARY 1919

The KPD had barely come to birth when it was dragged into a quarrel not of its own making. The USPD People's Representatives had resigned on 29 December, firstly in protest against Ebert's order to the Minister of War to use force to free Otto Wels from his captivity by the People's Naval Division; and secondly because of his failure either to set up a popular militia in place of the old standing army or to take any measures of nationalisation.[1] It was logical that the Independents in the Prussian government should also resign; they did so on 3 January. There was now a purely SPD government in power both in Prussia and in the *Reich*. The Berlin chief of police, Emil Eichhorn, was regarded by the SPD as a 'danger to public safety' and a sympathiser with the revolutionaries, whether Spartacists, rebellious sailors or *Obleute*.[2] He was also a member of the USPD. The resignation of the USPD ministers therefore seemed a good opportunity to get rid of him. On 4 January he was dismissed. But he refused to go, relying on the support of a wide spectrum of the Berlin left, including the central executive of the Berlin USPD, the *Obleute*, and the Spartacists. The *Obleute* decided on the evening of 4 January to dig their heels in: the retreat had gone far enough, so far and no further. What was the KPD *Zentrale* to do?

Its initial reaction was that any steps taken in defence of Eichhorn should not go beyond the limits of a protest demonstration.[3] Looking back a year later, a 'participant in the action' recalled the *Zentrale*'s attitude at the time: 'Everyone present agreed that it would be folly to strive towards the formation of a government; a government on a proletarian basis would not have lasted longer than a fortnight.'[4] Hence the party's slogans were: revocation of Eichhorn's dismissal, disarming of the counter-revolution, arming of the proletariat, formation of a Red Guard, but not the overthrow of the government. However, under the twin impulse of the enthusiasm of a 150 000-strong Berlin demonstration on 5 January and the impatience of the USPD leftist Georg Ledebour the mood changed. Liebknecht and Pieck now joined Ledebour in pressing for an attempt to seize power. The Berlin garrison was only waiting for a sign, it was said, and would readily join the workers in overthrowing the Ebert government.[5] A joint meeting of the Revolutionary Shop Stewards, the Berlin USPD and (for the Spartacists) Liebknecht and Pieck decided to attempt a seizure of power, and set up a Revolutionary Committee with 52 members to act as a provisional government and direct the insurrection. In fact this committee did no more than call for a fresh demonstration next day[6] and draw up a proclamation 'provisionally taking over governmental functions'[7] which was used in a vain attempt to occupy the War Ministry by persuasion, but never made public.

This rash step towards a seizure of power was by no means approved by all the communist leaders. The Liebknecht–Ledebour government proclamation had not even been submitted to the *Zentrale* for discussion. Karl Radek, whose utterances carried some weight since he represented the successful Russian Revolution, pointed out that it would 'be senseless to risk armed conflicts which could only end with the disarming of the organised workers' and proposed to the *Zentrale* that it call off the protest strike. Rosa Luxemburg replied to him that although it would be wiser to retreat in the face of superior force the KPD could not give the signal itself. It was up to the Independents to capitulate first.[8] Jogiches in contrast wanted a public disavowal of Liebknecht's action.[9] But Rosa's arguments prevailed. Meanwhile the Free Corps units pressed into service by Gustav Noske were on the march. Noske's intentions were made clear by the government's proclamation of 8 January accusing the Spartacists of bringing terror and anarchy and announcing 'the hour of decision is drawing near'.[10] The reply of the extreme left was defiant: 'General Strike! To arms! Into the streets for the last battle, for victory!'[11] The RSB (League of Red Soldiers), the Spartacists' military organisation, also called for armed resistance.[12] But the forces at the disposal of the insurgents were hopelessly inadequate; the decision of the People's Naval Division to stay neutral in the conflict was a bitter blow.[13] By 12 January Noske's troops (comprising both republican units and Free Corps) had retaken all the buildings seized a few days earlier (the

printing press, the Berlin police headquarters, the offices of
Vorwärts), shooting many of the rebels on the spot, after their
surrender. The Revolutionary Committee vanished as an
organised body (it met for the last time on 9 January); Radek
wrote a second appeal to the *Zentrale*, using Levi as his postman.
(It was too risky for him to go in person, since government troops
were already in the city.) The only option open was a last-minute
withdrawal, he said, and the evacuation of the buildings still held
by the insurgents.

> You have enough sense to realise that this fight is hopeless:
> Levi and Duncker have told me so . . . There is nothing to
> forbid the weaker party from withdrawing in the face of
> superior forces. In July 1917 when we were infinitely stronger
> than you are today we held the masses back, and when we failed
> we led them into a retreat, instead of a hopeless battle.[14]

Rosa Luxemburg and Leo Jogiches agreed that the fight was now
hopeless, but Rosa at least felt that it would be dishonourable to
withdraw now; if the party carried on, it would be able to
underline the faults of the other, larger groups like the
Revolutionary *Obleute* and their failure to provide a revolutionary
leadership. In the *Zentrale* Luxemburg and Pieck won the day
against Radek and Levi, and instead of issuing the call to break
off the struggle they sent a letter to the *Obleute* withdrawing from
the Revolutionary Committee 'in order to regain freedom of
action'.[15] The two main themes which resounded in Rosa's last
articles for *Die Rote Fahne* were revolutionary honour (the workers
were forced to take up arms by Ebert–Scheidemann's
provocations; the KPD could not desert them if it wanted to avoid
losing 'the moral credibility of the German revolution within the
International') and the absence of leadership ('Germany has so
far been the classic land of organisation . . . But what are we
experiencing today? At the most important moments of the
revolution this renowned "talent for organisation" has failed . . .
in the most pitiful manner.' 'The leadership has been deficient.
But a new leadership can and must be created by and from the
masses.'[16]) The last article of her life (14 January) admitted the
defeat (it was entitled 'Order Reigns in Berlin'), but was imbued
with revolutionary optimism. 'The masses . . . have made this
"defeat" a member of that series of historic defeats which are the

pride and strength of international socialism. This is why the future victory will flourish on the soil of this "defeat".'[17] Liebknecht's last article, 'Despite Everything' (15 January), was in a similar vein, though couched in more apocalyptic language: 'The German working class has not yet ended its road to Golgotha – the day of redemption is at hand, the day of judgement for Ebert–Scheidemann–Noske and the capitalist wirepullers who are still hiding behind them.'[18] The same day Luxemburg and Liebknecht were arrested by the Free Corps. Shortly afterwards the two unquestioned leaders of Spartacism were murdered by their captors, a crime for which a military court later handed out the derisory sentences of two years in one case, four months in another. There were also many acquittals.[19] Wilhelm Pieck, arrested along with Luxemburg and Liebknecht, was spared by the soldiers, perhaps because he was less prominent, and succeeded in making his escape two days later.[20]

'Order' now reigned in Berlin. It remained for Ebert and Noske to restore its benefits to the other parts of Germany which had risen up in mid-January in solidarity with Berlin. What the contemporary bourgeois and Social Democratic press described as 'communist putsches' were in the main just protests against repression and solidarity actions. The list of cities affected is long: Dresden, Stuttgart, Leipzig, Brunswick, Duisburg, Essen, Halle, Hamburg, Düsseldorf, Cuxhaven, Bremen. In Bremen, home of the wartime left radicals, the communists were stronger than anywhere else in January 1919, and they combined with the USPD to set up a 'socialist republic' which lasted 25 days, until 4 February, and briefly expropriated the means of production and transport.[21]

THE CAMPAIGN FOR 'SOCIALISATION' AND INDUSTRIAL DEMOCRACY

Simultaneously a mass movement developed in the heart of the Ruhr, but its motivation was not limited to the Berlin events. The objective of the Ruhr movement was apparently more easily attainable than a seizure of power: 'socialisation'. On 9 January the Essen Workers' and Soldiers' Council, which included representatives of all three left-wing parties, decided to put in hand the immediate socialisation of the mines in

Rhineland–Westphalia, and set up a Commission of Nine to do this, consisting of three Social Democrats, three Independents and three Spartacists. On 11 January the Workers' and Soldiers' Council occupied the building of the mine-owners' association and appointed a 'People's Commissar for Socialisation', an SPD member called Dr Ruben. These initiatives were approved by a regional conference of Workers' and Soldiers' Councils held on 13 January. The SPD (who were in the majority) saw the promise of socialisation as a way of calming the excited miners down, and making sure there were no further strikes. The strikers were asked to return to work, as 'the mines have now become the property of the people'.[22] Artur König, who signed on behalf of the KPD, was not surprisingly disavowed by the Essen branch of the party.[23] Nevertheless, the appeal succeeded, and the miners returned to work. Only in turbulent Hamborn was there further strike activity.[24] The Ruhr was not left long, however, to conduct discussions on socialisation. On 12 February General Theodor von Watter, newly appointed commander of the local army corps (the Seventh) sent the Free Corps unit of a certain Captain Lichtschlag to reconquer the mining district of the Ruhr; the reply of the radicals, given at the Mülheim Conference of 16 February, was to call a general strike. At its height the strike involved 52 per cent of the miners in the Ruhr. It developed rapidly into an armed conflict, which the Free Corps Lichtschlag won without difficulty. The miners had less than 1000 men under arms.[25] The USPD leaders took fright and started to negotiate with General von Watter. In return for a promise that the Free Corps would leave the region, they agreed that the workers' militia would surrender its arms and the strike would be called off (22 February). Of course, the Free Corps unit had no intention of leaving, and two days later it resumed its offensive.[26]

At this point (24 February) a general strike broke out in Central Germany, launched by a regional conference of miners at Halle, under the impulse of two Left Independents, Wilhelm Koenen and Bernhard Düwell. A quarter of the delegates were communists, a half USPD.[27] The main aim of the strike was, as in the Ruhr, 'socialisation' and 'democratisation'. Democracy was to be achieved in the mines and factories by giving 'immediate recognition' to the 'elected Factory Councils and . . . the District Miners' Council'.[28]

The workers of Central Germany took up the call with

enthusiasm: on 26 February the strike spread to Leipzig (the local factories voted by 40 000 to 5000 in favour), to Erfurt, and to the local railway network.[29] By 1 March it covered the whole of Thuringia, momentarily cutting off the Weimar National Assembly from all connection with the outside world. The SPD parliamentarians felt the ground shaking beneath their feet and called on the government to start the socialisation process, and to set up Factory Councils.[30] But worse was to come: Berlin itself returned to the charge. The Plenary Assembly of Workers' and Soldiers' Councils of Greater Berlin called almost unanimously for a general strike on 3 March, and even the SPD members were forced to accept the decision. The demands were: recognition of the Workers' Councils, implementation of the 'seven Hamburg points' for the democratisation of the army, adopted in December by the Congress of Councils and abrogated by Noske on 19 January,[31] freeing of political prisoners, ending of the state of siege, setting up of a revolutionary workers' guard, dissolution of Free Corps units, and the restoration of political and economic relations with Soviet Russia.[32]

With two strike movements proceeding at once in important industrial centres – Berlin and Central Germany – not to mention the continuous effervescence in Bavaria after the murder of Kurt Eisner in February the moment seemed to have arrived for the 'second revolution' which would bring power to the proletariat. The *Zentrale*, still under Jogiches's guidance, held to the idea that a general strike would achieve more than an attempt at armed insurrection.

> Workers! Now you have found the way to terrify the bourgeoisie! If you go to the ballot box . . . you are betrayed. If you reach for weapons . . . the bourgeoisie has the welcome opportunity to mow you down . . . But now you are immune to attack. The strike is the strongest weapon . . . Nothing can scare us, least of all the terror of the Noske guards . . . Keep up the strike.[33]

By the same token, the *Zentrale* was resolutely opposed to any armed conflict with the Free Corps, and blamed the People's Naval Division, who had left the workers in the lurch in January, and would do so again, for getting into a private quarrel with von Lüttwitz's men, who had been called into Berlin by Noske.[34] But it was in vain that the KPD told the workers not to be led astray into 'military putsches'.[35] In the conditions of the time, a non-violent general strike was an impossibility. There were conflicts with the police, shops were pillaged, and exchanges of fire took place with the Free Corps. The Independents proposed to extend the strike to cut off supplies of water, gas and electricity, and the SPD delegates, having lost the vote on this, walked out of the strike committee and appealed for a return to work (6 March). In the next few days, 'order' was once more restored by von Lüttwitz's troops and finally the strike committee, now exclusively USPD in composition, since the KPD had withdrawn earlier in protest against the presence of SPD members on it, recommended a return to work (8 March). There followed the fearful revenge of the military, spurred on by Noske. His proclamation of 9 March was clear enough: 'Any person found bearing arms and fighting against the government's troops is to be shot immediately.'[36] His own figure for the ensuing slaughter is 1200 deaths; the later communist estimate was 3000, including 29 sailors shot after coming to collect their pay 'because they looked intelligent'. Leo Jogiches disdained flight and was arrested and shot 'while attempting to escape', on 10 March.[37] For Berlin it was the end of all hopes for a 'second revolution'. The strike in Central Germany had also collapsed by then (7 March). The communist press was prohibited, and the party headquarters had to be transferred from Berlin, first to Frankfurt (19 March), then on to Leipzig (8 April). For a month the KPD's printed propaganda was limited to leaflets and certain local newspapers.

THE END OF THE COUNCIL MOVEMENT

The KPD party conference of 29 March at Frankfurt-am-Main took place at a time when the strike movement was in a trough between two waves. The massive Ruhr strike of April had not yet started; the impending storm in Munich had not yet burst; Berlin and Central Germany were back at work under martial law. Paul Levi reported on the *Zentrale*'s work since the founding congress. It was no time for self-congratulation. The party organisation had collapsed, there was 'very little chance of getting in contact again' with outlying districts, and the main task for the future must be to pick up the threads again. The party was faced with obstacles both from within and without. Within, there were the putschists, who 'only live off the nervousness of the masses'. Without, there were the Independents, 'who waver between humiliating submission to Ebert and issuing general strike calls'.[38] However, Levi was relatively optimistic about the prospects for revolution.

> Developments are moving towards a general strike all over Germany. This cannot be coordinated nationally by a central authority but must grow out of the overall movement . . . Our task is to give the strikes a political character by issuing the appropriate slogans. But there should be no call for a seizure of power: the proletariat is not ripe for this.[39]

Levi's attitude to the strikes which kept breaking out in Germany emerges clearly from a letter he sent to Lenin two days previously: 'We are doing nothing to encourage partial strikes, and in some individual cases we are doing everything possible to hold back the people from giving the government any chance of shedding blood. We can hold back the proletariat from this (though not the government). But not from striking: the bitterness is so great that the workers literally run out of the factories by themselves.' In any case, he added, the KPD would not put the brake on the strike movement 'because the general uprising in Germany will most probably grow out of an increasingly rapid succession of partial uprisings'.[40] This letter is revealing, because it indicates a tendency to equate a strike with an uprising and accordingly to ignore the need to prepare for armed struggle. The other members of the Spartacist *Zentrale* seem to have shared Levi's assumption that a general strike covering the whole of Germany would somehow lead automatically to a German 'Soviet Republic' or 'Republic of Councils'. Therefore there was great excitement when in early April it seemed as if the partial strikes were beginning to coincide. The first Leipzig issue of *Die Rote Fahne* (11 April) noted that there were simultaneous strike movements on the Ruhr, in Stuttgart, Magdeburg and Brunswick, and, above all, that a Council Republic had just been proclaimed in Munich. The paper appealed to the masses to follow the example of Hungary and Bavaria and set up a German Republic of Councils. 'The great day of the emancipation of the oppressed has dawned. Victory is near, perhaps only a step away

. . . Workers, proletarians . . . listen to the summons.'[41] The combination of the news from Hungary and Munich with the apparently irresistible wave of strikes in Germany seems to have led Levi temporarily to lose his sense of reality.

For there was another possible outcome to the movement, and a much more likely one: that the succession of local strikes and uprisings would be defeated in detail by Free Corps units moving from one city to another, or simply fade away when unendurable hunger forced the workers back into the factories. In retrospect Levi was able to forget that he had ever advanced an optimistic perspective: 'The movement ended with the great action of March 1919, the death of a thousand proletarians in Berlin and the shattering of the party's organisation . . . March 1919 meant the end of an epoch for the KPD and the German revolution. Till then the masses wanted action: afterwards their enthusiasm disappeared.'[42]

The most famous episode of the German Revolution came after this: the Bavarian Council Republic. The story has often been told[43] and here we shall only pick out what is relevant to the analysis of communist policy. The local leader of the KPD, Eugen Leviné, had been sent by the *Zentrale* to Munich to reorganise the party, and, ironically, get rid of leftist adventurers. He performed the task successfully, and the Munich KPD warned the proletariat on 16 March against hasty actions, on the ground that 'the seizure of power is for communists impossible while we only have a minority of the working class behind us'.[44] Leviné was acting entirely consistently both with his ideas and the policy of the *Zentrale* when he refused to take part in the Republic of Councils set up on 7 April by a curious coalition of Social Democrats, Independents, Anarchists and unattached leftists. 'Conditions in Germany are not yet ripe for a Soviet republic, least of all in Bavaria.'[45] 'This artificial construction will collapse like the bursting of a soap bubble or the fall of a house of cards . . . Workers, your representatives will have to take care to choose the right moment to proclaim the slogan: All Power to the Workers', Peasants' and Soldiers' Councils!'[46] Leviné adjudged the moment to have come six days later, when the supporters of the former government mounted a counter-putsch against the Council Republic (13 April). In the course of defeating the putsch from outside, the communists overthrew the existing republic and founded what they saw as a 'genuine' Council Republic, governed by a 15-member Action Committee dominated by themselves. Nothing had changed in the balance of forces since 7 April; what had happened was that, like Liebknecht and Luxemburg in January, Leviné considered it a matter of revolutionary honour to engage in this hopeless struggle alongside the most militant section of the proletariat. 'An honourable death and experience for the future is all we can salvage from the present situation', he told his party comrades.[47] Two weeks later, when defeat was certain, Ernst Toller of the USPD persuaded the Factory and Soldiers' Councils to elect a new Action Committee, with no communist members, to try the path of negotiations with the deposed SPD government of Johannes Hoffmann, which was waiting quietly in Bamberg for its restoration by the Free Corps (27 April). The communists explained this desertion by referring to the unripeness for socialism of the Munich working class,[48] and they called on the Bavarian Red Army to save the Council Republic, which it did on 29 April by snatching power back from the USPD. But the Munich episode had to end, whether by negotiation or by military defeat, and on 1 May the Ehrhardt Brigade fought its way into the city and proceeded to an exemplary punishment of the participants. The courts played their part too: the poets Ernst Toller and Erich Mühsam received heavy prison sentences; Leviné was condemned to death and shot, after uttering a phrase which was to become proverbial: 'We communists are all dead men on leave.' Several hundred others were killed without a trial.[49]

With the reduction of Munich there was no longer any doubt that the wave of revolution had subsided. Signs of a return to stability in Germany were unmistakable. The second (and last) Congress of Councils, held between 8 and 14 April, was dominated by the SPD delegation, which was determined to subordinate the Councils to the National Assembly and limit them to purely economic functions; the local power of the Councils had long since vanished in most parts of Germany; the newly-elected town councils simply dissolved them or cut off their funds. By mid-May this was happening even in the Ruhr.[50] The KPD did not waste its time in trying to resuscitate the Workers' Councils. Its support for them had always been conditional: they had to be genuine organs of workers' power and not parallel bodies anchored in a parliamentary constitution and limited to economic functions. This distinction was expressed by the use of of the phrase '*political* Workers' Councils'. As RF editorialised in February, 'The proletariat must . . . concentrate political power in the hands of political Workers' Councils.'[51] Councils of this kind, if they had ever existed, would have genuinely deserved to be described as Soviets. The conception was expounded repeatedly at the party's congresses over the next two years and in the theoretical journal *Die Internationale*.[52] The KPD struggled vainly until August 1919 to persuade the Workers' Councils to 'come out of the shadows and give a thought to their tasks and duties'.[53] Then it gave up, withdrawing in the course of August and September from those few Workers' Councils where it retained a representation.[54]

PAUL LEVI'S FIGHT AGAINST PUTSCHISM IN THE KPD

By May 1919 the first post-war revolutionary wave had subsided. The summer of 1919 was a time of transition from the apocalyptic hopes, general strikes and armed uprisings of the immediate post-war period to a new era marked by depression in the revolutionary camp but also by a growth in agitation for purely economic objectives, which lasted from mid-1919 to late in 1920.[55] Political stabilisation in Germany coincided with a recovery of exports, a rise in industrial activity and a fall in unemployment.[56]

Moreover, the 'great inflation' was just starting to gather momentum, gently and gradually as yet, but still noticeable enough to set in motion social groups which had previously stood apart from the German revolution: lower ranking officials and agricultural workers. This meant a reorientation in the party's work; at the same time the continuing three-way split among the proletariat between USPD, KPD and SPD necessitated a return to the existing trade unions, as the organs of working-class unity. But the fierce opposition of the left radicals in the party to these changes meant that the fight with them had to be taken up as an urgent priority.[57] What was needed in the meantime was to avoid at all costs a repetition of the disastrous uprisings of January in Berlin and Bremen, March in Hungary, April in Munich. This was the objective to which the *Zentrale* now devoted almost all its feeble strength under Paul Levi's leadership.

Ostensibly Levi's circular of 11 June 1919 to party organisations was concerned with the Versailles Settlement. But after outlining the danger of military dictatorship if negotiations with the Entente failed, the circular went on: 'It is not the task of the proletariat to make any attempt to get to power itself and thus take away from the bourgeoisie the frightful responsibility for the peace treaty . . . In this situation any action that would signify a struggle for power must be unconditionally avoided.'[58] Two days later another circular underlined this. A putsch from the right in response to Versailles was more likely than one from the left, wrote Levi. It would be wrong for the Spartacists to attempt a revolution at that time: 'Revolution is not a mad, blind process of running amok but a clear weighing up and examination of the given social forces . . . To undertake isolated local putsches would be merely to provide victims for the butcheries of the military dictatorship. This is the clear lesson from the events of the months gone by.'[59] And again on 19 June: 'Now is not the moment for the proletariat to enter into action . . . Hold back! Do not let yourselves be provoked!'[60] And a day later: 'The workers can wait calmly, despite all provocations, until their day has come.'[61] Levi also announced the voluntary liquidation of the RSB, the League of Red Soldiers, the nearest thing the KPD possessed to a military organisation. The only action he was prepared to contemplate was 'a historically necessary offensive of the proletariat'. Anything else was simply an invitation to the military to shed more proletarian blood.

There were a number of formidable obstacles to pursuing this policy of restraint. First, there was the elemental character of the movement: as we have seen, the communist party was never the sole driving force behind the so-called 'communist putsches' of 1919. It was a relatively small and uninfluential group.

Second, there was the lack of any discipline holding the party together: the KPD at this stage was in effect a federation of autonomous sections, some of which were controlled by people with views far removed from the Spartacist tradition. It took Levi and his supporters in the *Zentrale* almost a year to establish firm control over the party. The third obstacle he had to face was lack of clear backing from the Communist International. This was partly a practical matter. In the first year of its existence the Comintern hardly had an organisation at all, and the influence of the leading Bolsheviks was exerted through public statements which communists abroad were free to take account of or reject. There was an important exception: the presence of Karl Radek in Germany meant that the KPD had a fairly authoritative Bolshevik on the spot. He was originally sent out in December 1918, arriving just too late for the First Congress of Councils but in time for the KPD Founding Congress, and he stayed in Germany for over a year, though his activities were somewhat curtailed from February 1919 by imprisonment. Radek had the advantage of combining the two different worlds of German communism and Russian Bolshevism. His role as animator of the Bremen left radical faction during the First World War made him at least by proxy one of the founders of the KPD; his political collaboration with Lenin both before and after the seizure of power made him a Bolshevik by courtesy at least. But Radek's political line in 1919 was in fact usually the same as Levi's and his close involvement in the German scene made him aware of the obstacles in the way of the revolution.[62]

The same could not be said of the Russian Bolsheviks, whose great prestige as leaders of the first socialist revolution made the Germans listen to their proclamations with great attention. The view in Moscow at this time was coloured by a boundless revolutionary optimism. Already in November 1918 Lenin's reaction to the news of the collapse of Germany had been that the German socialist revolution was about to commence. The tragic events of the months of January and March 1919 should have dampened this optimism but did not. 1919 was the 'year of the red mirage'[63] and the usually sober Lenin was not exempt from the illusory belief that capitalism was about to collapse. In July 1919 he prophesied 'with confidence' the victory of the world Soviet republic 'by next July'.[64] Zinoviev, writing in the first issue of the Comintern journal, which came out in May 1919, asserted that within a year people would have started to forget that there had ever been a struggle for communism in Europe, for in a year's time, the whole of the continent would be communist.[65]

Thus Levi's detestation of 'putschism'; his doubts about the experiments in Hungary and Bavaria; and his obsession with clearing the left radicals out of the KPD before they did any more damage, were not ideas shared in Moscow. Radek was the Bolshevik closest to him at this time. But even Radek defended Béla Kun's seizure of power in Hungary,[66] and Lenin and Zinoviev welcomed any action which lessened the pressure of

Civil War and Allied intervention on Soviet Russia. Lenin did not come out against the left radicals till 1920; theorists of left radicalism like Gorter were able to write in the official journal of the Comintern; and Sebald Rutgers (another Dutch communist) was put in charge of the 'Amsterdam Bureau', set up after the First Comintern Congress to coordinate communist work in Western Europe. These differences of opinion did not matter very much in 1919, owing to the autonomy enjoyed by the member parties of the Comintern. But they were an important factor in the later hostility in Comintern circles to Paul Levi and in the gentle approach taken by the ECCI to his arch-enemies, the left communists who founded the KAPD in 1920.

In the long run the Levi line was victorious in the party, simply because it corresponded more closely with reality. The collapse of the Council movement, an accomplished fact by the summer of 1919, cut the ground from beneath those who wished to continue boycotting all parliaments and local assemblies: it meant there *summer 1919* was no alternative now (short of the Hamburg Left's largely imaginary Factory Organisations). The Soviet in Budapest, the Council in Munich, had both been overthrown. And above all, the masses had lost their enthusiasm for experiments. The recovery of the German economy and the new problem of inflation resulted in day-to-day sectional conflicts and a tremendous expansion of the traditional trade union movement. The leftist slogans 'Out of the Old Trade Unions' and 'Into the One Big Union' lost their appeal.

THE DEFEAT AND EXPULSION OF THE SEMI-SYNDICALIST OPPOSITION

In August 1919 the 'leftist' mood was still uppermost in the party; by October things had changed. The Levi *Zentrale* received a rough ride at the Frankfurt Conference of August. The core of the opposition, represented by the districts of Bremen and Hamburg, was supported on issues of organisation by the majority of the delegates at the conference, and a resolution from Laufenberg calling for the representation of organisations according to the strength of their membership was accepted over Levi's objections (the leftists were well entrenched in the largest districts). On the trade union question Levi offered a compromise: isolated individuals were to be discouraged from leaving the reformist unions, but larger groups were advised to take this step and form their own 'Workers' Unions' independent of the ADGB. The opposition would not accept even this compromise position.[67] The Frankfurt Conference then declared itself incompetent to take definite decisions because improperly constituted, and voted to call a new conference on the basis of one delegate for every 3000 party members.[68]

If this voting basis had been retained, Levi would probably have lost in October as well, at the so-called 'Heidelberg' Congress, held at various places late in that month.[69] He owed his success to the decision to give voting rights to members of the *Zentrale*, who were present *ex officio* and had not been elected from the districts.[70] The decisive vote on Laufenberg's resolution was 23 to 19, and the majority against Laufenberg included all members of the existing KPD *Zentrale*.[71]

In his opening speech at Heidelberg Levi derived the necessity of expelling the left opposition directly from the task of overthrowing capitalism. The task of the proletariat, he said, was clear: 'to create the nucleus of a party of revolution – the communist party'. But the party as it stood was incapable of this, because it was in a state of disintegration, having fallen into a severe illness, the 'sickness of Syndicalism'. Levi summed up the 'syndicalist' doctrines of the opposition in three points: (1) it saw the revolution as a purely economic process; (2) it rejected political means of struggle as harmful; and (3) it saw the general strike as 'the Alpha and Omega of the revolution'. The Marxist view, in contrast, was that the revolution could not be made mechanically with a single patent recipe. 'The revolution is the organic process of the liberation of the whole proletarian class, with *all* means, in all ways, and at *all* places.' A political party was needed to accomplish this task. Levi asserted that the Hamburg Left's doctrines led straight to the dissolution of the party, quoting their statement that 'the communist party propagates the proletarian unity organisation and the Council System in order to abolish itself as a political party when this demand has been achieved. With the realisation of the proletarian class organisation (i.e. One Big Union) the communist party will cease to exist alongside it as a party.'[72] He characteristically concluded by annihilating his opponents with a Latin tag: *Tune cede malis, sed contra audentior ito* (Yield not to evil, but go to face it with a bolder step).[73]

Wolffheim, in reply, denied the charge that he rejected the role of the party. 'We demand both the *Union* and the Party', he said. But he insisted that the Hamburg tendency would continue to propagate the idea of an *Union*, the aim of which would be the organisation of the dictatorship of Workers' and Factory Councils. Laufenberg added that Radek's letter to the Party Congress called for party unity and was thus in contradiction to Levi's plan to throw the opposition out.[74] He then raised the significant accusation that the *Zentrale* 'has a peculiar leaning towards the USPD, shown in their letter to them about a joint demonstration on 7 November in celebration of the Russian Revolution'. This was true in fact where Levi was concerned. He felt that a mass communist party could only be achieved if the KPD entered into a more comradely relationship with the USPD; the expulsion of the 'Syndicalist' opposition would assist this process. Levi's 'Theses on Communist Principles and Tactics' guaranteed the removal of the 'Syndicalists' by including a provision that 'members of the KPD who do not share these views must leave the party'.[75] With the adoption of the theses, the opposition walked out, and were subsequently expelled (23 October). Twenty-five delegates in all had to leave this Congress. They came largely from North Germany (Hamburg, Hanover, Bremen, Lübeck) and Berlin, although there was a scattering of individuals from other places (Saxony, the Rhineland).

This split in the KPD(S) was the work of Paul Levi rather than the Comintern leaders. Radek, despite agreeing on all the points of principle involved, and despite having written a pamphlet to this effect,[76] sent a letter to the *Zentrale* appealing to it not to split the party over a minor issue of tactics.[77] Lenin was also inclined to play down the issue of anti-parliamentarism (he had in his time after all boycotted a Russian parliament) and wrote to the KPD *Zentrale* shortly after Heidelberg that 'given agreement on the basic issue . . . the restoration of unity in the German party is both possible and necessary'.[78]

The Heidelberg bloodletting cut the party's strength by approximately 50 per cent. The expelled comrades do not fall very neatly into a single political category. Levi managed to persuade himself and his supporters that they had expelled the 'terrorists' and 'Syndicalists' from their ranks. But most of the opposition rejected these descriptions. They were in fact 'left communists', who wished to preserve what they thought was the Spartacist tradition of resistance to centralisation and bureaucracy. The KPD was beginning to resemble the SPD, they claimed, it was becoming 'an organisation for the domination of the masses by their leaders.'[79] Instead of centralisation they advocated a federal party structure, based on 'Factory Organisations'. At the same time they advocated the replacement of the old trade unions by a universal union of workers without distinction of craft or industry. The General Workers' Union of Germany (AAUD) was founded in February 1920 by the left communists to give effect to this idea.[80] They strenuously denied that they were against political parties, however. For a long time they refused to leave the KPD, and it was only the KPD's evident inadequacy during the Kapp putsch which persuaded them to form their own party, the KAPD (Communist Workers' Party of Germany) at a congress held on 4 and 5 April 1920. The KAPD was not intended as 'a party in the traditional sense' but as 'an organisation directed to freeing the proletariat from all forms of domination by leaders'.[81] According to the KAPD party programme 'the radical removal of all leadership politics is the prerequisite for the rapid advance of the proletarian evolution'.[82] This was clearly far removed from Bolshevism or traditional Social Democracy, but the KAPD's existence as a party and its advocacy of the dictatorship of the proletariat differentiated it equally clearly from Syndicalism.[83] The KAPD in fact formed part of an international movement of left communism, which had its theoretical roots more in Holland than in Germany. It owed more to the Dutch theorists Pannekoek and Gorter than to the Germans Wolffheim and Laufenberg, whose ideas of alliance with the German bourgeoisie under the slogan of National Bolshevism soon made them as unwelcome within the ranks of left communists as they had been in the KPD(S).[84]

THE UNEASY RELATIONSHIP WITH THE USPD

With the removal of the left communists from the KPD the stage was set for the campaign to win mass support. Levi hoped that the outcome of the Heidelberg Congress would help to overcome the anti-Spartacist prejudices of the masses of workers who had so far preferred to stay with the USPD. He also considered that the pressure of events would drive the USPD itself closer to communism. In late November 1919 he drew up a detailed analysis of the German situation, which was probably intended for Lenin's eyes. In it he pointed to the succession of defeats suffered by the working class, the latest of which was the complete collapse of a general strike called on 4 November to protest against Noske's dissolution of the last surviving institution of the November 1918 revolution, the Greater Berlin Executive Council. Now a 'triumphant counter-revolution' faced a 'defeated revolution'. But this would lead to a radicalisation of the USPD. The left wing of that party was 'now essentially with us' and would 'throw out the right'.[85] This was an accurate prognosis, in the short term. The Leipzig Congress of the USPD (30 November–6 December 1919) voted to leave the Second International and enter the Third International 'alone if necessary' but preferably in association with 'the social-revolutionary parties of other countries'.[86] It unanimously accepted an Action Programme involving a future 'dictatorship of the proletariat based on a system of Workers' Councils'. The right wing of the USPD appeared to be 'only a small group of leaders'.[87] In Radek's opinion, the Independents were 'on their way to becoming a communist party'.[88]

In the longer term, this was too optimistic. In fact the right-wing leaders of the USPD – such people as Wilhelm Dittmann, Luise Zietz and Rudolf Hilferding – did not see any need to change their policies. Moreover, the Comintern's newly-established West European Secretariat (and Levi too, though his version was milder in tone) thought that the USPD should enter bilateral negotiations with Moscow rather than trying to bring in 'social-revolutionary parties of other countries'.[89] A fuller statement from the ECCI was sent on 5 February 1920, although it was only received by the USPD on 9 April, having been delayed for unclear reasons. It was harsh and uncompromising, and demanded the correction of numerous 'mistakes' made by that party, as well as 'decisively rejecting' any 'cooperation with the right-wing leaders'. The leadership of the USPD would have to be 'cleaned up' and the only route to the Third International was 'amalgamation with the KPD'. The letter emphasised, however, that the ECCI did not envisage the mechanical transfer of Russian experience to German conditions, offering to 'amend and extend the programme of the Third International on the basis of Marxist theory and the experience of the revolutionary struggle throughout the world.'[90]

Meanwhile, the left of the USPD had made a great tactical error by organising a mass demonstration in front of the *Reichstag* building on 13 January 1920 in defiance of a government ban (and without even consulting the KPD). This could only mean an attempt to intimidate the German parliament into abandoning the Factory Council Law, which was being discussed inside, and the USPD did not have the strength to enforce its threats. The security police opened fire with machine-guns, killing 42 people and wounding 105. The government declared a state of siege, and the USPD were forced into a condition of semi-legality for a month. The KPD naturally suffered as well, though it had had no part in the demonstration, and it charged the USPD left with 'weakness and lack of political judgement'.[91]

Another point of difference was the USPD's pacifism. The KPD line on foreign policy at this time was a kind of *politique du pire*: Germany was an oppressed nation, and a conflict between Germany and the West could only favour the revolutionary movement. The removal of the Hamburg group from the party had not entirely obliterated this way of thinking, which found expression in a refusal to accept the provisions of the Versailles Treaty. On 2 February 1920 the Western allies delivered to the German government a list of leading German 'war criminals' from Hindenburg downwards, who were to be handed over for trial. This request was refused, and the USPD condemned the SPD Chancellor, Gustav Bauer, for his failure to act against German war criminals. They advocated the 'sacrifice of a few individuals for the sake of peace'.[92] This view was not shared by the KPD, which felt that if the crisis got worse and rival national capitalists came to blows the workers could only gain. By advocating conciliation of the Entente, the Independents were 'betraying the revolution'. 'The USPD are bending their efforts to maintaining the Ebert government', said Thalheimer at the Third Party Congress, 'whereas it is clear that a Ludendorff government is a far more revolutionising fact than an Ebert–Bauer government.'[93] Ernst Meyer said that to concede the demand for the delivery of the 'war criminals' would merely 'strengthen foreign chauvinism and weaken fraternal parties in the Entente countries'. Moreover, it was 'the duty of party comrades to underline the treachery of the Right USPD and the failure of the Left USPD'.[94]

The Third Congress of the KPD(S), which met on 25 and 26

February 1920 in Karlsruhe and Durlach, emanated a general atmosphere of pessimism about the German situation. Meyer, who delivered the main political report, noted 'a lack of revolutionary will among the German workers', including a tendency to emigrate. Clara Zetkin denounced emigration as 'treachery to the revolution'. According to Fritz Heckert, the workers were weary 'and this is reflected in our party'.[95] Zetkin's was one of the few voices to hint at a favourable evolution of the crisis: 'the workers are exhausted at the moment; but the Promethean spark of revolution slumbers in the masses and our task is to blow it into a flame'. One consolation was that the 'left communists' were in no better condition: the evolution of Laufenberg and Wolffheim towards 'National Bolshevism' horrified many of their comrades and seemed to open a prospect that the opposition group would disintegrate. However, an application for re-entry to the KPD from the Bremen district organisation was rejected, on the ground that it had failed to break with the Hamburg National Bolsheviks.[96]

The final resolution of the Third Congress called on the German government to establish diplomatic and economic relations with Soviet Russia, warning nevertheless that 'if the capitalist countries continue to exist in the West the economic advantages of this will not fall to the popular masses . . . but be soaked up by the capital of the Western countries'. This was a hint that the slogan of alliance with Soviet Russia was not sufficient in itself for the KPD (as it was to be in future years). The main task, concluded the resolution, was 'to replace this government, which is only a figleaf for the Ludendorff clique'.[97]

The business report, read by Hugo Eberlein, was not encouraging. Most of the larger KPD districts had split off after Heidelberg. Those that remained had one thousand or two thousand members each, except for Chemnitz (16 000), Hanau (5000) and Stuttgart (5300). The loss of the left communists had halved the size of the KPD (it was now roughly 57 000 strong) and made it a sect, with little hope of affecting the course of events. It is true that the party's strength in Chemnitz and Stuttgart was unimpaired. But the western edge of Saxony and the urban enclaves of rural Württemberg were not the whole of Germany. The decisive events of the first crisis of Weimar democracy, around the Kapp putsch of March 1920, were played out rather in Berlin – where the KPD was now virtually non-existent – and on the Ruhr – where by Eberlein's admission 'all attempts to make contact had failed' in February 1920.[98] The majority of the Ruhr communists went over to the left opposition after the Heidelberg split. Only the groups in Hamborn and Dinslaken had stayed with the party.[99]

THE CRUSHING OF THE KAPP PUTSCH

The defence of the Weimar Republic against the Kapp putsch, the most militant action by the German working class in the whole Weimar epoch, and initially the most successful, was undertaken independently of the communist party. The detailed history of these days of March 1920 has been written by Erhard Lucas. His work largely confirms the impressionistic picture painted by Rosenberg's broad but sure brush 40 years before. The Kapp putsch split Germany into five sections: Bavaria was under the unchallenged rule of the right, elsewhere there was a varied spectrum ranging from the 'successful proletarian rising' in Rhineland–Westphalia, with the formation of the 'Red Army of the Ruhr' by USPD militants and the temporary defeat of the Reichswehr, to the Kappist heartland of East Prussia. In between came the SPD-dominated north and south-west of Germany, and the motley array of conflicting forces in Saxony and Thuringia.[100] The only area where the KPD provided the driving force in the anti-Kapp resistance was the Erzgebirge, around the city of Chemnitz.

Even so, it is of interest to see how it handled this situation, as the alternatives which came to the surface in 1920, such as isolation or cooperation with other socialist parties, defence of the bourgeois republic or advance towards proletarian dictatorship, 'workers' government' or Soviet republic, were of continuing significance. A deeply divided *Zentrale* confronted the Kapp putsch. Paul Levi, the figure of greatest authority in the party, was in prison at the time, having been arrested as part of the Bauer government's policy of harassment of the extreme left. In his absence a tendency to sectarianism came to the fore. On the worthlessness of the bourgeois republic there was universal agreement; and it was assumed by the *Zentrale* majority, led by Thalheimer, that the working class shared their views. A party circular of November 1919 clearly implied this:

After a year of existence the bourgeois republic has lost its
illusory youthful charm in the eyes of the proletarian masses
. . . The maintenance of the bourgeois republic, which the
Scheidemanns have inscribed on their banner, is precisely what
is impossible . . . The impending military coup d'état must be
opposed with a revolutionary offensive towards the communist
republic, the republic of Councils.[101]

Shortly before the putsch this circular was recommended as a
guide to action by the *Zentrale*, and it added 'a certain weariness
has taken hold of the workers in general. The possibilities for
action are very slight and . . . we must avoid actions which go
beyond our resources.'[102]

With this background, it is easy to understand the tone of the
KPD's proclamation of 14 March 1920 that the proletariat 'would
not lift a finger for the democratic republic', which was merely 'a
paltry mask for the dictatorship of the bourgeoisie'. It advised
against a general strike, on the ground that the workers were too
demoralised by recent defeats to respond to the call.[103] This was
an inadequate response for a revolutionary party to make, even
so, and a clear underestimate of the fighting capacity of the
German workers. They did not listen to this appeal to passivity; it
was clear by the end of that day that Kapp was coming up against
a well-nigh unanimous working-class resistance. Quickly the line
was changed; the next morning a KPD appeal to strike was on the
streets: 'For the general strike! Down with the military
dictatorship! Down with bourgeois democracy! All power to the
Workers' Councils!'[104] The KPD's original error arose out of its
lack of contact with the masses, especially in Berlin, where the
party headquarters was a group of officers without soldiers
(membership in Berlin had fallen from 12 000 to 800 as a result of
the Heidelberg split).[105]

Where the KPD was still a mass party after Heidelberg the
instructions of the *Zentrale* were simply ignored. The Chemnitz
district organisation, led by Heinrich Brandler, immediately
acted to set up Workers' Councils, arm the workers and arrest all
suspected Kappists in the city.[106] Here the USPD had always been
insignificant; the KPD faced its rival the SPD directly. The
Executive Council set up on 15 March to run the city consisted of
ten KPD members, nine SPD, one USPD and one Democrat.
According to Brandler it exercised authority over a radius of 50

km from the city, but was unable to link up with other parts of Saxony. In Dresden the SPD still had the leading position, and their constitutionalist path was hardly threatened by the local communists, who boycotted the resistance to Kapp under Otto Rühle's influence. Leipzig was a stronghold of the USPD, and initially responded strongly to the general strike call. But once Kapp had resigned, the USPD and SPD jointly appealed to the workers to hand in their weapons and go back to work. The Chemnitz SPD also demanded an end to the general strike on 18 March, and the communists, aware of their isolation, accepted this, though they made sure that the workers retained their arms.[107] At the same time, but quite independently of Brandler and against his wishes, an unconventional communist called Max Hölz was organising a guerrilla band in nearby Falkenstein. Hölz's men roamed through Saxony storming prisons and attacking army units, pillaging shops and robbing banks to feed themselves and the local poor.[108] This 'adventurism' was not to the taste of the KPD leaders, and Hölz's escapades were officially condemned at the Fourth Party Congress.[109]

On 17 March the idea of a 'purely socialist government', or 'workers' government', was advanced by Carl Legien, the chairman of the Free Trade Unions, as a way of preventing the return of the situation of creeping counter-revolution which had existed under the Bauer coalition government. The leftists in the KPD *Zentrale*, led by Paul Frölich, at first opposed any collaboration with the Social Democrats in support of such a government (at the *Zentrale* session of 21–22 March).[110] Only on 26 March 1920, rather too late to make any difference, was a declaration by the *Zentrale* published in *Die Rote Fahne* to the effect that the KPD would act as a 'loyal opposition' to a 'workers' government' if it could be formed.[111] By then the idea of a 'workers' government' had been abandoned by the SPD and the Free Trade Unions, partly because of the refusal of both Däumig (on the left of the USPD) and Crispien (on the right) to 'negotiate with traitors to the working class (i.e. the SPD leaders and Legien)'.[112] This left the road open for a simple return to the old order, which was of course the preferred solution of the SPD, as it would allow the workers to be disarmed and their weapons to be returned to their rightful owners, the *Reichswehr*, and legitimate constitutional authority to be re-established.

But first it was necessary to break the will of the militant proletarians of the Ruhr. The 'Red Army of the Ruhr' had grown up spontaneously in the fight against the *Reichswehr* during the Kapp putsch; now it decided to fight on against the restored SPD government and its military instrument General von Watter. The KPD had little influence here, but it threw what influence it had into the scales in favour of this hopeless struggle by one region of Germany against the might of the army.[113] The party appealed on 4 April for the general strike on the Ruhr to be extended to the rest of the *Reich*, but in vain.[114] The 'grenades and shrapnel of Watter and Müller' swept away the miners' resistance and the *Freikorps* men exacted a bloody revenge.[115]

The party failed miserably in March 1920. Everyone was aware of this, but there was no agreement on the precise nature of its mistakes and on the lessons to be drawn for the future. The Central Commission (ZA) had a leftist majority, and on 30 March it condemned the 'loyal opposition' declaration by twelve votes to eight as having an inevitably 'diversionary effect at a moment when the struggle was in full swing'.[116] The Fourth Party Congress (14–15 April 1920) was sharply divided on the issue. The majority of delegates were inclined to reject the idea of a 'purely socialist government'. Karl Eulert saw such a government as 'reactionary and anti-working class'; Edwin Hörnle said it would only have 'compromised the proletariat'; Clara Zetkin said it provided the Independents with an alibi for passivity; Ernst Meyer blamed the 'loyal opposition' declaration for destroying the workers' will to fight, not in Berlin (where the general strike had already ended on 25 March) but in the rest of the country.[117] There were equally powerful voices on the other side, however. Thalheimer defended the declaration as 'absolutely correct'. It was 'the maximum that could be got out of the struggle politically'. He had 'no illusions about the political role of a purely socialist government', its tendency to revert to an Ebert–Noske regime, but he saw USPD participation in it as destroying the illusions of the masses. Pieck, who was mainly responsible for the declaration, explained its background, and drew on the authority of Trotsky to suggest that this was similar to Bolshevik tactics in June 1917 in Russia when they called on the Menshevik and SR-dominated Soviets to take power into their own hands. Finally, Levi rose to justify the declaration as an orderly withdrawal in conditions of 'defeat and weakness', although he added that he would not have used the phrase 'loyal opposition' himself.[118]

Armed resistance and armed repression, March 1920

1   *A detachment of the 'Red Army of the Ruhr' (top)*

2   *Pro-Kapp troops firing on demonstrators in Berlin (bottom)*

The opponents of the declaration had a big majority at the Fourth Congress (37 to 6)[119] and they appeared to have support in Moscow too, since Radek published a fierce article claiming that the *Zentrale* had replaced the SPD's 'parliamentary cretinism' with a 'governmental cretinism' of its own.[120] Béla Kun, writing in the Vienna journal *Kommunismus*, described belief in a 'purely working-class government' consisting of socialists as a 'reactionary utopia'.[121]

However, a month later Lenin intervened, and with such effect that the debate on the 'loyal opposition' declaration was concluded in a sense favourable to Levi and his supporters. In an appendix to his famous pamphlet *Left Wing Communism: An Infantile Disorder*, Lenin asserted that the declaration of 26 March 1920 was 'quite correct both in its basic premise and its practical conclusions'. The basic premise was that 'at present there is no objective basis' for the dictatorship of the proletariat because the 'majority of the urban workers' support the Independents. Although he went on to criticise the way the declaration had been formulated, it was clear that he had come down on the side of the Levi *Zentrale*.[122] For the present the message was that the KPD must now address itself to the task of winning mass support.

THE CAMPAIGN TO WIN THE USPD FOR COMMUNISM

In 1920 the Spartacists had behind them the tradition of opposition to the First World War, the prestige attaching to their close association with the Bolshevik leaders, and the moral authority of being the main target of the persecutions of early 1919. But they did not have the ear of the masses. This fact was underlined by the Reichstag elections of 6 June 1920. The Fourth Congress had unanimously approved participation in these elections, although there was a continuing division of opinion on whether it was right to have boycotted the National Assembly elections of January 1919. Levi had worked out a conventional election platform full of 'positive demands to secure practical work in parliament' but the delegates struck these out and the KPD(S) went before the electorate with a flaming affirmation of its revolutionary commitment, reminding the voters that 'the elections could not in any case achieve the goal of the removal of capitalism' and that 'the decision will lie outside parliament. The purpose of participation [in the elections] is to bring home to the German proletariat what its task is. Arm the working class! Disarm the bourgeois military formations! Power to the Workers' Councils! Closest cooperation with Soviet Russia!'[123]

This brought in 442 000 votes and the election of two communists to the *Reichstag* (Clara Zetkin and Paul Levi). The KPD's 1.7 per cent contrasted with the USPD's 18.8 per cent and the SPD's 21.6 per cent. Outside Chemnitz (9.2 per cent) the party was still a sect. The true verdict of these elections was against the SPD and in favour of the USPD, whose newspaper summed up the results accurately enough in these words: 'Independent Social Democracy has become the party of the German working class in the centres of German industry.'[124] The KPD's future task was to ally the political steadiness and indubitably communist character of Spartacism with the access to the German workers possessed by the Independents without succumbing to their vagueness on key issues. The USPD was the political home of a large number of workers who could be won over to communism. But what was to be done with the rest of them, and especially the leaders? Communists had different views on this problem.

One line of approach, favoured by the more radical Spartacists, was to break up the USPD from within and to win over the left-wing elements in it as individuals. As Meyer said at the Fourth Congress, 'The Left USPD can only be driven into action with kicks', and he recommended the method 'used in Saxony': 'There we said: either you go with us or we lock you up.'[125] This ultimatist attitude was countered by Levi with the argument that 'the left wing of the USPD is not our enemy but emotionally and at heart on our side. The fight must be waged exclusively against the right wing.'[126]

Levi was therefore advocating a splitting of the USPD rather than a straight fusion between the two parties. In this he did not differ from the Comintern leaders. No one was so optimistic as to believe the whole USPD could be brought over. However, considerable tact was used to persuade the USPD as a whole to send a delegation to Moscow, representing both wings of the party, for direct negotiations. A Bolshevik emissary, Alexander Shliapnikov, reassured the USPD executive on 7 May that, notwithstanding the letter of 5 February, the ECCI did not regard the expulsion of particular right-wing leaders as a prerequisite for opening discussions on entry into the Comintern.[127] This did not of course mean that the Hilferdings and Kautskys would not be expelled later on or in the course of the negotiations. The KPD itself was less inclined than Shliapnikov to observe the amenities of diplomacy. On 17 June it decided to demand from the USPD both acceptance of the Conditions of Admission and 'proof of revolutionary inclinations in the shape of the expulsion of right-wing leaders'.[128] There was also that irritating gad-fly on the left, the recently-formed KAPD, to be dealt with. The KPD *Zentrale* was strongly opposed to the admission of this party to the Comintern, whether it accepted the Conditions or not, 'because there is no room in Germany for two communist parties'.[129] This rivalry was not felt so strongly by the ECCI, which on 2 June sent an open letter to the KAPD suggesting that it could be admitted to the Comintern provided certain of its leaders were expelled. Wolffheim and Laufenberg (the 'Hamburg tendency') were unwelcome because their 'National Bolshevism' led them into alliance with German Nationalists, while Otto Rühle (from Dresden) had made himself impossible by his rejection of the very idea of a political party.[130] But the KAPD also had to 'submit unconditionally to the decisions of the Second Congress of the Comintern' and these were likely to favour participation in trade unions and parliaments, hostility to which was the KAPD's main *raison d'être*.

The price of the USPD's admission to the Comintern was the abandonment of its distinctive but vague socialist rhetoric, exemplified in Dittmann's election manifesto of 20 April 1920, which endeavoured to combine an emphasis on the ballot box with 'the activity of the masses, who must continually work to influence the shaping of political conditions'.[131] Condition No. 1 would soon put a stop to this: 'All propaganda and agitation must be of a genuinely communist character . . . The dictatorship of the proletariat must be advocated.'[132] Lenin's 19 Conditions of Admission (which became 21 by the addition of two more at the Second Congress) were severe enough to imply an immediate split in all the non-communist parties which desired to enter the Comintern. Trotsky underlined the point: 'From this day on, from this Congress on, the split in the world working class will proceed with tenfold greater rapidity. Programme against programme; tactic against tactic; method against method.'[133] This applied as much to the USPD as it did to the French and Italian Socialist Parties.

Of the four delegates sent to the Second Congress by the USPD, Crispien and Dittmann opposed the Conditions, and Däumig and Walter Stoecker upheld them. The Conditions thus served to guarantee a split. But the Statutes, also adopted at the Second Congress, had an even greater significance for the future. The Statutes were the instrument by which international discipline was maintained, in other words the submission of the other parties to the decisions of the Russian-dominated ECCI (Executive Committee of the Communist International). The ECCI was raised to the position of 'directing body of the Comintern in the periods between its World Congresses'. Statute No. 8 secured Russian domination:

> The chief work of the ECCI falls on the party of that country where, by a decision of the World Congress, the Executive Committee has its seat. The party . . . shall have five representatives with full voting powers on the EC. The EC conducts the entire work of the Comintern from one congress to the next . . . and issues instructions binding on all parties and organisations belonging to the Cominterm.[134]

As Paul Levi reported back to his party in August, 'the ECCI conducts communist affairs between congresses and has been handed a tremendous amount of power'. He drew attention to the danger that 'setting excessively sharp conditions of an organisational kind would shift the struggle away from the *political* to the *organisational* sphere'.[135] Levi also criticised the decision to admit the KAPD delegates to the debates of the Congress. The Bolshevik reaction to these criticisms was to claim that the KPD *Zentrale* was becoming divided into a right and left faction, with Levi and Jakob Walcher acting as leaders of the right against Frölich and Meyer, seen as being on the left. Levi in particular was reproached for his excessive fear of putschism, which led him to advocate passivity, thereby destroying the revolutionary *élan* of the party. The association of the KAPD with the KPD would provide a counter-weight to Levi's rightist tendencies, it was suggested.[136] One may discern here the beginnings of the tension between Moscow and Paul Levi which resulted a few months later in his resignation and eventual abandonment of communism. At this stage, however, the attempt to drive a wedge between the 'rightist' leader of the party and his more left-inclined colleagues failed owing to the absence of a concrete issue over which factions in the party could line up.

With the end of the Second Comintern Congress and the return home of the German delegations from the USPD, KPD and KAPD (August 1920), the main question of the next few months was the fate of the USPD. Would it join the Comintern *en bloc*, accepting the 21 Conditions and ridding itself of a few right-wing leaders? Would it split, leaving a pro-communist minority to join the KPD? Or would the split favour the communists, compelling the non-communists to set up their own party on the ruins of the old one? This question was decided by the successful agitation of the Left USPD in party meetings up and down the country during September and October. The elections to the Party Congress resulted in victories for the supporters of affiliation to the Comintern in most of the larger regions, such as Berlin, Halle-Merseburg, Lower Rhine and Hamburg.[137] By the time the USPD Congress convened in Halle, on 12 October 1920, it was clear to everyone that the left would have a majority. When Zinoviev, the representative of the ECCI, disembarked in Germany he was met by Curt Geyer (Left USPD), who announced triumphantly: 'We have the majority.'[138] The oratorical duel between Zinoviev and Hilferding at Halle therefore had little impact on the outcome. Apparently no more than ten delegates changed their minds after listening to Zinoviev's long and eloquent speech.[139] By 237 votes to 156 the USPD Congress voted to accept the 21 Conditions and begin the process of fusion with the KPD(S). The defeated right took with them most of the apparatus, the press and 300 000 members; 400 000 stayed with the left USPD and two months later joined the communist party; the remainder (about 200 000) ceased to engage in political activity.

3 Forcing the Pace of Revolution

THE UNIFICATION CONGRESS

Seen from Moscow, the result of the Halle Congress was highly satisfying; but it contained an obvious danger. The sudden entry of hundreds of thousands of former Social Democrats into the party might tend to dilute it. Hence the ECCI continued to hanker after the inclusion of the 'genuine revolutionaries' of the KAPD as a ginger group within the larger body. On 25 October a letter was sent to 'the revolutionary workers of Germany', as assembled in the three parties of KPD, USPD (Left) and KAPD, calling on them to 'create a united party of German communists'.[1] The Fifth Congress of the KPD, held in November 1920, was also asked by Zinoviev (speaking for the ECCI) to 'show more toleration than hitherto to the KAPD . . . There are in the ranks of the KAPD good, serious, proletarian, revolutionary elements. We must at all costs attract them into our ranks and it is essential to meet them half way.'[2] Shortly afterwards (28 November) the ECCI admitted the KAPD to the Comintern as a 'sympathising party', though suggesting (not insisting) that its members join the official communist party and 'submit to international proletarian discipline'. In taking this course the ECCI was overriding the objections of the KPD, the USPD (Left) and the Bulgarian Communist Party.[3] It was clear from Levi's speech at the Fifth KPD Congress that he was more interested in attracting 'certain elements of the Right USPD' than the KAPD leftists, who should not be won back 'by abandonment of our principles'.[4] There was a clear division between the majority at the Fifth Congress (including Walter Stoecker, who appeared as a guest from the Left USPD) and the ECCI representative Shmit (Vasily Shmit, the Russian trade

54

unionist) who argued that the Bolsheviks had made the Russian Revolution jointly with the Anarchists.[5] This was convincingly rebutted by Thalheimer, who said that there was no reason why the KAPD 'Anarcho Syndicalists' should not help in the revolution, but they should do so from outside the party, just as the Anarchists had done in Russia.[6]

Thalheimer then went on to discuss the political situation, introducing a theme that was to be of great significance in determining the party's approach after the Unification Congress. 'Economic conditions in Germany are crying out for seizure of power by the proletariat', he said. The working class must 'steal a march on the counter revolution, it must entice it out of its nest and force it to fight . . . at the moment favourable to the working class.' He concluded with two slogans: 'Initiative! Revolutionary offensive!'[7] This was the first reference to the policy which was to result in the disastrous March Action of 1921. Hugo Urbahns (from Hamburg) underlined this by saying 'the subjective maturity of the proletariat is all that is missing. This maturity will not be brought about by educational work but by *action*. We must shake up the workers.'[8] Däumig added that the opportunity missed in July 1920 (when the advance of the Red Army on Warsaw failed to stimulate any uprising in solidarity in Germany) would not be missed again.[9]

Clearly Levi had managed to remove one putschist tendency only to see another emerging in its place. He ascribed Urbahns's argument to the fact that 'Hamburg is a relatively weak district'.[10] The final resolution passed by the Congress was couched in leftist terms: 'The task of the KPD is to exploit crises arising from the internal and international situation for revolutionary action.'[11]

The Sixth (or Unification) Congress took place in Berlin from 4 to 7 December 1920. Its task was to consummate the union between the Left USPD and the Spartacists, and it achieved this successfully. There was a certain amount of tension between the two groups, but the need for political unification prevented the implicit rivalry from coming into the open. Moreover, there is no evidence that the factional struggles which tore the KPD apart in later years had any connection with the disparate origins of the groups which went to make up the party. At the Unification Congress the former Independents allowed the much weaker KPD (there were 349 USPD delegates, 136 from the KPD) to be represented far beyond its numerical entitlement in the directing institutions of the new party, which was given the name United Communist Party of Germany (VKPD).[12] There were two chairmen, Ernst Däumig (from the USPD) and Paul Levi, and the VKPD *Zentrale* consisted of 8 former Independents and 6 former Spartacists.[13] The KPD representatives had the ideas, and the Marxist background, and they dominated the debates at the Unification Congress. As Ruth Fischer later wrote: 'They accepted the welcome but rough-hewn material from the USPD, which needed much polishing before it could be brought up to their high-class brand of Marxism.'[14] Of the 7 main speakers only 2 were from the USPD; and the party's theoretical journal, *Die Internationale*, continued to be dominated throughout 1921 by former Spartacists; a total of 3 out of the 67 signed articles published in that year were by former Independents. The Left USPD did, it is true, contain a number of intellectuals who later made their mark in the KPD, such as Arthur Rosenberg and Karl Korsch, but they had not yet risen to prominence. The people who came over to communism from the USPD in 1920 were largely working-class militants, veterans of the strike movement during the war, revolutionary shop stewards who had played a role in November 1918, and young workers who had fought against the Kapp putsch. They accepted the intellectual pre-eminence of the former Spartacists without jealousy.

The conflict between Levi and the leftists continued at the Unification Congress. His long opening speech unfolded a broad perspective of world economic crisis and a world revolution of which German events were only a part. But he stressed that the VKPD's task was 'one of unheard of magnitude and . . . difficulty.'[15] He replied to Fritz Rück's suggestion of a 'general uprising' with an uncanny anticipation of his criticism of the later March action: 'Every big action must at least be supported by the sympathy . . . of the proletarian masses, . . . and every action which begins without this moral support collapses before it has begun.'[16] But he had to contend with a general feeling that the conversion of the KPD into a mass party heralded the decisive struggle. Ernst Meyer said: 'The situation compels us to action, and the large numbers we now have give us a psychological awareness of our own strength.' Hans Weber, a leftist from the Palatinate, added, 'No more reflecting, considering . . . Enough of speech, we must act.' Arthur Rosenberg was the most explicit: 'The wave of revolution is moving towards Central Europe. Italy and Germany are ripe for the decisive struggle and we shall have to get ready for this . . . The unemployed can only be helped by the conquest of political power, dictatorship. . . . The final struggle for world revolution, that is our main task.'[17] Instead of an action programme, advancing specific demands, a 'Manifesto to the German and International Proletariat' was adopted, in which far-reaching concessions were made to the left's demands for action. The proletariat had been defeated in previous struggles, it said, because of the absence of a leading revolutionary party. Now there was one, the VKPD. 'A party whose organisation embraces hundreds of thousands . . . must recruit first and foremost by the deed, through action . . . The VKPD will be able to set off actions by the proletariat or put itself at the head of actions which have arisen spontaneously. Any of the situations of struggle that come about may grow into the struggle for power . . . Every partial struggle . . . can turn into a struggle for the whole thing.'[18] This manifesto was the work of Radek, the ECCI representative, who thus aligned himself with the left, and against Levi. Its formulations were a long way from Levi's own summary of the work of the Congress: 'The communists . . . must remember that they only constitute a fraction of the proletariat.'[19]

But Radek's attitude during the winter of 1920–21 was distinctly ambiguous. The constantly repeated theme of 'action' at any price, the assertion that 'the VKPD has sufficient strength to go over to action by itself where the events permit and demand'[20] was contradicted by a move towards a 'united front policy' (*avant la lettre*), for which Radek and Levi were jointly responsible. The 'open letter' of 8 January 1921 was a consistent continuation of Levi's tactics towards the USPD, and he prepared the way for it in an article in RF entitled 'Matters of Tactics'. The VKPD had certainly become a mass party by the fusion, he wrote, but 'this act by itself does not permit it to take sole command of the destinies of the German Revolution, without regard to other layers of the proletariat'. The masses would first have to be won over 'not only by propaganda but by bringing them into actions which allow them to grasp what is in their interest'.[21] Hence the open letter, addressed to the SPD, USPD, KAPD and the trade unions, proposed various campaigns to promote working-class objectives, all capable of being achieved within the capitalist framework, which the non-communist organisations were invited to support, but which the VKPD would go ahead with whatever the response.[22] Radek was entirely in agreement with Levi on the need for a broad appeal to all workers' organisations. The open letter may well have been his brainchild, at least he claimed authorship on two occasions.[23] He warmly defended the idea in the communist press.[24] But he was very much in a minority internationally. He was the open letter's sole defender at a session of the ECCI's Narrower Bureau on 21 February 1921. Zinoviev, Bukharin, Béla Kun and August Guralsky all opposed it, but were restrained by Lenin from issuing a formal condemnation. Instead the question of tactics was 'left open for discussion' as Zinoviev put it; a significant admission of divided counsels.[25] Nor was there unanimous support for the open letter from within the VKPD. When the ZA (Central Commission) of the party convened on 27 January the left faction (Ruth Fischer, Arkady Maslow and Ernst Friesland) described it as an 'opportunist move'.[26]

In so far as the open letter was addressed to organised bodies of proletarians it met with well-nigh universal rejection (the exception was the Syndicalist FAUD).[27] This was not unexpected. But the expected storm of indignation against treacherous leaders who refused to fight for working-class interests did not materialise either. The VKPD tried to push the movement forward by issuing an 'Appeal to the German proletariat' for the holding of mass meetings, to impose the open letter by pressure from below.[28] Meetings were held by metalworkers, railwaymen and miners, resolutions were passed, but the only immediate result was the expulsion of communists from the ADGB-affiliated trade unions. Heckert and Brandler were expelled from the Building Workers' Union, along with less prominent communists. The VKPD gained considerable sympathy from rank-and-file Social Democrats, but it was a long process to convert this sympathy into support. The ECCI was impatient for an immediate success; and by an unfortunate coincidence a series of unrelated events deprived the VKPD of Levi's leadership when it was most needed.

THE ITALIAN PROBLEM

The tension between Levi and the ECCI, which had been mounting since the Second Comintern Congress, reached breaking point shortly after the open letter was issued, over the apparently remote question of the split in the Italian Socialist Party (PSI). This had been one of the few socialist parties to enter the Comintern *en bloc* in 1919. But even then it was already deeply divided between the reformists under Filipo Turati and the main body of the party, which followed Giacinto Serrati in adopting a kind of verbal revolutionism without practical consequences. Subsequently a further division emerged, between a left wing, led by Amadeo Bordiga, which saw the main task as the creation of a purely communist party, and the Serratian centre, which sought to retain mass support by delaying the expulsion of the reformists until the rank-and-file could be split away from them.

The Comintern, while also wishing to retain a mass party in Italy, did not have inexhaustible patience. Serrati had accepted the 21 Conditions but seemed unwilling to apply them. Events in the autumn of 1920 made matters worse: the reformists were held responsible for the failure to exploit what seemed to be a revolutionary situation, and Serrati sent an unsatisfactory reply to an ECCI 'ultimatum' of August calling on him to 'cleanse the party'. Hence the ECCI's delegates to the PSI Congress held in Leghorn from 15 to 21 January 1921, Matyas Rákosi and Christo Kabakchiev, were instructed to make sure that the 21 Conditions were complied with and the reformists expelled. If Serrati did not accept this, he would have to go too. The divergence between the ECCI representatives and Levi on this issue seemed to be minute: he wanted 'to keep Serrati if possible' otherwise 'the masses would not be gained', whereas Kabakchiev was keen to attack Serrati from the outset. Both agreed that the 21 Conditions should be applied and the reformists expelled. Levi spoke in favour of this at the Congress itself, which he attended as a fraternal delegate from the German party: 'There are moments in the life of a party', he said, 'when it can no longer remain united, when paths separate.'[29] But how far to the right should the line between communists and non-communists be drawn? Was it advisable to exclude from the communist party not just Serrati but the mass of workers who followed him? In the event, the Italian Communist Party as constituted in 1921 consisted only of the Bordiga faction, with its 58 000 members. The 98 000 socialists who followed Serrati were left outside. Levi saw this as a proof that the ECCI representatives had displayed excessive rigidity, and he immediately published an article in *Die Rote Fahne* to that effect. He argued that but for Rákosi's ham-fistedness the successful merger of 1920 with the USPD could have been repeated in Italy.[30]

The real issue in this dispute was not the Italian party or Serrati but the behaviour of the ECCI emissaries, and, arising from that, the relationship of the member parties of the Third International to the Comintern leadership. The existence of the ECCI itself was not in dispute: in view of the impracticability of convening a world congress on every occasion when an important issue came up, there had to be some body with the authority to make decisions in the interval between congresses. That, at least, was the theory. In practice the ECCI representatives represented the prevailing opinion in the Bolshevik Party's Politburo, as interpreted at this stage by Zinoviev, with Radek his very able second, and specialist on Germany. But the German party's leadership was still self-confident enough in 1921 to question the decisions of the ECCI – and thereby the decisions of the Russians – not just on German affairs, but on any question affecting the communist movement as a whole. Levi took seriously the rhetoric of the Second Comintern Congress about the joint responsibility of all communist parties for each other. He saw Berlin as the centre not just of German but of Western European communism. The KPD was in his view specially qualified to give advice to other Western European parties, because it possessed an insight denied to the ECCI's Eastern European envoys (the 'Turkestanis'). But to criticise the ECCI was to criticise Moscow. This was intolerable. 'Needless to say, I have no blind allegiance to the ECCI', said Radek, 'but there is criticism and criticism.'[31] The Russian party could criticise other parties, but no one had the right to criticise the Russian party or the Comintern leadership, or, it seemed, its plenipotentiaries, least of all publicly. Levi was aware of this. 'Any attempt on our part to criticise mistakes will be interpreted only as opposition to the Comintern. This is not my intention at all', he said at the stormy *Zentrale* session of 28 January.[32]

Levi had no wish to criticise Soviet internal policy. Although he had his private reservations about this (inherited from Rosa Luxemburg) he was prepared to accept that people like Lenin and Trotsky could give useful advice on the way forward for the German Revolution. This is clear from his correspondence with Lenin. But commitment to the Comintern embraced more than just respect for leading Russian revolutionaries. It meant accepting dictation from the ECCI, and, even worse, the not particularly outstanding field agents it sent to Western Europe. Although Rákosi and Kun were invested with the full panoply of international communist authority, they remained members of a small Eastern European party which had just given a textbook example of how *not* to conduct a revolution. Levi had recently published a critical article attacking the Hungarian communists for taking power before the proletariat was ripe for this.[33] For him the Hungarian Revolution of 1919 was a putsch: the lesson to be drawn was not to repeat it elsewhere. For Rákosi and Kun (as also for Radek) the lesson was that Social Democrats could not be relied on, and that hard, pure communist parties with no Centrist admixture should be formed everywhere. Rákosi sought to impose this view in Italy, France, Czechoslovakia and wherever else necessary, through the authority of the Comintern rather than through political argument. Radek, with characteristic two-facedness, kept his doubts about Rákosi to himself and converted the issue at the earliest opportunity into one of discipline. He might have helped to avert the subsequent disastrous developments; but he preferred to please important people in the Russian Politburo like Zinoviev and Bukharin rather than allow his undoubted intelligence and sense of German realities to come into play.

Hence Radek responded to Levi's evaluation of the Leghorn split by insisting on an immediate session of the *Zentrale*, at which he attacked Levi in so personal a manner that he walked out: a written apology smoothed this over, but the issue remained and Radek's threat 'to draw the sword first, before you can attack us' remained hanging in the air.[34] At the *Zentrale* session of 28 January Radek tried to provoke Levi into open defiance, calling on him to express 'open, clear and unequivocal disagreement' which might 'bring the Executive to correct its errors'. Levi would not be drawn. Criticism, he said, 'would aggravate the malady instead of fostering the healing process . . . Not all illnesses require operations.'[35]

After this brief passage of arms the matter of Serrati was temporarily settled when Levi withdrew a resolution on the Italian question which called for 'renewed attempts to gather together the communist elements in Italy' and declared that 'no price would be too high to pay for the unity of Italy's communists,

with the exception of the price of the retention of the reformists
. . . within the party'.[36] Instead a compromise resolution drafted
by Radek and Clara Zetkin was adopted, referring to the
'Bordiga–Bombacci group' as the 'only communist party in
Italy',[37] but leaving the door open 'for a large part of the Serratian
workers to find their way to the communist party'.[38]

A week later the whole issue came up again. Rákosi arrived in
Berlin fresh from his Italian 'triumph' and told the Germans that
the resolution of 1 February was inadequate 'especially since Levi
has now publicly interpreted it in a Serratian sense.'[39] Thalheimer
and Stoecker took Rákosi's part and introduced a new, sharper
resolution attacking the 'Serratian group' as a whole not just for
failing to expel the reformists but for errors in the nationality,
trade union and agrarian questions. But Levi could still muster
enough support to have this rejected.

Thalheimer and Stoecker then exercised their undoubted
constitutional right to appeal from the *Zentrale* to the ZA, the
party's supreme body in the periods between congresses, and here
they were more successful. Rákosi presented a report in favour of
their resolution, explaining that 'a small, pure party is better than
a mass party' and adding 'this question is not only Italian. This
emerges from our negotiations with the French party, with the
Czechoslovak party . . . There are many people in the French
party who are undesirable.'[40] 'If this principle is applied in
France', countered Levi, 'it can be applied here. We also have
our opportunists. Friesland says I am one. But communism in
Germany will not survive the next split.'[41] Despite this appeal, the
ZA adopted the Thalheimer–Stoecker resolution by 28 votes to
23. Thereupon Levi, Däumig, Clara Zetkin, Otto Brass and
Adolf Hoffmann resigned from the *Zentrale*, on the ground that
they refused to take the responsibility for a policy of 'creating
purer parties by the method of mechanical splits'.[42] The meeting
then elected Brandler and Stoecker as joint chairmen and coopted Meyer, Frölich, Paul Wegmann, Hugo Eberlein and Max
Sievers.[43] The new *Zentrale* hastened to declare that there was no
disagreement of principle between it and those who had just
resigned. Why then had they voted for the Thalheimer–Stoecker
resolution? The answer was revealing: 'In order to show the
party's desire to cooperate loyally with the ECCI.'[44]

This was a decisive moment in the internal history of the KPD.
The new men in the leadership were less able to stand up to the

pressure exercised by the ECCI's representatives and less inclined to do so. Moreover, the loss of so many 'rightists' meant that the new *Zentrale* would lean more to the 'left'. The stage was set for the disastrous episode known later as the 'March Action'.

THE MARCH ACTION

The winter of 1920–1 was a very difficult period for the Soviet regime in Russia. These were the dying days of War Communism, with waves of working-class and peasant discontent beating up around the Bolsheviks, and fierce disputes within the party about how to overcome the evident crisis. Some people were inclined to see a successful German Revolution as a way of taking the pressure off Soviet Russia.[45] Béla Kun was sent to Berlin at the end of February with this message. He told Clara Zetkin on 8 March that Russia had to have the burden lifted from her shoulders by a movement in the West, and that the VKPD was now a strong enough party to undertake the task.[46] Lenin confirmed that this was the content of Kun's message a month later: 'The representative of the ECCI defended the foolish tactic, which was too much to the left, of taking "immediate action to help the Russians".'[47] Radek wrote on 14 March to the *Zentrale* in similar vein, outlining the background to the New Economic Policy, which was the way the Russians solved their problem without assistance from the European revolution, and adding 'spring and summer will be very hard. Help from abroad to raise confidence here is very necessary. The situation for you is clear . . . you must do everything to mobilise the party.' More cautious than Kun, he warned that 'one cannot mount actions suddenly and without preparation, like firing a pistol'.[48]

The German situation too was marked by a number of critical features in early 1921. It was not hard to build up a picture of imminent crisis. Curt Geyer did exactly this at the ECCI session of 22 February. Unemployment was rising again, he said, real wages had fallen, conflict between Germany and the Entente over reparations payments was imminent, the plebiscite over the future of Upper Silesia might well lead to armed conflict with Poland, and there was 'provocation of the workers by armed reactionaries especially in Bavaria'.[49] Even the moderate Geyer, who was later to join Levi in condemning the March Action, thought that 'the objective conditions for a decisive action are present'. This was an illusion. The 4 per cent level of unemployment by itself was not sufficient to stimulate action. The party's isolation had just been shown by the lack of response to the Open Letter; the crisis over reparations was just as likely to work in favour of the nationalists as the communists; Levi's slogan of 'Alliance with Soviet Russia' had fallen flat as a means of agitation; the conflict in Upper Silesia could do no more than add an extra element of confusion, since it was incumbent on the VKPD to tread the narrow path of proletarian internationalism and reject the nationalist blandishments of both Germans and Poles; the elections of 20 February to the Prussian Diet showed that the VKPD had gained the support of the majority of the working-class electorate in only one district – Halle–Merseburg.[50]

The 'crisis of March 1921' was therefore located in the offices of the ECCI in Moscow and in the VKPD leadership in Berlin rather than in Germany. Or, to be more precise, it arose out of the attempt to generalise critical events taking place in one German district – Halle–Merseburg – to the country as a whole. A critical situation had been developing for some time in the province of Prussian Saxony (i.e. Halle–Merseburg), in particular the mining district of Mansfeld. In February 1921 the employers had recruited a force of men from a detective agency to police the mines, but the mineworkers had been strong enough to throw them out. In March the attempt was renewed, this time officially. Otto Hörsing, the SPD governor of the province, announced on 17 March his intention to mount a police occupation of the industrial districts, including Mansfeld. The ostensible grounds were 'the constant thefts, sabotage and attacks on managers'.[51] The real reason was to disarm the workers, who had kept the weapons won during the Kapp putsch, and to bring an apparent 'no-go area' back under the control of the central government.

It seems that news of Hörsing's decision arrived at some point during a ZA session of 16–17 March 1921, originally summoned on the initiative of Béla Kun to discuss ways of mobilising the masses for revolutionary action. Everyone present at the meeting (except Heinrich Malzahn, representing the VKPD's trade union section) agreed that great working-class struggles were in the offing, irrespective of what happened in Prussian Saxony. Various arguments were advanced in justification of this view: the sanctions policy of the Entente, the plebiscite in Upper Silesia, the rejection of recent wage claims, the expulsion of communists from the factories (one might call this the argument from failure), the movement of agricultural workers in East Prussia. Previous struggles had failed, said Brandler, because of their isolated character. The nearest thing to a joint action by the German proletariat had been the fight against Kapp, which was a success. 'The state of affairs obliges us not just to wait passively but to intervene with political actions, to change things in our direction', he concluded, suggesting a number of eventualities in which the government might be overthrown: 'if it gets into an adventure in Upper Silesia [or] if Hörsing's decree is put into operation and our comrades in Central Germany take up the struggle'. If the latter event occurred, the VKPD 'would be compelled in the rest of the *Reich* to act in support of Central Germany, even before Easter'. Otherwise, the first day of the Easter holiday would be an appropriate moment to start the *Aktion*.[52] Frölich concurred, adding the significant words:

> What the *Zentrale* now proposes is a complete break with the past. Up till now we have been forced to adopt the tactic of letting things come to us, and making decisions once a situation of struggle had arisen. Now we say: we are so strong, and the situation is so pregnant with destiny that we must proceed to determine the fate of the party and the revolution ourselves.[53]

The leftists in the VKPD saw Hörsing's proclamation as a heaven-sent opportunity. It was unnecessary to provoke the enemy, as he had done the job for them. But in fact they had fallen into a trap. They started the March Action under conditions, and at a time, selected by the enemy, and with no idea whether they were attempting to establish a dictatorship of the proletariat, overthrow the Prussian government, mount a solidarity action with the Mansfeld miners, or merely prove to Moscow that the VKPD was a genuinely revolutionary party. On the evening of 17 March 1921 the *Zentrale* met to discuss the situation arising from Hörsing's 'provocation'. The majority supported Brandler's demand for action. Since the district of Halle–Merseburg was to be given the honour of leading off with a general strike its delegates were admitted to the meeting. But they advised caution, warning that a general strike would immediately

turn into an armed uprising in their district. Was this what the
Zentrale wanted? It seemed that it was: the next day the local KPD
paper the *Mansfelder Zeitung* called for a general strike in the area.
Guralsky, who was on the spot, had succeeded in persuading the
local party activists into this step.[54]

Meanwhile, in Berlin, the other two ECCI representatives, the
Hungarians Béla Kun and Josef Pogany, set to work to ensure
that the *Aktion* would begin without delay. The workers were
summoned to take up arms in *Die Rote Fahne* of 18 March, under
the banner headline 'Clear Answer!' The article was highly
inflammatory ('The law means nothing any more . . . Weapons
will decide the issue . . . Every worker should whistle at the law
and get himself a weapon wherever one is to be found.') and it
was reprinted the next day, the previous issue of the newspaper
having been confiscated by the Prussian authorities.[55] It was
written by Béla Kun himself, and further fiery proclamations
followed over the next few days, in which the necessity of armed
action was repeatedly stressed. Even so, nothing much happened
outside Mansfeld for several days: the *Zentrale*'s later claim that
the German workers reacted immediately to Hörsing's move, and
even outran the party's preparations, seems to have no
foundation. In fact, Eberlein had to be sent to Central Germany
on 22 March to promote a general strike by 'artificial methods'.
He endeavoured to get the workers in the mood for action by
organising sham kidnappings of local party leaders, by
dynamiting a munitions depot and by blowing up a workers'
cooperative society headquarters at Halle and blaming this onto
the reactionaries or the police.[56] Very little came of these plans,
mainly because of the unwillingness of the local party
functionaries to be drawn in. The most important result was
rather to discredit Eberlein and through him also the KPD, when
documents proving that Eberlein had actually made these
proposals fell into the hands of the SPD and were subsequently
published in *Vorwärts*.[56] Far more significant at the time was the
uprising of Max Hölz in the Mansfeld district. Hölz had already
raised the standard of communist revolt once, during the Kapp
putsch, in rather more favourable circumstances. Now he saw his
opportunity again. This remarkable man, who had no access to
the inner counsels of the VKPD, read in a newspaper that a
general strike had been declared in Central Germany,
immediately jumped on a train, and arrived early in the morning

of 22 March at the mining village of Kloster-Mansfeld, where he proceeded to organise the workers into fighting units, doing what the VKPD leaders advocated in theory but were unable to achieve in practice. His band of rebels, numbering about 2500, spent the time from 23 March to 1 April burning down public offices, plundering shops, robbing banks, dynamiting buildings and railway lines, and above all fighting the much more numerous *Sipo* forces (the Security Police, or 'Greens' as he calls them in his book).[57] The VKPD leaders were as suspicious of him as they had been in 1920, whereas the KAPD welcomed him as one of their own sort. While admitting this affinity, he continued to regard himself as an orthodox communist, despite his earlier expulsion from the KPD, and promptly applied for readmission after the March Action. After his release from prison in 1928 he went to Moscow, dying in exile in 1933 as a respected figure of German communism.

It was partly as a result of Hölz's activities that a general strike finally broke out, in Prussian Saxony, on 23 March.[58] At the same time there was a partial strike in Hamburg (by 10 000 dockers) and the KPD and KAPD together called for the extension of the general strike to cover the whole of the *Reich*, in solidarity with the workers of Central Germany and Hamburg (24 March).[59]

This appeal did not meet with a great response; one of the characteristic features of the March Action was the great unwillingness of the proletariat, whether communist or not, to obey the party's commands. In Berlin the movement was a complete fiasco;[60] in the Ruhr things went somewhat better at first, but even here the strike was limited to a few places and only lasted from 24 to 30 March. Heinrich Malzahn estimated the number of strikers at 200 000–220 000 over the whole of Germany, of whom 120 000 were already on strike in Central Germany before the general strike appeal came through.[61] Even in Central Germany there was a clear difference between the combativeness of the Mansfeld region and the 18 000 strong Leuna Works, and the passivity displayed by the city of Halle.[62]

So Central Germany and Hamburg stood alone, and they were soon brought to their knees by the overwhelming forces of the opponent. By 29 March most of the Hamburg docks were again in operation, and on 30 March a conference of leading party functionaries was called by the *Zentrale* to decide whether to call off the March Action. A pessimistic report was delivered by Franken, a communist trade unionist from the Ruhr, and he recommended that the hopeless struggle be brought to an end. Eberlein managed to persuade the majority of the *Zentrale* to keep the conflict going (against their better judgement) in the expectation of a movement among the agricultural workers of East Germany and a promised increase in the level of activity in Halle–Merseburg province.[63] This decision was then pushed through by Pieck and Heckert at a meeting of the party's trade union section (the *Reichsgewerkschaftszentrale*) over the fierce opposition of the trade unionists themselves. 'There is nothing left to do but heighten the action', explained Pieck.[64] Only on 1 April was a majority finally found within the VKPD *Zentrale* for calling off the general strike, in belated recognition that the March Action had been defeated.[65]

THE LOSS OF PAUL LEVI

While admitting the defeat, the leading group in the party drew the odd conclusion that the March Action had actually been a step forward, and they developed a whole theory out of this. As we have seen, there were hints even earlier, at the time of the Fifth Party Congress, that the proletariat could only act if it was galvanised by some bold stroke. 'Objectively' the economic situation called for revolution; 'subjectively' the proletariat was unready for it. The way forward, according to Thalheimer and Béla Kun, was the 'revolutionary offensive'. 'The VKPD has seized the revolutionary initiative, it has introduced a policy of *revolutionary offensive* . . . It is not there to put a brake on the masses, but to whip up their enthusiasm.'[66] This theory was intended to be of European rather than merely German significance.[67] The ECCI in Moscow did not do anything to oppose this new departure at the time; in fact it encouraged the KPD by its proclamation of 6 April: 'You have acted correctly! You have turned a new page in the history of the German working class. Arm for new struggles; examine your experiences in the struggle and learn from them.'[68]

Paul Levi, the party's former leader, disagreed strongly with this estimate. He was convinced that the *Zentrale*'s tactics in the March Action had been disastrous (and he was kept fully informed by dissident party members). When it became clear that

Karl Liebknecht

Rosa Luxemburg

Clara Zetkin

Paul Levi

Karl Radek

Heinrich Brandler

3   Five early leaders of the KPD and Karl Radek

the ZA supported the *Zentrale* over the March Action, and even proposed to 'hold fast to the line of the revolutionary offensive',[69] Levi decided on a fateful step: the publication of a pamphlet, entitled *Unser Weg*, publicly exposing the background of the KPD's decision to engage in the March Action. In *Unser Weg* Levi denounced the *Zentrale* with all the oratorical power and biting wit at his command. He submitted the text of the pamphlet to Clara Zetkin, before sending it to the press. Although she described it as 'absolutely excellent' she went through it with a blue pencil toning down or excising the most wounding passages, especially those of 'international' significance, e.g. the attack on the ECCI's representative in Germany, not named by Levi, but described as the 'Turkestani' and thus clearly enough identified for those who recognised the reference.[70] Zetkin, with her innate party-mindedness, was far more able than Levi to distinguish between what was, and was not, acceptable in Moscow, even though on the actual issue (and all previous disputes too) she stood with him.

One may either view it as a tragedy that a man of Levi's calibre should have been lost to the communist movement by his inability to follow the path of quiet negotiations behind the scenes with the top people in the International; or one may see in this an inevitable development, symptomatic of the *true* relation between the headquarters of the Communist International and the International's constituent sections. In the latter case the meaning of these events is simply that no person of independent judgement could survive in the communist movement. In favour of the first view is the point that Levi himself tried to follow the course of a private appeal, by writing on 27 March to Lenin himself.[71] But he was too impatient: before Lenin had had a chance to reply (essentially in his favour), before the whole policy of the revolutionary offensive had been disavowed at the Third Comintern Congress, Levi issued his destructive pamphlet (12 April 1921).[72]

The argument of *Unser Weg* was that the party had allowed itself to be dragged into an Anarchist adventure, 'the greatest Bakuninist putsch of history so far'.[73] After describing, with copious examples, the way the party had advanced purely propagandistic slogans, with no real content, along 'Berlin' (or 'Fischerite') lines in the weeks after Levi and his supporters resigned, he went on to document the abrupt change from complete passivity to pure putschism, and to show how this was caused not by any change in the concrete German situation such as a Lenin might have picked out (here Levi includes an analysis of Lenin's arguments for seizing power in 1917), but by the arrival of an emissary from Moscow.[74] The acting leader of the party, Heinrich Brandler, far from opposing the demand for action, defended it by talking nonsense 'for which he deserved to be sent to a lunatic asylum'.[75] The action itself arose not from Brandler but from 'a single brain, which hasn't the slightest understanding of German conditions' – he did not mention Béla Kun by name – and, even after the action's failure was obvious, it was continued 'by people who sent their own flesh and blood to die for a cause they recognised was lost, so as not to endanger their position in the *Zentrale*'. Levi demanded that such people should 'never publicly go before German workers again'. Here he had in mind Hugo Eberlein, who as military expert was responsible for the measures of provocation which disfigured the March Action. 'Anyone who believes that he can drive the workers into action with dynamite or beatings has no place in a communist party.' Failing severe chastisement of the putschists, Levi predicted, the KPD would collapse into an insignificant sect within three months. He was wrong. But his final and most controversial point was the most penetrating of all, and in retrospect perfectly accurate. 'The ECCI bears at least part of the blame for this catastrophe.'[76] As a result of its isolation from Western Europe it had adopted the method of despatching confidential emissaries to the West. These people were not of top quality – the best cadres were urgently needed at home – but second-raters, 'miniature statesmen, of whom one has the impression that they want to show off their brilliance . . . I wish the Turkestanis no evil, but they . . . would do less harm if they tried their tricks in Turkestan.' (It was an open secret that Béla Kun had been sent to Turkestan in disgrace by Lenin for the indiscriminate slaughter he ordered in the Crimea after the defeat of Baron Wrangel's White Guard army in November 1920.)[77] Kun and the other Comintern emissaries not only influenced the policy of the non-Russian communist parties, but served as a channel of direct and secret communication with Moscow, bypassing the national party leaderships and undermining mutual confidence between them and the ECCI. 'The ECCI works like a Cheka projected beyond the Russian boundary: an impossible situation.' Though what Levi said was true, the logic of his argument led away from the Communist International. If he rejected the intervention of the ECCI he was rejecting the international discipline which was supposed to distinguish the Third from the Second International. Moreover, the whole tone of *Unser Weg*, with its references to 'Turkestan' and 'a Cheka' was liable to give offence to the Russians.

Levi was immediately expelled from the party by the Zentrale (15 April) for 'giving open support to the enemy', a decision upheld by the ZA on 4 May by 38 votes to 7. 'The road of Levi leads towards the USPD', predicted Ernst Meyer (correctly, but where else could he go?). Maslow described him as 'the German Serrati'.[78] Friesland 'regretted that Levi was only expelled for breaking discipline: a whole *Weltanschauung* divides us from him'.[79]

Despite the strong support at the top for Levi's expulsion, one may distinguish two different views on the question. Maslow and Fischer, on the left, were delighted at the removal of such a leading 'rightist'. Then there was the 'loyal majority', people like Meyer, Pieck, Brandler and Walcher who despite their doubts about the March Action had already made their decision on grounds of international discipline. According to Pieck, 'the worst thing of all is this: Levi has sown distrust of the representatives of the ECCI'.[80] Loyalists of this stripe were to constitute the leading group in the KPD for the next few years, carrying out a policy approved by the Comintern but diametrically opposed to a 'revolutionary offensive', until the crisis of 1923.

The coalition against Levi and 'Levitism' in the KPD was thus made up of different elements, and it might have been possible to split it. Between the left and the Levites there could be no compromise; Eberlein too, though not identified with the left faction, was rendered unacceptable by his close practical involvement in the March Action. Those who opposed Levi for reasons of party discipline could perhaps be brought round, since no difference of principle separated them from him. But the Comintern's stress on discipline, and its horror at Levi's deliberate revelation of these delicate disputes, made a compromise impossible. His expulsion was confirmed in turn by the ECCI (29 April) and by the Third Comintern Congress which met in the summer of 1921. He was only prepared to return to the party on his own terms. The KPD, he said, would first have to be cleansed by a public discussion of the issues involved in the March Action. 'If there is something to be learned . . . the necessary condition for this is that the masses know and discuss the mistakes as freely and publicly as possible.'[81]

Although united in rejecting Levi's criticisms, the left and centre of the KPD differed deeply on most other issues. It is at this point, in the early part of 1921, that one may locate the crystallisation of the ultra-left tendency which was henceforth to be a constant theme in party history. An 'ultra-left temptation' is inherent in the situation of any communist party. A communist party by its nature is committed to revolution; revolution is not conceived of in any other way than as a violent overthrow of the capitalist state during which the non-communist parties inevitably become enemies because there are only two sides to a barricade. With revolution about to break out, anyone who supported any other tactic was *ipso facto* an opportunist. This simplified view of the world appeared to the left communists who set up the KAPD in 1920 to justify the rejection of trade unions and parliaments; now the VKPD leftists used it to rule out any cooperation with the Social Democrats on the lines of the open letter of January 1921. Despite the fact that the party left's strongholds were the cities of Berlin and Hamburg, with their strong concentration of non-communist proletarians, the leftists were able to ignore the embarrassing fact that the influence of the KPD on non-communist workers was non-existent. The pathetic failure of Berlin during the March Action (and the refusal of more than a small section of the Hamburg proletariat to follow the party's lead) demonstrated the VKPD's lack of influence clearly enough. Arkady Maslow and Ruth Fischer were the leaders of the ultra-left faction, along with Ernst Friesland; other figures of considerable importance later on, who already appear in the Berlin Left in 1921, were Artur Rosenberg and Ottomar Geschke. In Hamburg there were the contrasting personalities of Hugo Urbahns and Ernst Thälmann. Socially the ultra-left was a mixture of proletarians and intellectuals; but one thing they did have in common, which may help to explain their attitude negatively: none of them had been educated in the early Spartacist tradition. Either they came from outside Germany (Ruth Fischer from Austria, Maslow from Russia, Friesland too was in Russia until the end of 1918) or they entered the VKPD in 1920 after passing through the Left USPD (this does not apply to Geschke or Urbahns). Hence their lack of sympathy for the task assigned to the communist movement by Rosa Luxemburg: 'It must work forward in a consistent direction between twin dangers: between abandoning its mass character and abandoning the final goal, between relapsing into a sect and turning into a bourgeois reform movement, between Anarchism and opportunism.'[82]

4 The Reflux of Revolution

THE EMERGENCE OF THE UNITED FRONT POLICY

The ultra left and the VKPD majority were not able for long to bask in the sunshine of the ECCI's approval. The change in attitude was indicated by Karl Radek – often the bell-wether of Comintern tactical turns – in an article of 10 May 1921, in which he criticised the VKPD *Zentrale* for speaking of an 'offensive' when the March Action was really a 'defensive offensive'.[1] This argument opened the way to the compromise formulation of the Third Comintern Congress: 'The March Action was not an offensive but a response to Hörsing's police provocation.' According to Trotsky this decision was not arrived at without severe disagreements within the Russian Politburo.[2] The German left and its 'theory of the offensive' was upheld by Zinoviev and Bukharin and opposed by Lenin, Trotsky and Kamenev. The Russian delegation to the Third Congress was similarly divided, and only preserved its public unanimity thanks to a compromise resolution. Lenin was keen to bury the theory of the offensive quickly, and he exposed his objections in detail to Zinoviev on 10 June:

> It is stupid and harmful to write that the period of propaganda has gone by and the period of action has begun . . . It is necessary to fight unceasingly and systematically to win *the majority of the working class*, at the outset *within the old trade unions* . . . All those who have not understood that the tactic of the Open Letter is obligatory must be *expelled* from the International within a month. I see clearly that it was a mistake on my part to have agreed to the admission of the KAPD. This must be corrected as rapidly as possible.

The March Action had not been a putsch, Lenin continued, but a 'heroic defence by the revolutionary workers'. Due proportion had to be maintained, however: the figure of one million participants advanced by 'optimists' like Brandler was far too high. Only 100 000 workers had taken part. Levi had committed a 'grave error' by describing the March Action as a putsch. He should be punished by temporary suspension from the party, with a chance of re-entry after six months. 'But politically', added Lenin, 'Levi is right as against the *Zentrale* on many points.'[3]

The background to this change of tactics by the Comintern leaders was the simultaneous change in the overall economic and political conjuncture. Whereas in 1919 and 1920 the capitalist world had been in the throes of economic crisis, 1921 saw a gradual stabilisation. Trotsky was one of the first Bolshevik leaders to admit this, and his views carried great weight at the time. 'The situation is no longer as it was', he said in June. 'Now we see and feel that we are not so immediately close to the goal, the conquest of power, the world revolution. In 1919 we said it was a question of months, and now we say it is a question perhaps of years.'[4]

The VKPD sent a large delegation to Moscow for the Third Comintern Congress, which took place in June and July 1921. Lenin received a number of the German communists privately, along with Béla Kun. He made no secret of his scorn for the arguments in favour of the theory of the offensive. The VKPD was compelled to withdraw its theses on the March Action. It could take some comfort from Zinoviev's back-handed compliment that 'on the whole it had nothing to be ashamed of'[5] and Radek's statement that the March Action, with all its errors, was 'a step forward' because the party 'has shown the will to struggle and come out of it hardened and steeled'.[6]

The Third Comintern Congress was the scene of impassioned public debate between the different German factions – the KAPD representative, who naturally attacked everyone else, Heckert for the KPD majority, Zetkin for the minority, Ernst Thälmann for the KPD left. Heckert boldly defended his faction against Lenin's attacks, accusing him of elementary misunderstandings in a manner quite unthinkable in subsequent years.[7] He blamed the errors of March not on the *Zentrale* but on 'deliberate sabotage by the elements who represent the opposition at this Congress'.[8] The clearest statement from the left was Thälmann's: he described the March Action as an expression of 'the revolutionary impatience of the masses'.[9]

Trotsky replied that the Russian delegation's 'Theses on Tactics' 'contained the maximum of concessions to the tendency represented here by many comrades, including Thälmann'. He directly rebutted the analysis of the overall situation given by the VKPD majority, saying that, far from driving towards crisis, 'the international situation was moving in the direction of a compromise' before the March Action. Moreover, if the Action were to be repeated 'it might actually ruin this splendid party. The philosophy of the offensive is the greatest political danger . . . and in its practical application the greatest political crime.'[10] The very large left faction at the Congress of 1921, led by the VKPD, was unrepentant. Five parties made a declaration accepting the Theses on Tactics 'in principle' but contesting Trotsky's interpretation of them. He was thus clearly identified as the chief Russian opponent of the left.[11] But behind Trotsky stood Lenin, and with his support the compromise of the Third Congress was forced through. The accent was now to be placed on the need to secure mass support.

The decisions of the Third Comintern Congress had several important consequences for the German communists. First, there was the definitive removal of the KAPD from the scene. The ECCI's toleration of that party was now at an end: it issued an ultimatum giving it the choice of merging with the VKPD within three months, or being expelled from the International.[12] The KAPD preferred the second alternative. Second, there was the renewed move towards a policy of 'united front'. The slogan itself was not launched until December 1921, but the policy was implicit in the decisions of the Third Congress, and in the open letter of January 1921, now described by Lenin as 'perfectly correct tactics'.[13] Paradoxically, this was exactly what Levi had fought for, and continued to advocate outside the party in his journal *Unser Weg*.[14] But now it would be applied without him. The conditions set by the ECCI for his return were harsh, involving cessation of all organisational activity, folding up *Unser Weg*, and six months of 'good conduct and celebration of Bolshevik omniscience', as he put it in a letter to a friend.[15] He might have been prepared to agree to this earlier in the year; but by August 1921 he had come to consider that the Communist International was dominated by people he termed 'semi-Anarchists'. He concluded 'In Germany Lenin is . . . the grey theory, Béla Kun the practice of the Comintern.'

Actually Levi was quite wrong here. The so-called left majority
of the VKPD were concerned mainly to save face when they
insisted on a positive evaluation of the March Action: the policy
subsequently pursued by Meyer, Brandler and the rest showed
that they too had learned the lesson of March, perhaps too well.
Only the ultra-leftists around Fischer and Maslow were for a
continuation of the old policy. They had support in Moscow from
Radek, who warned the party against the 'dangers of
opportunism' in a letter to the Jena Congress of the KPD[16] and
sent an article to RF[17] attacking Clara Zetkin. It was in these
personal terms that the struggle within the KPD was conducted; it
could not be otherwise, since all sides were committed to
implementing the tactics laid down by the Third Comintern
Congress, and could therefore have no differences of principle.
Hence the refusal of the ZA by a majority of one vote to allow the
election of Zetkin and Malzahn to the *Zentrale* (4 August) did not
mean that the 'Moscow compromise' had been abandoned. The
intervention of Lenin [18] and the ECCI[19] in separate letters to the
Jena Congress was sufficient to bring about the adoption of a
united front programme. Levi was unable to imagine that this
change of heart was genuine.[20] It was made less convincing than it
might have been by the insistence of the dominant faction in the
KPD on pursuing its personal vendettas.[21] But the election of
Ernst Meyer as party chairman was to prove a solid guarantee
that the united front tactic would be vigorously prosecuted.

The meaning of this for Germany is indicated by the Jena
Congress's manifesto. It called for (1) the confiscation of the
possessions of the old princely dynasties, (2) the control of
production by factory committees, (3) the transfer to the
capitalists of the burden of reparations payments, and (4) a
genuine dissolution and disarming of all the illegal fighting
organisations of the bourgeoisie (e.g. *Orgesch, Einwohnerwehren,
Stahlhelm*) and the formation of self-defence forces of industrial
workers, employees and agricultural workers.[22]

On this basis the KPD hoped to achieve a united front with the
Social Democrats. A further impulse was provided by the
assassination of Matthias Erzberger (26 August), which brought
home to all democrats and socialists the danger presented by the
right-wing military organisations; in addition, the elections of
September 1921 to the Thuringian Diet gave the workers' parties
(i.e. SPD, USPD and KPD) an overall majority and therefore
raised in a new form the old (pre-1914) problem of parliamentary

coalitions. In October the KPD put forward a four-point programme which stuck close to the SPD-dominated trade unions' demands, calling in particular for the 'taking over of tangible assets' [*Erfassung der Sachwerte*], which implied bringing under state control all those real, as opposed to nominal objects of value unaffected by inflation, including shares, land and industrial plant. The official trade union version was unsurprisingly more moderate, involving 'the transfer to the *Reich* of 25 per cent of share capital'; the KPD in contrast advocated 'the taking over of assets with a gold value [*Goldwerte*], i.e. the confiscation of a part of capitalist property to the benefit of the state'.[23]

This suggestion had been made once already by the KPD *Zentrale*, at the Jena Congress, but the party's ultra-leftists had convinced the majority of the delegates that it was a 'state-capitalist slogan' unworthy of communists. The fact that it could now be put forward officially and made the basis of a united front campaign was some indication of the distance travelled by the party since August, under the leadership of Meyer and Friesland.

However, at this juncture a dispute broke out again with the ECCI. The real issue was the right of the KPD leadership to conduct its policy independently, and in particular to be free from the interference of the representatives of the ECCI on the spot, who continued to bypass the proper chain of command. The problem was the same as in February and March. Then it was Kun; now it was Felix Wolf (Nicolas Krebs). Karl Radek supported him in the background with menacing public missives to *Die Rote Fahne*. The decision on relations with the ECCI had already been taken in effect in February 1921 when Levi, Zetkin and others lost the vital vote and resigned from the *Zentrale*. Levi had not come back, of course; those who, like Zetkin, had returned, by that very fact resigned themselves to accepting the ECCI's dictation. Accordingly, the crisis of December 1921 was a crisis over Ernst Friesland rather than a general crisis of the party. No one else in the top leadership was prepared to join him: and at the decisive session of the *Polbüro*[24] on 12 December five potential supporters of Friesland explained that they could not adopt a position which would be construed as an attack on the ECCI.[25] In the last analysis, then, it was loyalty to the International which prevented the KPD from insisting on its right to judge the issues independently.

It was therefore the ECCI, not the KPD, which made it impossible for the united front to be extended to allow cooperation with Levi's splinter group the *Kommunistische Arbeitsgemeinschaft* (KAG) and ultimately fusion with it; it was the ECCI which prevented a thorough purging of the sins of March 1921 and above all the removal of Hugo Eberlein, a man deeply and publicly compromised now that the so-called *Vorwärts* revelations had come out.[26]

On 20 December 1921 Friesland sent out an 'appeal to members of the party' against 'the pernicious influence exerted by certain members of the ECCI'. It was signed by 128 functionaries; in addition, 74 party members demanded the resignation of those responsible for the March provocations. Things were now too hot for Eberlein, who was compelled to take refuge temporarily in Moscow, and he never subsequently played a leading role in the party. But that was all that was achieved. Friesland was expelled (27 December), joined the KAG, and the crisis died down. As Thalheimer said, though putting it rather too strongly, 'this was the departure of leaders without followers'.[27] The people who left with Friesland were of a particular kind: they were trade union leaders formerly in the Left USPD, who had joined the KPD in 1920: Richard Müller and Paul Wegmann (former Revolutionary Shop Stewards during the November Revolution), Paul Neumann, Heinrich Malzahn and Fritz Winguth (all in the Metalworkers' Union) and Otto Brass. The major part of the *Reichsgewerkschaftszentrale* (i.e. the central trade union headquarters of the KPD) departed with Friesland.[28]

ERNST MEYER AND THE HEYDAY OF THE UNITED FRONT

The loss of the 'right' might have meant an increase in the influence of the 'left': this fear certainly existed among the KPD majority. But nothing of the kind happened, for several reasons: perhaps the fundamental one was the recovery (admittedly only temporary) of the German economy. Unemployment continued to decline; productive activity continued to pick up; whatever Radek might say, Levi was right about this in 1922. Varga's reports in the international communist press (he was already the Comintern's official economic analyst) confirmed the recovery. 'The general picture of the German economy from a purely business standpoint is very favourable.'[29] The situation was not one of acute crisis, even if it could be claimed that a collapse was just round the corner. Politically and internationally 1922 was the heyday of 'fulfilment' as conducted by the Chancellor Josef Wirth and his Foreign Minister Walter Rathenau, economically it was a period of capitalist offensive, with rapid inflation giving rise to a progressive fall in real wages, and increasing attacks by the employers on the eight-hour day; the situation cried out for patient day-to-day work by the party to win the working class on the basis of a minimum programme of the defence of living standards and working conditions. Against these facts the ultra-left could make no headway. The 'united front' was appropriate to the epoch. A second vital factor was Lenin's decision to throw the weight of his influence against Maslow. In his letter of 14 August 1921 to the Jena Congress he recommended that Maslow be 'sent to Russia for a year or two to be transformed by useful labour'.[30] The KPD refused to exile him in this way, but Lenin's attitude had been made clear enough. Thirdly, the strength of the ultra-left appeared greater than it was in reality because it was highly localised: at this stage the ultra-leftists controlled only Berlin–Brandenburg district (Fischer, Maslow, Rosenberg) and the *Wasserkante*, i.e. in effect Hamburg (Urbahns, Thälmann). The Hamburg communists seemed especially subject to the temptations of ultra-leftism because they were permanently and hopelessly in a minority within the local working class. Finally, the majority leadership of the KPD showed unexpected backbone in pushing through their conception of the united front in the face of accusations of opportunism. Ernst Meyer in particular successfully stamped on the intrigues of August Guralski, yet another of the ECCI's emissaries.[31]

However all these factors were only of temporary significance. The limits of united front activities were always narrowly circumscribed in the minds of the leading Russians. The united front, it was explained 'did not signify a compromise among socialist parties . . . but a gathering together of the working class for the struggle for its most immediate interests . . . and when the KPD becomes the leading factor in it this must grow into a struggle for power.'[32] Hence the campaigns were supposed to show results, not in terms of success for the agitation, but in terms of an accretion of communist influence. The united front was pursued during 1922 on two levels, one could say: at the level of the working-class movement and at the level of national politics. Within the working-class context there were some successes to show by the end of 1922.

First, there was the rebirth of a Factory Council movement, outside the framework of the legally recognised Factory Councils.[33] In November 1922 a *Reich* Congress of Factory Councils brought together 846 delegates, 657 of whom were communists. The fact that almost 200 non-communists were present was remarkable, in view of the ADGB threat to expel anyone who took part.[34] Another way of breaking into the non-communist sections of the working class was to set up Control Committees (*Kontrollausschüsse*) to try to control prices locally and fight against speculation. By July 1923 there were 800 of them, but they were subsequently made illegal, and did not survive. There were Committees of Unemployed too, which gained importance in the second half of 1923 when unemployment began to increase dramatically. The united front also meant united action within strikes, such as the February 1922 railway workers' strike in defence of the right to strike denied them as state officials, supported by the KPD alone, and continued by large numbers of non-communist workers in defiance of their own organisations; then there was the Metalworkers' strike in South Germany (March to May 1922). All these varied activities strengthened the influence of the KPD, so that by the time of Eleventh Congress of the ADGB, held in June 1922, they were able to secure more than one eighth of the delegates – 90 out of 691 – although the USPD had 132, which brings the KPD's 'success' back into proportion, when one recalls that this was the rump USPD left behind after the majority had gone over to the communists in 1920. Still, this was the high-water mark of communist influence in the Free Trade Unions during the Weimar Republic. The previous ADGB Congress had had only seven KPD delegates. Moreover, this degree of representation may have reflected a much higher level of communist support within the membership, if we are to go by the elections for the Berlin Metalworkers, at which the KPD got 30 000 and the USPD 31 000 votes, and the USPD filled the delegation with its own people rather than in proportion to the voting figures.[35] August Enderle in fact claimed that 'the real influence of the communists extended to at least a third of the membership'.[36] The success of the party in the *economic* forms of the united front was impressive enough for even Ruth Fischer to write 'this tactic brought complete success'.[37]

But there was also the overall political aspect to consider, and here the picture was grim. Walter Rathenau was the architect of the 'policy of fulfilment of the Versailles Treaty' which the Wirth government had been pursuing for a year to the disgust of the extreme right. On 24 June 1922 he was murdered by members of the 'Organisation Consul' a nationalist gang of ex-army officers. This murder set off mass demonstrations all over Germany against the monarchist reaction and for the republic. Here was an obvious case for the application of the proletarian united front in the field of national politics. The problem was that the defence of the republic was no longer the defence of the achievements of the November Revolution: all that was left of November was a bourgeois republic; hence the KPD was in danger either of committing itself to demands that did not go far enough, or outrunning the development of events and scaring off the socialist parties. The SPD demanded on 27 June that the KPD should undertake not 'to attack the democratic republic in acts, words, or in writing'. The KPD refused, and the SPD politicians were only induced to remain in the meeting by the pleas of the trade union representatives.[38] By the Berlin Agreement of 27 June 1922, the working-class parties and the main trade union associations (KPD, SPD, USPD, ADGB and AfA – the Salaried Employees' Union, *Allgemeiner freier Angestelltenbund*), agreed to work in any way they could for the defence of the republic, a purge of monarchists from the army, the police and the courts, the dissolution of all anti-republican armed groups, and a political amnesty. A joint appeal to the German working class was issued to that effect. The response was tremendous, culminating in a massive demonstration on 4 July, and clashes with the police: these developments were not to the taste of the SPD, which broke off relations with the KPD (8 July) and went over to a purely parliamentary effort, negotiating with the German People's Party, a largely monarchist group, over a 'Law for the Defence of the Republic'. Inadequate though the proposed law was, it was made much worse by the bourgeois majority in the German parliament, who converted it into a law against communism rather than right-wing terrorism. The KPD was finally forced to join the extreme right in voting against the bill (18 July) while the

SPD and USPD voted in favour. One of the first measures taken
by the government when the bill became law was to prohibit RF
for three weeks.[39]

The Rathenau campaign was a disaster for the KPD. As
Wilhelm Koenen write in *Inprekorr*, 'it ended in the most
miserable and shameful way imaginable: what could have led to
the conquest of positions of power for the workers has now at the
end brought only a strengthening of bourgeois power.'[40] But it did
have one positive aspect: it marked the beginning of the
movement of Proletarian Hundreds (*Hundertschaften*), the first
attempt to solve the military problems facing the workers on a
mass basis rather than through conspiratorial organisation. But
this was not apparent at the time. For the present, and certainly
as an example of the united front tactic, the Rathenau campaign
was a miserable failure. According to Pieck 'the party had
insufficient strength to bring the masses to undertake any serious
action for its demands against the will of the Social Democratic
party and trade union leaders'.[41] Between 8 July, when the ECCI
sent an official letter rejecting the Fischer–Maslow criticisms of
the campaign as 'hysterical' and stating that the KPD's line was
'completely correct',[42] and 18 July, when Zinoviev sent a highly
critical letter to the German party,[43] the failure had become clear
to Moscow. Zinoviev accused the KPD of feebleness, or failing to
conduct an agitation independent of the SPD, and of
overstressing the defence of the republic at the expense of the
proletariat's class interests. At this point, therefore, the chairman
of the ECCI was inclined to agree with the criticisms made by the
German left, and the clear consequence was pressure exerted by
the ECCI upon Meyer. From the moment of the failure of the
Rathenau campaign, Meyer was finished as leader of the KPD.
This did not mean his immediate dismissal: he had after all
committed no breach of discipline. As with Levi, indirect methods
were used – the construction of an anti-Meyer faction within the
Zentrale – but in this case they were unsuccessful, since Meyer was
able to appeal from the *Zentrale* to the ZA. At the *Zentrale* session of
18 July, Guralski, the Comintern representative, condemned the
KPD's defence of bourgeois democracy in association with Social
Democrats, and was able to persuade a majority of members to
drop Meyer's version of the united front. But on 23 July, when
the ZA met, the attacks of Guralski were rejected by most of those
present. The reasons for this temporary setback for the

Comintern's representative were firstly that on any realistic estimate revolution was *not* just around the corner, and secondly that Guralski was one of the ECCI's least impressive agents, his speech on this occasion being nonsensical and self-contradictory, culminating in the phrase: 'the attitude of the *Zentrale* [during the Rathenau campaign] was on the whole correct, on the whole it had a line, but the mood was wrong'.[44]

This victory over Guralski should not be viewed as an indication of the relative freedom of action still possessed by the KPD in 1922. It was, rather, a unique occurrence, unparalleled in the previous year: in 1921 first Levi and then Friesland, without the wholehearted backing of their colleagues, were unable to resist the Comintern and had to resign. Meyer was sent to Moscow to represent the German party in the ECCI until after the Fourth Comintern Congress. The immediate reappointment of Brandler as party chairman after his return to Germany under the Rathenau amnesty (August 1922) was no doubt a sign of the party's confidence in him, but it was also an indication that he was better fitted to smooth over disputes with the left than Meyer had been. Meyer's position was now in fact untenable: if the ECCI's objective was to hold the German party together, and if the majority of the *Zentrale* shared this objective (as expressed by Pieck, when he told the ZA 'we accepted the resolution of 18 July attacking our own policy because we wanted to avoid a party crisis'), then the hatred of the leftists for Meyer was a good reason why he should be dropped. At the next party congress, the Leipzig Congress of January 1923, his name was dropped from the list of candidates for the *Zentrale* presented by the outgoing *Zentrale* itself, and there was no possibility of his continuing as party chairman.[45]

'WORKERS' GOVERNMENT' AND RUHR INVASION

The removal of Meyer did not mean that the united front tactic was now dead and buried. His successor, Heinrich Brandler, was just as strongly in favour of it, and he regarded the formation of 'workers' governments' resting on the activities of workers outside parliament as the appropriate form of this tactic for Germany. By 1922 the problem of 'workers' governments' was being posed at local rather than national level, owing to the differential political development of the more industrialised areas of Germany. In Saxony in particular there had been a potential 'workers' government' since November 1920, when the elections resulted in a majority for the left-wing parties, producing a Diet in which 40 socialist and 9 communist deputies faced a bourgeois minority of 47. At that stage the KPD had replied to the Social Democrats' request for support with the words 'A pretended workers' government can only be a caretaker for the affairs of the capitalist class.'[46] Despite this jaundiced view the party did not use its nine votes in the Diet to overthrow the SPD government. In September 1921 a similar situation arose in Thuringia (28 socialist and communist deputies against 26 of other parties). The USPD proposed a workers' government; the KPD would not enter it, but agreed to give support from outside 'provided it carried on a consistent proletarian policy'.[47]

The elections of 5 November 1922 to the Saxon Diet again resulted in a victory for the 'working-class parties'. The SPD, into which the USPD had now merged, received 41 seats, the KPD 10 (with a 50 per cent increase in votes), and the bourgeois parties 46. The Saxon SPD, under strong pressure from its left wing, as represented by Dr Erich Zeigner and Georg Graupe, the trade union leader, offered to form a workers' government which would work for the realisation of the Ten Demands, previously laid down by the Saxon KPD as a condition of entry (20 November 1922).[48] The *Zentrale* in Berlin did not feel it could decide these matters by itself, since, as Böttcher put it, 'participation in the Saxon workers' government is the first practical experiment in Western Europe for the whole International'. Hence the decision was passed to the ECCI.

The possibility of using a 'workers' government' as a base for the formation of working-class strongpoints depended very much on how far the SPD was prepared to go. Among the KPD's Ten Points there were demands for a compulsory loan of 30 per cent of all property (point 2) and for the calling of a Congress of Factory Councils to which all important legislative proposals were to be presented (point 9). This was too much for the Saxon SPD. The decision of Moscow, therefore – a decision which had to be imposed on a reluctant Thalheimer and Meyer, who were both prepared to drop points 2 and 9 – was that the KPD must break off the negotiations.[49] There was no doubt that this decision was in the spirit of the united front, as strictly interpreted by the

Comintern. The point was underlined when the Saxon SPD government as finally constituted turned out to be so moderate that it could dispense with communist support and rely on the Centre Party's votes.

The Fourth Comintern Congress, which held its sessions in November and December 1922, was dominated by the debate on the united front tactic, and once again the German party held pride of place in the discussions. It was in Germany that the problem of the united front was posed most acutely, and also in Germany that the inner-party conflicts on the issue were most serious. The Comintern's leaders continued to view the prospects of revolution in a rather pessimistic light: as Radek put it, 'although world capitalism has not overcome its crisis, large sections of the proletariat have lost confidence in their capacity to conquer power in the foreseeable future . . . The conquest of power is not on the order of the day. The proletariat is still in retreat.'[50] In reply to attacks by Hugo Urbahns on this position, Radek commented that the German working class as a whole was 'not ready to struggle for power, and the communist party's immediate task was to organise the defence of the proletariat against the capitalist offensive'. Hence there were dangers both in 'Otzovism' (i.e. rejection of parliamentary and trade union action in the certain expectation of revolution) and in passivity.[51]

However, the Soviet delegation was not unanimous. Bukharin and Zinoviev still inclined to the side of the German left, especially to the left's interpretation of the 'workers' government'. Zinoviev asserted that 'we understand by ''workers' government'' nothing other than the application of the dictatorship of the proletariat. Even if a workers' government were to come into existence, we could not avoid civil war.'[52] Meyer immediately protested against this view in the name of the KPD majority leadership, saying that, far from being a synonym for the dictatorship of the proletariat, the workers' government was 'a slogan we advance in order to win over the workers to a common struggle against the bourgeois class . . . If the slogan is followed by the majority of the working class, this will lead either to dictatorship of the proletariat or to long phases of sharp class struggle, i.e. civil war in all its forms.'[53]

The German delegation to the Congress had to permit the ultra-left minority delegates to speak, in view of the support they enjoyed both at home and within the ECCI, and it was inevitably

Ruth Fischer who took the platform to contradict Meyer on all points. She sharply criticised the KPD leadership for its behaviour over the Rathenau campaign, when it had 'offered negotiations, cooperation at the summit' with the Social Democrats, and its 'tendency to give a revolution a "western" hair-style, to create democratic intermediate stages between what we have now and what we desire'.[54]

The final resolutions of the Fourth Comintern Congress did not decide the question of the workers' government either way: the workers' government, the Congress resolved, is not 'the necessary form of transition towards the dictatorship of the proletariat, but it may constitute a point of departure for the conquest of that dictatorship'. The resolution enumerated no less than five different types of workers' government, starting with a 'liberal workers' government', a coalition between the bourgeoisie and counter-revolutionary workers' leaders (Great Britain), and ascending through 'workers' and peasants' government' to 'workers' government with communist participation', and finally, the acme of perfection, 'a genuine proletarian workers' government in its purest form, which can only be embodied in a government of the communist party'.

At the Leipzig Congress of the KPD (28 January to 1 February 1923) the left was so strong that it was impossible to preserve the atmosphere of relative unanimity which had prevailed at Jena. Such a vigorous confrontation of opposing standpoints had not been seen since the KAPD crisis. The strength of the leftist minority was such that the *Zentrale* had to allow the leftists to deliver counter-statements to each of the main official speeches by the leadership. Ruth Fischer took the floor to mount a general attack on the party's policy over the previous seventeen months – i.e. as far back as the Jena Congress of 1921 – accusing it of a 'tendency to passivity, opportunism, and revisionism'.[55] The worst mistake of the Meyer *Zentrale* had been the failure to raise the question of a general strike during the Rathenau campaign of 1922. Fischer was contradicted sharply by Kleine-Guralski, the permanent ECCI representative in Germany, soon to increase his influence further by being elected to the *Zentrale*:

Unfortunately we do not have a serious right or a serious left. Our right is a typhus bacillus and our left is a slight chill with a bit of a temperature in a healthy body. All doctors will confirm that a typhus bacillus with a slight chill can be dangerous. The left wants to protect the party against opportunism by surrounding it with barbed wire. But if the barbed wire is so dense that it cuts you off from the masses, that is wrong . . . The Berlin organisation is not worse than others, it is politically better educated, but I must say this: your lines of barbed wire bar the way to the VSPD and are forming a KAPD among you.[56]

Though they were a strong minority, the leftists were unable to force any changes in the party's policy. The voting on the main issue, the *Zentrale*'s 'Theses on the United Front and Workers' Government', was 118 to 59. The left had control of two strong local organisations (Berlin–Brandenburg and Wasserkante–Hamburg), two medium ones (Middle Rhine and Hesse–Frankfurt), and one minute one (Lusatia). This amounted to a total of 70 delegates out of the total of 219 at the Congress. (70 people voted for resolution 21, calling on party members to leave religious organisations, which was introduced as a test of the left's strength.) The Brandler line was therefore the party line in the following months.

The Leipzig Congress, so concerned both to fight old battles again and to lay down conditions for future workers' governments, made very little of the international crisis, which was at that moment reaching an acute stage with the Franco-Belgian occupation of the Ruhr on 11 January and the Cuno government's response of passive resistance. Neither the Brandler *Zentrale* nor the Fischer–Maslow group had any hesitation in dissociating themselves from the wave of outraged German national feeling which, according to them, was artificially blown up by the capitalists and their government. A delegate from the Ruhr asserted that passive resistance was practised by the officials at the coal-mines, but that no miner would have gone on strike if the coal-owners had not offered to make up their wages. 'Our counter-propaganda', he said, 'and the mistrust of the workers themselves prevented them from being misused for these nationalist purposes . . . We communists in the Ruhr can be proud that we were first to say to the worker: your enemy is not the Frenchman, your enemy is German and French capitalism . . . Our fight is not against one alone but both: against the criminal machinations of the Cuno government and French militarism.'[57]

The KPD had voted against passive resistance in the Ruhr at the end of the *Reichstag* debate of 13 January. Frölich declared: 'we feel ourselves to be the brothers of our French comrades at this moment. No national united front. Instead, the united front of the proletariat. The only thing that can save the German people is the overthrow of the government.' A similarly internationalist note was struck in the political report of the *Zentrale* to the Eighth Congress, presented by Meyer:

> The Ruhr occupation is a result of the *sabotage* of reparations by the Cuno cabinet, which has failed to fulfil promises of wood and coal deliveries. But the heavy industrialists around Stinnes are ready to settle with the French capitalists and industrialists. The nationalist agitation deployed in press and parliament is only a cover, a smokescreen behind which private attempts at settlement are being made between German and French industrialists. The German people are simply being used as a bargaining counter. What Rosa Luxemburg said in the Junius pamphlet is true here: the vital interests of the nation are identical with the class interests of the proletariat and the best means against invasion is as sharp a class struggle as possible. The interests of the German proletariat demand, first and foremost, a fight against the German capitalists and the Cuno cabinet. For the main enemy is in our own country. In the *occupied* area, the resistance of the Rhenish-Westphalian proletariat will be directed equally against both enemies.[58]

Far from countering this internationalism with a National Bolshevist policy, as has sometimes been suggested, the left insinuated that the *Zentrale* was itself deviating in that direction: Urbahns poured scorn on the idea that the Ruhr conflict could be turned into a war of revolutionary defence and national salvation.[59] The strength of the left opposition at the Leipzig Congress persuaded the ECCI's delegates, Radek and the Bulgarian Vasily Kolarov, to work out a compromise, which Brandler accepted, willingly or unwillingly. The workers' government was described as 'an attempt by the working class, within the framework . . . of bourgeois democracy, and basing itself on proletarian organs and proletarian mass movements, to conduct a working-class policy'. So far this statement was on Brandlerite lines. But the theses continued: 'The workers' government is not a "simplified revolution" or a "substitute for dictatorship'' . . . but a period of struggle, of violent struggle, by the proletariat against its bourgeoisie.' Moreover, it was not a 'necessary stage in the struggle for political power . . . but a possible stage'.[60] These were perhaps merely verbal concessions to the left, but Radek also insisted that the left opposition should be represented in the new *Zentrale*. The ECCI was keen to avoid a split in the German party, and tried to bridge over the differences by having Arthur Ewert, Rudolf Lindau and Hans Pfeiffer elected to the *Zentrale*.[61] None of these were prominent leftists, in fact Ewert was hardly one at all, but Lindau and Pfeiffer at least were sufficiently acceptable to the left to secure a well-nigh unanimous vote in their favour. The rest of the candidates were chosen on a purely factional basis, with the left minority putting forward its own candidates – Ruth Fischer, Ottomar Geschke, Iwan Katz and Artur König – and seeing them voted down.

The KPD leadership which confronted the Ruhr crisis was thus firmly in Brandler's hands until June 1923, and the removal of Meyer from the *Zentrale* made no difference. Brandler simply continued Meyer's policy, which was to work for a workers' government resting on extra-parliamentary mass action, but with a parliamentary aspect as well. This might well mean that the KPD voted for an SPD government, or even entered one as a coalition partner. It certainly did not mean that a revolutionary seizure of power was on the agenda.

5 The Failed October

THE CONFLICT BETWEEN HEINRICH BRANDLER AND THE KPD LEFT

The year 1923 was one of great opportunities and difficult decisions for the KPD. Germany was subject to two simultaneous and interconnected crises: the foreign policy crisis of the Ruhr occupation and the internal crisis of rampant inflation. The Cuno government's decision to resort to passive resistance resulted in a 'patriotic strike', in the sabotage of railways, the cutting of electric cables, mass arrests by the occupying authorities, and other acts of repression, sometimes going as far as the shooting of resisters. German nationalist feeling was greatly exacerbated. The KPD tried at first to stand aside from all this; but the situation pulled the party along. The working class was affected by the rise in prices and growing unemployment, and street demonstrations broke out, suppressed by the occupying forces. On 31 March the 53 000 Krupp workers at Essen tried to prevent French troops from requisitioning the lorries with which their food supplies were transported; the French opened fire leaving 13 people dead and 40 wounded.[1] The party distributed the blame for this incident equally between 'French militarists' and 'German nationalist provocateurs', and intervened to keep the workers calm 'and frustrate Fascist provocations'.[2] On 13 April, at Mülheim, the workers seized the town hall and set up a Workers' Council, which distributed food and tried to form a workers' militia. The impulse was provided not by the KPD but by Syndicalists. In fact the party did all it could 'to hold back the starving and embittered unemployed from acts of despair' and blamed 'criminal provocateurs' for the clashes with the police. The 'Mülheim massacre' of 18–19 April, which brought the restoration of order, was conducted jointly by the Nazis and the *Schupos* (security police), who had received permission from the

91

French occupying authorities to enter the area. Eight workers were killed, about 50 wounded.[3]

The working class of the Ruhr was gradually forced into a conflict with the occupation forces which made nonsense of the KPD's original policy of rejecting passive resistance, expressed so strikingly in the 23 January editorial in *Die Rote Fahne*, headed 'Smite Poincaré and Cuno on the Ruhr and on the Spree', which concluded that 'the battle of the Ruhr is a conflict between two bourgeoisies on the back of the German working class'. This approach was continued in March with a conference of Factory Councils at Essen (11 March) 'to discuss measures against French imperialism and German capitalism', followed by an international conference at Frankfurt a week later, which called for a fight against war and Fascism. Brandler delivered a pessimistic address to the Frankfurt Conference, claiming that the tide of revolution was 'receding not rising' and that the main task was to 'rally the proletariat together'. For the Fischer–Maslow group, the Ruhr conflict was a fresh stick with which to beat Brandler: the Berlin Left asserted misleadingly that he had kept the Ruhr question off the agenda at Leipzig (in fact they had never tried to put it on the agenda).[4]

It was August Thalheimer, Brandler's closest associate, who first hinted at a possible change of policy and a softening of the principled internationalist line of January. In an unsigned article published in February he asserted that 'the roles of the French and German bourgeoisies are not the same. The German bourgeoisie has emerged as objectively revolutionary, against its own wishes.' He concluded, admittedly, by saying that the KPD must struggle against 'both the imperialist infiltrator on the Ruhr and the German bourgeoisie, with the aim of laying the burden of the Ruhr conflict on the shoulders of that bourgeoisie'. Even so, the implication was clear: victory over the French occupier in the Ruhr 'war' was a legitimate communist goal.[5] He underlined this point on 1 March, when he called for 'energetic resistance in the Ruhr' and 'at the same time a sharp struggle against the Cuno government with the aim of overthrowing it, as an obstacle to the successful struggle against the external enemy'.[6] This last argument bore an unfortunate resemblance to the contemporary reasoning of Ludendorff and Hitler.

The Thalheimer line provoked immediate opposition both at home (in the Frankfurt branch of the party, a left stronghold) and abroad (in the Communist Party of Czechoslovakia, where communists from the German-speaking minority had a very sharp nose for anything that smacked of German nationalism). The leftist Dr Joseph Winternitz ('Sommer') rebuked Thalheimer a month later for abandoning 'the clear communist line of the Leipzig Congress on the Ruhr occupation' and charged him with moving towards National Bolshevism.[7] The views of the left were summed up like this: 'The *decisive* blow against French imperialism can only be struck after the overthrow of the German bourgeoisie by the German working class in alliance with the proletariat of France and Russia.'[8]

At this time, therefore, the left opposition viewed the struggle over the Ruhr as a diversion: the main task was to overthrow the German bourgeoisie. The way to do this, according to the left, was to avoid any alliance with the SPD. The question of a socialist alliance was by March 1923 of vital importance, at the local level, since there had been a very strong swing to the left among the Social Democrats of Saxony. An emergency congress of the Saxon SPD, held on 4 March, rejected the party executive's advice to seek a coalition with the Democrats, and voted overwhelmingly for Georg Graupe's resolution in favour of negotiations with the KPD on the basis of its programme for Saxony, published two days before.[9] Even though it proved impossible to form a coalition cabinet, both the *Zentrale* and the local KPD leadership recommended propping up a minority SPD government. On 19 March the Saxon KPD districts decided by 21 votes to 7 (Dresden and Chemnitz, Brandler's stronghold, in favour, Leipzig opposed) to vote in the Diet for a government of left Social Democrats.[10] Dr Erich Zeigner (SPD) was elected prime minister of Saxony two days later with communist support.[11] On the face of it, this was a big step towards the kind of opportunist combination the ECCI had ruled out in 1922: the Saxon SPD persisted in rejecting the KPD's demand for the convocation of a congress of Factory Councils, yet the KPD voted for the Zeigner government. However, the fact that the agreement with the SPD foresaw 'the formation of Proletarian Hundreds' and 'measures of defence against Fascism' indicated that here at last the pressing need for the workers to arm themselves against the growing Nazi movement was being recognised. Fischer and Maslow ignored this aspect, concentrating instead on what was immediately obvious: the Saxon KPD was getting too close to the Social

Democrats. At the District Congress of the KPD for Rhineland–Westphalia North, held at Essen on 25 March, the confrontation between left and right in the KPD reached a new level of acerbity. 'Either we should have made sure a congress of Factory Councils took place, or we should have told the SPD: do your own dirty work', said Ruth Fischer.[12] The District Directorate (BL) of the Berlin KPD had already resolved that 'Communists will under no circumstances vote for a Social Democratic prime minister or a Social Democratic minority government.'[13]

The groundswell of left-wing opinion within the party was so strong that the *Zentrale* only won its vote at Essen by 68 to 55, although Rhineland–Westphalia was under the control of Albert Stolzenburg and Walter Stoecker, strong supporters of Brandler. Once again the ECCI intervened to prevent a split. Some members of the left (not the most prominent) were prevailed upon to disavow the extremism of Maslow and Fischer,[14] and Zinoviev as chairman of the ECCI sent a letter inviting representatives of the *Zentrale* and the left opposition to arrive in Moscow by 22 April for a conference.[15] At this conference, which took place towards the end of April, a compromise was sought and found by the ECCI, after discussions with both Brandler and Paul Böttcher (for the *Zentrale*) and Maslow, Fischer, Thälmann and Gerhard Eisler (for the left opposition). It was agreed that four leading leftists should be coopted to the *Zentrale*; and a resolution was issued condemning 'rightist' and 'leftist' errors, and concluding that 'the struggle against left tendencies could only be conducted with success if the *Zentrale* of the KPD first of all eliminated the reasons for the left's revolutionary mistrust by fighting against right-wing elements'.[16]

On the Ruhr issue, the (leftist) idea of propaganda for the occupation of the factories was rejected since the situation in Germany was 'not revolutionary'. The German proletariat was being ground between two millstones, the German and French bourgeoisie, said the ECCI resolution. The KPD's tactics in Saxony were described as correct, but the party was criticised for failing to place the struggle for a workers' government in Saxony within the context of a similar struggle over the whole of Germany. 'The Saxon SPD government might find it was compelled to lead the masses in a struggle against the bourgeoisie; this would face the KPD with great tasks.' A policy of National Bolshevism was hinted at:

The German bourgeoisie can no longer carry the banner of the struggle for national liberation in Germany, it is neither capable of fighting the Entente, nor does it want to. The task of the KPD is to open the eyes of the broad petty bourgeois nationalist masses to the fact that only the working class, after it is victorious, will be able to defend German soil, the treasures of German culture, and the future of the German nation.

There was to be no special discussion organ, as the left had demanded, but the rival positions could be presented in a monthly supplement to *Die Rote Fahne*; no emergency congress of the party need be called.

This agreement was essentially a holding operation, allowing Brandler to keep control of the party. On all the disputed points the ECCI leaned to the right. The admission of four leftists to a *Zentrale* of 21 people could not make much difference to party policy while Brandler remained in charge.

THE TWIN CRISES OF PASSIVE RESISTANCE AND INFLATION

The crisis in the KPD could be held in check by ECCI's palliative measures; the crisis in the country, on the other hand, progressively deepened and worsened; the year 1923 was one of great inflation. The value of the mark plummeted; prices rose to astronomical heights; money wages failed to keep pace. Hence real wages declined. The weekly real wage of a skilled worker had been falling since 1921 (from 78 per cent of the 1913 level to 68 per cent in 1922). In July 1923 it reached 48 per cent.[17] Unemployment was not a problem in the early months of 1923, but it increased progressively from July onwards.[18] There was also a considerable degree of short-time working.[19]

The political consequences of the German crisis were many and varied. It stimulated the growth of a left wing within the reunited SPD, the nucleus of which was not surprisingly formed by re-entrants from the Rump USPD. These Left Social Democrats advocated a united front with the communists, and as we have seen they were able to take control of the SPD in Saxony in March 1923. There was also a strong shift to the left in the Thuringian SPD. But even the section of the SPD which was furthest to the left, as represented by Paul Levi (ex-KPD, ex-USPD) and Kurt Rosenfeld (ex-USPD), remained divided from the KPD by its refusal to take measures which smacked of a dictatorship of the proletariat.

The year 1923 also saw a growth of autonomous working-class organisations standing at least formally outside the party and trade union framework, though always strongly under communist influence. A movement of 'wild' Factory Councils flourished, outside the legal limits laid down in 1920. It culminated in the strike of August 1923 against the Cuno government, set off on 11 August by an assembly of Berlin Factory Councillors at which 12 000 people were present.[20] Apart from the Factory Councils there were Action Committees, Control Committees and, above all, Proletarian Hundreds, organs of working-class self-defence which may date back to the Rathenau campaign of 1922, although the first quoted example was set up at Chemnitz in March 1923.[21] Within a few weeks of their appearance in Chemnitz there were Proletarian Hundreds in all the urban areas of Germany, encouraged by the KPD especially after the Mülheim massacre of mid-April. They were anathema to the right SPD, and Carl Severing, the Prussian Minister of the Interior, soon prohibited them on his territory (12 May). The Prussian example was followed by most of the other states. In Saxony and Thuringia, on the other hand, they were encouraged, even receiving funds from the local state governments run by left-inclined SPD members. The aim of the Proletarian Hundreds, as the communist Paul Böttcher explained in June, was 'defence against Fascist attacks'. They were 'not a KPD party army, but an organ of the united front movement'. He warned against the KPD left's call for the arming of the Hundreds; this would not succeed, he said, as the working class was not yet ready to struggle for power. Only when the workers had reached this stage of political maturity could the question of armaments be posed.[22]

The other main consequence of the Ruhr crisis, rather underestimated at the time although with hindsight one might regard it as the more significant development, was the rise of an extreme German nationalism directed as much against indigenous working-class organisations as against the foreign occupier. The response of the communists to this danger was two-edged: they proposed both a fierce fight against 'Fascism' and an attempt to enter into alliance with it on the basis of the 'liberation of Germany from French imperialism'. The ECCI is sometimes held responsible for this 'Schlageter line', introduced by Karl Radek in a speech of 20 June. Using the death of the nationalist fanatic Leo Schlageter at the hands of a French firing squad as his text, Radek appealed to the 'hundreds of Schlageters' to recognise that 'Germany can only be freed from the bonds of slavery with the working class, not against it'.[23] One might have expected an outcry from the KPD; but there is no evidence of any opposition to the Schlageter line within the party. The Brandler leadership implemented it; and Ruth Fischer addressed these remarks to the German nationalists in July: 'The giant who will liberate Germany is there: it is the German proletariat, of which you form a part, and with which you must align yourself.'[24] Despite all the indications of crisis in Germany in the summer of 1923 the Moscow leaders of the Comintern still did not see the conquest of power there as an immediate task. Zinoviev declared at the Enlarged ECCI in June 1923: 'Yes, Comrades, Germany is on the eve of revolution. That does not mean that we only have to wait a month or a year . . . Perhaps much more time than that will be needed, but in the historical sense Germany is on the eve of the proletarian over-turn.'[25] A number of aspects of the German situation tended to suggest that Zinoviev was right to foresee partial defeats before the final success. A movement for a general strike in May 1923 in solidarity with a sectional strike by Ruhr miners was a failure: the *Zentrale* was forced to call it off on 29 May for lack of support – 310 000 workers at most came out. There were many strikes in June and July, but they were all partial, sectional strikes for economic reasons. Brandler's appeal 'To the Party', published in RF on 12 July 1923, was later described by Trotsky as the single piece of evidence which alerted him to the presence of a revolutionary situation in Germany. ('When a Brandler writes like this, something is afoot.') It is hard to see how Trotsky could have drawn this conclusion from Brandler's pessimistic tone. The Cuno government was on the verge of bankruptcy, said Brandler. An internal and external crisis was on the horizon, but its three manifestations were: separatism in the Rhineland, the secession of Bavaria from the *Reich* under extreme right-wing pressure, and the Black *Reichswehr*'s preparations for civil war against proletarian Saxony and Thuringia. The prospect was one of severe defensive battles against the counter-revolution. 'If the Fascists put one striker in

ten against the wall, the communists will put one in five Fascists
there.' Weapons (in short supply) would be acquired in the course
of combat, in which the workers would rely on their superior
numbers. All this would be done in alliance with the Social
Democrats and non-party workers. An 'Anti-Fascist Day' was
announced for 29 July. It was to take the form of mass
demonstrations all over the country.[26]

Every state government in Germany, except those of Saxony,
Thuringia and Baden, prohibited the Anti-Fascist Day.
Brandler's impulse was to give way, despite the urgings of Ruth
Fischer and the left opposition. Fischer proposed to hold the
Berlin demonstration anyway.[27] Brandler replied that it could
only go ahead if adequate protection were available. He decided
to ask the advice of the ECCI on this important problem and sent
a telegram to Moscow. Zinoviev and Bukharin were for ignoring
the government prohibition and going ahead; Stalin was for a
temporary retreat – 'The Germans should be restrained and not
spurred on', he said – and Radek agreed with Stalin. It was
decided that the 29 July demonstration should be abandoned.
'We fear a trap', explained the Presidium of the Comintern in a
telegram sent by Radek on 26 July to the *Zentrale*.[28] Indoor
meetings were held instead, and the workers flocked to them in
their hundreds of thousands (200 000 in Berlin). In Saxony,
where outdoor demonstrations were permitted, 60 000 turned up
to the city of Chemnitz.[29] Moreover, the left of the SPD now
moved a step closer to cooperation with the communists. The
Weimar Conference of 29 July, attended by 30 SPD *Reichstag*
deputies, called for the overthrow of the Cuno government,
opposed any participation in a 'Grand Coalition' and demanded
'as much cooperation as possible with the communists to achieve
immediate proletarian objectives'.[30] Not only was the KPD's
influence on Social Democrats increasing, the workers were
tending to abandon the SPD at elections. This at least is the
message of the Diet elections in the small rural state of
Mecklenburg–Strelitz in July. A total of 12 800 people voted for
the SPD, 11 000 for the KPD, whereas in 1920 there were only
2300 votes for the extreme left (in this case the USPD) against
23 000 for the SPD. In the absence of any elections on a national
scale (they were not held until May 1924) it is impossible to know
whether the electors of Mecklenburg–Strelitz were representative
of the whole country. In any case, those who directed the party's

policy continued to be cautious. Radek wrote on 29 July that the moment for the attack had still not arrived. The first task of the party, he said, was 'to organise the majority of the active sections of the working class under its banner. We must continue to bear in mind that we are momentarily the weaker side . . . We must avoid anything that might allow the enemy to defeat us in detail.'[31] At the ZA session of 5–6 August, Brandler said the task was to prepare for a 'defensive revolutionary struggle', to form a united front which would lead to action for a 'workers' and peasants' government'. These proposals were accepted, though seven people abstained. Brandler later claimed that this was not an opposition on principle but a personal demonstration against his leadership. However Hugo Urbahns at least gave a reason: 'A peasant is a capitalist. Therefore the slogan of a workers' and peasants' government is incorrect.'[32]

The strike movement of 9 to 14 August against Cuno was in a way a successful continuation of Brandler's defensive united front policy. It was widespread enough to be called a general strike in Berlin and Halle–Merseburg, and it was partly led by the KPD, through the Committee of 15 Factory Council Representatives for Greater Berlin, which issued a call on 10 August for a 'workers' and peasants' government'. However, the main feature of the movement was its spontaneity: the Full Assembly of Berlin Factory Councils on 11 August voted unanimously 'without distinction of tendency' for a three-day general strike. Apart from the KPD, the other major working-class organisations, the ADGB, SPD and the USPD remnant, would have nothing to do with this venture.[33] They preferred to travel the road of peaceful negotiations with the Cuno government; later that day, however, the danger that it would lose control over the masses impelled the SPD to withdraw its parliamentary support from Cuno. This combination of pressure 'from below', i.e. from the masses acting largely under communist leadership, and 'from alongside', i.e. from the SPD fraction in parliament, compelled Cuno's resignation.

REVOLUTION IN THE OFFING

The general strike of mid-August was in fact the high-point of the mass movement in Germany in 1923. Roughly three million workers took part.[34] It was accompanied by severe clashes between demonstrators and police: these led to 30 deaths on 12 August, 110 on 13 August. If ever there was a revolutionary situation in Germany in 1923 it was in mid-August. But the linked crises in foreign policy and economics were about to be brought to an end by Cuno's successor, Stresemann. Germany in 1923 was not gripped by a crisis of capitalism insoluble within the bourgeois framework. The country had been brought to its knees by two specific, and avoidable, policies: Cuno's passive resistance on the Ruhr, and three years' excessive use of the printing press to solve financial problems. Hence the twin decisions of August, to negotiate with France over reparations and to stabilise the German mark, were effective in restoring confidence in the business world and among the middle classes. There remained the problem of the workers, who were still suffering the full effects of the inflation (it was not to be brought to an end until 20 November, by which time one dollar was worth 4000 billion marks). Repression was one answer. Severing's police force took measures against the Committee of 15 which had set off the strike. The *Reich* Committee of Factory Councils was prohibited on 16 August. But the best answer was the entry of four SPD members into the Stresemann cabinet: Robert Schmidt, Rudolf Hilferding, Wilhelm Sollmann and Gustav Radbruch. This, combined with immediate wage increases to cancel out some of the effects of the inflation, was enough to reassure the non-communist majority of the working class, and pull them out of the strike movement.[35] On 14 August the KPD decided that the strike would have to be called off. The later measures against the Factory Councils set off merely token protests.[36] Radek commented:

> It is possible that Stresemann despite everything means a stage has been reached at which the movement will stand still for a certain period. The German communists will use this time to organise better and win over the majority of the working class, creating forms of united action which will allow them to penetrate to the petty-bourgeois masses.[37]

In taking this view he was in line with Brandler, but not with the men in the Russian Politburo. Zinoviev wrote on 15 August: 'The crisis is coming! Decisive events are imminent. A new chapter is opening . . . The KPD must rapidly orient itself towards the approaching revolutionary crisis . . . The stake is immense. The moment when boldness is all is drawing near.'[38]

Given the subordination of the KPD to the Russian Communist Party, normally exercised through the ECCI, it was for Moscow to decide. A meeting of the Politburo on 23 August 'discussed the question of the German revolution in all its details', as Zinoviev later asserted.[39] It was joined for the occasion by Radek, Pyatakov, Shmit, Kuusinen and Tsyurupa – all representatives of the Comintern apparatus and Russian experts on Germany – and the two permanent KPD representatives in Moscow, Jakob Walcher and Edwin Hörnle, and it decided that the time had come for the communist insurrection. Stalin's caution was outweighed by the enthusiasm of Trotsky and Zinoviev. Radek was as usual carried along by the tide.[40] A committee of four (Radek, Pyatakov, Josef Unshlikht and Vassily Shmit) was appointed to supervise the preparations. No decision was made as to the date of the revolution or the precise method.

In Germany, meanwhile, the *Zentrale* was still unaware of the vital step taken in Moscow. The crisis appeared in fact to be lessening. The SPD's policy of class collaboration had just registered a success with the agreement of 23 August with the employers whereby wage increases would be paid in advance of expected price rises. Thalheimer wrote at this time that the coming of the Stresemann government signified the unwillingness of more than a minority of the working class to fight for a 'workers' and peasants' government', let alone a proletarian dictatorship. 'Politically and organisationally', he added, 'we still have a long road to travel before the conditions are ripe to secure victory for the working class . . . The future will bring a right-wing dictatorship under the cover of the present government and in partial collaboration with it.'[41]

Trotsky's 'appeal to the proletariat of all countries', issued the same day as Thalheimer's article, struck a different note.

The situation in Germany is becoming ever more acute. Unless all the signs are deceptive, revolution is approaching. The German proletariat . . . will not just have to face the armed forces of the German bourgeoisie, but there is a danger that at the same time as the bourgeoisie attacks . . . the Entente bourgeoisie and its vassals will forget their conflict with the German bourgeoisie and rush to its assistance.[42]

Trotsky was thus already thinking about the next stage but one, the defence of a revolution against foreign invasion. Thalheimer's conception, on the other hand, was of a revolution which grew out of the workers' defensive reaction to the coming of a right-wing dictatorship. It was scarcely compatible with the idea of a planned insurrection by communist cadres just decided on by the Russian Politburo. There was a contrast between the pessimism of the KPD *Zentrale* (which had just warned that the proletariat would have great difficulties in procuring weapons)[43] and the revolutionary enthusiasm which had evidently taken hold of Moscow.[44]

Brandler was now summoned to the Soviet capital, along with no less than three leftists (Maslow, Thälmann and Fischer) who were no doubt there to stiffen his revolutionary backbone. The Moscow discussions lasted through September: Brandler hesitated, Zinoviev thumped the table, Trotsky tried to lay down a precise date, arguing in essence that what was right for the Bolsheviks in October 1917 must be right for the KPD in October 1923,[45] Maslow and Fischer suggested that the sooner the seizure of power took place, the better. Brandler objected to fixing a timetable, and restated his doubts about the prospects for a proletarian revolution. He was overruled, and a plan was worked out, based on the entry of the KPD into coalition cabinets in Saxony and Thuringia. The proletariat, it was decided, would 'concentrate its strength in Saxony, taking as its starting-point the defence of the workers' government, into which we enter'. This last manoeuvre was not conceived as a provocation to the *Reich* government (though this was how it turned out) but as a way of getting hold of weapons, through control of the police force.[46]

In the aftermath of the October débacle, Zinoviev was to assert that the KPD's entry into the Saxon coalition cabinet was turned into a 'banal parliamentary combination' by Brandler, whereas it was intended to be 'an episode in the struggle, a revolutionary strategy'.[47] This was a distortion of the truth. Zinoviev himself persuaded Brandler to take this step, against his better judgement. Brandler thought that entry into a coalition 'workers' government' of this kind should be preceded by a mobilisation of the masses.[48] He even expressed his doubts publicly, in a speech to a congress of the Polish Communist Party in September: 'This time the proletariat will sacrifice not 20 000 of its troops as in 1918–19 but many hundreds of thousands . . . It would face not only 500 000 well organised and armed Fascists but 500 000 other opponents from the *Reichswehr* and elsewhere.'[49] But still he submitted, returning to Germany at the beginning of October with the task of preparing the entry of communists into the Saxon cabinet and launching an uprising within the next four to six weeks. An official message sent by the ECCI to the *Zentrale* on 1 October summed up the Moscow decisions: 'We must enter [the Saxon government] on condition the Zeigner people [the Left Social Democrats in Saxony] are actually willing to defend Saxony against Bavaria and the Fascists. 50 000 to 60 000 have to be armed immediately. Ignore Müller. The same in Thuringia.'[50]

This telegram swung the balance in the KPD *Zentrale* towards insurrection. The day before, it had rejected a suggestion that if circumstances were ripe in Saxony a rising should be attempted. Now the whole policy of the party was reoriented, away from public agitation, and towards secret preparations for the impending rising. 'All the party's functionaries were turned into technicians, political work was practically given up.'[51]

The military preparations involved the creation of a secret apparatus, with much assistance from a team of Russian advisers, led by a Civil War veteran known as General P. S. Skoblevsky.[52] An intelligence service, a terror unit and a red army were to be set up. The red army was to be based on the existing Proletarian Hundreds.[53] Germany was split up into six military districts, each one entrusted to a party official backed by a Russian military adviser. Skoblevsky was assisted by a party Military Council under Ernst Schneller. Then there was a 'Revolutionary Committee' headed by Guralski-Kleine, operating alongside Skoblevsky's military organisation but with no clearly defined role. The intelligence and terror units were coordinated by Nicolai Krestinsky, the Soviet Ambassador in Berlin, and the representative of the Comintern's 'Department for International Liaison' (Russian initials OMS), Jacob Mirov-Abramov. Finally, there was the four-man ECCI committee appointed two months before to supervise the whole operation.[54]

There was therefore a great deal of organisation, but very little actual preparation. Although the number of fighting men in the Proletarian Hundreds is given as 100 000,[55] not all of them had weapons. A figure of 11 000 rifles was advanced at the ZA meeting of 3 November 1923;[56] Walter Zeutschel, a participant who later left the KPD, claims there were 50 000,[57] but he is not a very reliable witness. Brandler recalled that 'money was given out for the purchase of weapons but weapons were not acquired'.[58]

The strategy of relying on the communist stronghold in Central Germany, sealing off Bavaria, and sending all units to Berlin to wage the decisive battle[59] was the best that could be devised in the circumstances. It properly took into account the great differences which separated the German regions. These had emerged with great clarity at the time of the Kapp putsch: reactionary Bavaria faced socialist Saxony and Thuringia; in Berlin no one group had the upper hand. But this was not to be a re-run of the Kapp putsch; the whole proletariat, socialist and communist, would not rise a second time in a defensive struggle against military dictatorship, which could then turn into an onslaught on capitalist society. The issues were more confused now. Social Democrats in the central government such as Rudolf Hilferding were fighting the Fascist danger in their own constitutionalist way; the Left Social Democrats of Central Germany, like Zeigner, saw joint proletarian action as a means of self-defence against the Fascists in Bavaria, not a step to communist revolution; and when the KPD tried to impose its more far-reaching aims, the Social Democratic masses preferred to follow their own leaders. Since the KPD was committed to joining Zeigner's cabinet by decisions arrived at previously in Moscow the party could not insist on the Ministry of the Interior, the key to controlling the police. Instead Brandler became Assistant Secretary (*Ministerialdirektor*) in charge of the State Chancellery (12 October).[60] It was his job to find secret stores of weapons and then hand them over to the Proletarian Hundreds. This was in fact impossible. There were no weapons available. 'The workers had cleared out the arsenals in Saxony and Thuringia at the time of the Kapp putsch, and . . . the March action . . . Every time the police wanted submachine-guns they had to apply for them from the military camp at Döberitz . . .'[61] Brandler was already aware of the problem on 12 October, when he told the *Zentrale*: 'The armaments situation is catastrophic . . . Our duty is to temporise and not take part in isolated conflicts.'[62]

A DISASTROUS DÉNOUEMENT

The entry of the KPD ministers into the Saxon government quickly brought things to a head, but in an unexpected and unwelcome way. The local military commander, General Alfred Müller, who was supposed to be being 'ignored', issued an order the next day, banning all Proletarian Hundreds 'or similar organisations' in his district.[63] The KPD Finance Minister Paul Böttcher replied with a public speech demanding 'the immediate arming of the Proletarian Hundreds'.[64] This was merely rhetoric: it scared the bourgeoisie but did not arm the workers.

The party's position was not strong. Agitation was made harder by the cat and mouse game the authorities were playing with RF: it was confiscated on 26 August, and forced to suspend publication between 4 and 11 September, 24 September and 9 October, and 11 October and 20 October. Editorials in the Chemnitz *Kämpfer* were no substitute. In any case, the main contribution of the communist press to the October 'preparations' was to print discussion articles on the 'theory of civil war' and 'partisan struggle'. Time slipped by in those October days, a period during which the KPD failed to mount any effective counter-action to the gradual encroachments of the national civilian and local military authorities. After all, the Moscow plan did not provide for a defensive struggle. Two blows fell on 13 October: the *Reichstag* passed Stresemann's Enabling Act, which allowed the government to take all necessary measures to meet the political and economic crisis, and General Müller issued his decree banning the Proletarian Hundreds in Saxony. On 16 October he removed the Saxon police from the control of the Zeigner cabinet and placed them directly under the *Reichswehr*, i.e. himself. A similar situation existed in Thuringia, though events there lagged several days behind: the communists entered the Thuringian government on 13 October; a general strike was prohibited by General Walther Reinhardt, Müller's counterpart in Thuringia, on 17 October.

The whole of Germany had been in a state of emergency since 27 September: this meant in practice that the regional military commanders exercised executive powers in their areas.[65] When Zeigner refused to dissolve the Proletarian Hundreds (Müller's final ultimatum, 17 October; Zeigner's reply in the Saxon Diet, 18 October), the Stresemann cabinet decided to send the army into Saxony and Thuringia (19 October). The actual entry of *Reichswehr* formations into Saxony took place on 21 October; here was the moment at which communist strategy would be put to the test. 21 October, far from being a date set in Moscow, was forced on the KPD by the rapid development of the crisis in relations between Saxony, the *Reich* authorities and the local *Reichswehr* commander. Now was the time 'to place the left SPD leadership before the alternative of either jointly fighting against the bourgeoisie or refusing to do so' in which case it would be 'unmasked' and the workers would lose their 'last illusion'.[66] The news that the *Reichswehr* was preparing to intervene arrived on 20 October. But before undertaking any counter-action, the KPD leaders decided to test the temperature outside the party and put the matter to a conference of Factory Council representatives, called originally for a quite different reason, and due to convene at Chemnitz the next day. The Chemnitz Conference was a disaster. Brandler told the meeting that the Left SPD's hope that the *Reich* government would protect Saxony against Bavarian Fascism was vain. The only hope for the Saxon proletariat was an immediate general strike, for which the Conference must vote unanimously, and straight away. The Left Social Democrats were not enthusiastic. The *Reich* government had on 20 October justified the intervention on the ground that it was directed against the Bavaria of Kahr and Hitler not the Saxony of Zeigner: Zeigner was not being deposed. Moreover, it was for the government and Saxon Diet to decide on resistance, not an *ad hoc* congress of Factory Councils. Georg Graupe, the SPD Minister of Labour, declared that if the general strike proposals were even discussed by the meeting he would have to leave it.[67] The general strike idea was given a 'third class funeral' by being handed over to a subcommittee. 'The communists also voted for this in order to preserve a unified fighting front.'[68] After the meeting, on the evening of 21 October, the *Zentrale* agreed to call off the planned insurrection (unanimously, according to Brandler and Thalheimer). The Left Social Democrats were neither compelled to fight nor unmasked as cowards. The decision to retreat was made by the *Zentrale* at Brandler's suggestion. Radek and Pyatakov could not be consulted because they had not yet arrived in Chemnitz. When they did, the next day, they upheld the decision.[69] Radek tried to salvage something from the wreck by proposing a general strike which would not turn into an armed insurrection. Both factions within the KPD rejected this. Ruth Fischer called for a strike *leading* to insurrection; Brandler declared that in the present situation any general strike would be bound to turn into an armed insurrection, hence nothing could be done. No agreement was reached, so in practice the result was inactivity.[70]

Only in one place did the communists rise in armed revolt in October 1923: Hamburg. The precise reason for the Hamburg insurrection will probably never be known. The most plausible account is that Hugo Urbahns, the Political Director of the Hamburg KPD district, arrived at the Chemnitz Conference after it was over, and, learning of the decision to abandon the planned uprising, sent a comrade named Inselberger back to Hamburg with orders to 'report on the situation'. He himself travelled first to Dresden, then back to Hamburg, where he went straight to bed (22 October). When he awoke the next morning the rising had started. This is Urbahns's own version.[71] At his trial the prosecution did not contest his assertion that he did not order the uprising. They relied instead on the general tone of KPD propaganda in the preceding weeks.[72] If Urbahns did not start it, who did? The answer appears to be: certain local communists who were eager to go into action. On 21 October the Hamburg dockers resolved on a general strike, to be called if the *Reich* government intervened in Saxony. The next day the news of intervention arrived. The local trade union leaders called on the Berlin headquarters to proclaim a nation-wide general strike, but insisted that Hamburg should not jump the gun (22 October). The KPD representatives Esser and Rühl refused to accept this decision. The same day the communist military leaders Hans Kippenberger and Albert Schreiner, and their Russian adviser General Moishe Stern (alias Kleber), prepared a plan for an insurrection, which was put into effect early the next morning. There were no weapons to be had, so early on 23 October an estimated 1 300 communists attacked 26 police stations, capturing 17 of them, and took the weapons stored there. These were used over the next few days in sniping at the police from behind barricades. But the expected mass support did not materialise. Even the striking dockers stayed out of the fight. On the other side stood 6000 well-armed police and soldiers. The struggle was hopeless. Only in the working-class suburb of Barmbeck (where Ernst Thälmann was in command) did fighting continue until 25 October. Elsewhere the rising was ended on 24 October. There were 21 dead and 175 wounded among the insurgents, 17 dead and 69 wounded among the police and soldiers. 102 prisoners were taken. These proportions are a tribute to Hans Kippenberger's cleverly executed retreat, on which he later reported to the ECCI.[73] The courts handed out two death penalties and 430 years in prison for offences arising out of the Hamburg insurrection. The whole story was later transfigured into a romantic legend, notably by the Russian journalist Larisa Reisner, and it helped to consolidate Thälmann's hold on the party leadership in the later 1920s, since as a prominent Hamburg communist he played a considerable part in the rising (though he did not start or lead it).[74]

After the defeat of the Hamburg rising, Radek repeated his suggestion ('strike without armed insurrection'): this was adopted by the *Zentrale* on 25 October[75] and put into effect on 29 October, when the Saxon KPD and SPD, and the trade unions, jointly called on the Saxon population to resist Stresemann's second intervention into Saxon affairs (he had just dismissed the Zeigner government and replaced it by a *Reich* Commissioner, Dr Rudolf Heinze) by a three-day general strike.[76] This joint socialist–communist resistance was however sabotaged by Zeigner himself, who resigned the very next day as Prime Minister of Saxony, under pressure from his Berlin colleagues Wilhelm Dittmann and Otto Wels, who had travelled down to Saxony to impress on him the SPD party executive's view of the situation. A purely Social Democratic government was then formed under Dr Karl Fellisch.[77] The strike of 29 October was intended to cover the whole of Germany, but in most places it was only weakly supported. Only in Hanau did it last three days, as planned.[78] In Berlin, Ruth Fischer rejected the whole idea, claiming that the masses were too disheartened by events in Saxony and Hamburg to respond to any calls from the KPD.[79] She was right. The psychological effect of this sudden end to the hopes of the militants of 1923 was well described by the Comintern journalist who wrote under the pseudonym 'R. Albert' for the Paris *Clarté*:

A million revolutionaries waiting for the signal for the attack: behind them the millions of unemployed, starving, desperate people . . . The muscles of this crowd were already taut, fists were clenched on their weapons . . . And nothing happened: the bloody buffoonery of Dresden, a few drops of blood on the streets of industrial Saxony – 60 dead in all – and the jubilation of a bankrupt Social Democracy which had emerged from the adventure a passive mass, ponderously faithful to its past betrayals.[80]

The emotions are well caught here; the facts were slightly different. The allegedly jubilant Social Democrats in fact withdrew from the Stresemann cabinet on 2 November in protest against the removal of Zeigner; their usefulness to the bourgeoisie was now in any case exhausted, with the defeat of the revolution. Stresemann too had almost played out his role, with the successful settlement of the Bavarian problem (9 November) and the issuing of a new and stable currency, the *Rentenmark* (16 November). There was no obstacle to a further move to the right. Stresemann was replaced by the conservative Centre Party politician Wilhelm Marx (23 November), General von Seeckt's order banning the communist party and its press was made the same day, and shortly afterwards the eight-hour day in heavy industry and mining was ended by an extension of working hours to 59 a week (14 December). Not just the KPD, but the whole German working class, suffered a crushing defeat in 1923.

6 Communist Defeat and Capitalist Stabilisation

RECRIMINATIONS IN MOSCOW

The fact of defeat was as apparent to the KPD as it was to non-communists. Less apparent was its definitive character. Was this merely a temporary setback? Was the revolutionary wave still mounting? Much of the party's propaganda gave this impression. Zinoviev's series of articles, 'Problems of the German Revolution', started in *Pravda* on 12 October and reprinted in *Inprekorr*, continued right up to 30 October, without any hint that the 'German revolution' had suffered a decisive defeat. Brandler's resolution of 4 November 1923, which was adopted by the ZA by 40 votes to 13, proclaimed that 'armed insurrection remains on the agenda'. But it was also asserted that the German situation had changed, in the sense that the November Republic had come to an end. Fascism was now victorious, Brandler claimed, in the form of the dictatorship of General von Seeckt. This conclusion, though incorrect, was understandable; it was an attempt on his part to put the best possible face on the catastrophe. He went on to claim: 'Fascism has only defeated the bankrupt November republic. It has not yet achieved a victory over the working class.'[1]

With failure came the search for an explanation. Were there objective reasons for the débacle of October? Or was it a failure of leadership? It seems that Zinoviev, the chairman of the ECCI, was at first disposed to absolve Brandler's leadership from blame. On 2 November he wrote that the German party's tactics had been correct.[2] But in a postscript to his lucubrations on the German revolution he reproached Brandler and the Brandler *Zentrale* for having failed to arm the workers; or raise the question of nationalisation in Saxony; or arrest speculators; or set up

110

Workers' Councils.[3] These criticisms were transmitted officially by the ECCI to the KPD some time in November or December, in a fiercely hostile letter, ending with the words: 'No, comrades, that is not the way one prepares a revolution.'[4]

Zinoviev was not alone in his views. The well-nigh universal reaction of the Russian leaders was to condemn the policy of the KPD in 1923, and that meant condemning its leaders. Even Trotsky, despite his political closeness to Radek, his respect for Brandler, and his doubts about Zinoviev's conduct of Comintern affairs, was certain that there had been an opportunity for revolution in Germany in the summer of 1923, that the Russian Politburo had correctly diagnosed it, and that the KPD had failed the supreme test:

> If the KPD had abruptly changed the pace of its work and profited by the five or six months that history accorded it for direct . . . preparation for the seizure of power, the outcome . . . could have been quite different . . . But the German party continued . . . its propaganda policy of yesterday, even if on a larger scale. It was only in October that it adopted a new orientation. But by then it had too little time left . . . and at the decisive moment the party retreated without giving battle.

However, Trotsky refused to blame individuals. It was the fault of 'routine' and 'automatism', he said.[5]

Only Radek, who was after all jointly responsible for the October retreat, continued to defend Brandler and the 'right' in the KPD. In order to strengthen his hand he gave the impression that Trotsky agreed with him. 'These theses', he said at the January 1924 session of ECCI, 'were drafted by comrades Trotsky and Pyatakov and by myself.'[6] Trotsky did not contradict him at the time (he was not present at the session) but he later referred to Radek's theses as erroneous.[7]

On 27 December the Russian Politburo passed a resolution condemning Radek and the KPD right. This resolution laid down the line of policy the ECCI was to follow in the next few months towards the factional struggles in the German party: 'The Politburo . . . bases its policy on support of the great majority of the Central Committee [i.e. the *Zentrale*] of the KPD and on collaboration with the Left, while criticising the errors of the Left . . . and the gross errors of the Right.'[8] This reference to a 'majority' independent of left or right must be understood in the light of Brandler's abandonment some time in November by the 'centre', a group who argued that retreat was inevitable, as Brandler claimed, but should have been a planned withdrawal with skirmishes rather than an abject flight. Whereas on 3 November the ZA had adopted Brandler's resolution by 40 votes against the 13 of the left, on 7 December 17 members of Brandler's former majority voted with Fischer and Maslow.[9]

The change was not unconnected with the publication in the meantime of an article by Zinoviev directly attacking the Resolution of 3 November.[10] There was also Zinoviev's official letter, already mentioned, attacking Brandler for converting his entry into the Saxon government into a 'banal parliamentary combination with the Social Democrats', which arrived at about this time. It was a clear hint that Brandler was no longer supported in Moscow, and it helped to persuade Remmele, Eberlein, Stoecker, Koenen and, needless to say, Kleine-Guralski to come out against him.

The KPD leadership was thus split into three factions, and each faction now issued contrasting theses on the reasons for the October defeat.[11] According to the centre group, the situation in Germany in October 1923 was 'objectively revolutionary to a very high degree', and the KPD's retreat was a consequence of tactical and strategic errors committed by the Brandler leadership. These could be summed up as: a failure to begin military preparations early enough (they should have been started at the time of the invasion of the Ruhr); a deliberate holding back of the masses in September and October so as to husband their strength for the decisive blow; a failure to use the party's position in the Saxon government to mobilise the masses; an overestimation of the proletarian vanguard's will to fight. The retreat without fighting any rearguard skirmishes was also a mistake, because it shattered the confidence of the masses in the party. Even so, the centre group thought the future would see a 'grand action by the proletarian masses'.

The left's theses were not very different, except that they condemned in addition 'the reformist tactic of the united front and the search for an alliance with the Left Social Democrats'. Finally, Brandler and Thalheimer continued in their theses to defend the October retreat. They blamed the failure of the German October on 'objective causes, which cannot be ascribed to mistakes of tactics on the part of the KPD . . . The majority of the working class was *no longer* prepared to fight for the democracy of November (1918) . . . and *not yet* ready to enter the lists for the dictatorship of the Workers' Councils and for socialism.' The one mistake they admitted was the belief that the working class had been already won for socialism: a mistake made both by the *Zentrale* and the ECCI, they said. It was wrong to have set such an early date for the insurrection, and technical deficiencies in the preparations stemmed from that initial mistake. Thus the centre and left theses differed only in nuances of formulation, whereas the Brandler–Thalheimer version was diametrically opposed both to the other two and to the predominant view in the ECCI. A meeting of the ECCI Presidium opened on 11 January 1924 in Moscow to discuss the October defeat and the situation in the KPD. The three German factions were all represented, but the Brandler faction alone was in the dock. The attacks of the centre and the left were followed by Zinoviev's summing up. Brandler's attitude in October had been 'a symptom of rottenness'; the leadership must be changed, and it should pass to 'the present majority in the *Zentrale* (i.e. the Centre group) together with the Left of the party'.[12] The problem was then placed in the hands of a commission, consisting of Maslow and Thälmann (for the left), Remmele, Koenen and Pieck (for the centre), and Kuusinen (for the Comintern apparatus). This produced a resolution half-way between the left and centre versions of the German events, and the meeting finally adopted it unanimously, overriding the objections of Brandler and Radek, who did not feel strong enough actually to vote against.[13]

There is nothing mysterious in Brandler's downfall. He was the scapegoat for the KPD's failure in October; once Zinoviev, head of the Comintern, had turned against him, he was finished. Radek, who upheld Brandler to the end, was never of equal political weight, not being a member of the Russian Politburo. There is no evidence that the crisis in the Bolshevik Party played any part in these events. Brandler and Thalheimer did not lift a finger to defend Trotsky in January 1924, on Thalheimer's own admission.[14] Of course, if (*per impossibile*) the Russian party crisis had ended in victory rather than defeat for Trotsky, Radek's stock would have risen again and efforts would have been made to keep the left out of the leadership of the KPD. But it is not even certain that the left would have lost this battle. As it was, the rise of

Maslow and Fischer was neither hindered nor helped by changes in Moscow.

The change in personnel also implied a change in KPD policy. But the record shows that an abrupt turn 'to the left' occurred under Brandler, even before the January decisions. The theses of 3 November, representing the views of the Brandler *Zentrale*, prepared the way for a swing to the left by stressing the betrayals of the SPD and rejecting any future dealings with SPD leaders. In fact 'a life and death struggle' was announced against the 'Social Democratic accomplices of Fascism'.[15] In future the united front would be set up only from below. It remained to draw the practical conclusions from this policy. The ECCI resolution of 21 January 1924 endeavoured to do this: the immediate tasks of the party, said the ECCI, were to agitate for the *dictatorship of the proletariat* (i.e. no longer for the workers' and peasants' government), to make technical preparations for decisive struggles and 'to create Proletarian Hundreds in reality, not just on paper'. The united front was implicitly ruled out as unnecessary, since 'the KPD is strong enough to achieve victory against all other parties'.[16] Trade union policy was also altered: strikes were now to be organised independently of, and if necessary against the wishes of, the officials of the ADGB. The slogan 'save the trade unions' in its previous interpretation was declared incorrect. The trade unions could only be saved by 'revolutionising them through the Factory Councils'.[17] Zinoviev set the tone for the new attitude towards the SPD in January 1924:

> The essence of the matter consists in this, that General Seeckt is a Fascist like others, that the leaders of German Social Democracy have become Fascist through and through, that they have in fact formed a life and death alliance against the proletarian revolution with General Seeckt, this German Kolchak. That is the reason why our whole attitude towards Social Democracy needs revising . . . The slogan 'unity from below' must become a living reality.[18]

THE TRIUMPH OF THE KPD LEFT

On 19 February the ZA of the KPD met in Halle, with the Moscow decisions high on the agenda. It acted as expected, sharply condemning the Brandler group and electing a new

Zentrale, consisting of five members of the centre group and two of the left opposition. Remmele was elected chairman, Thälmann vice-chairman.[19]

The centre–left coalition of February 1924 was unstable. The centre group was not very strong within the party, and its influence rested on the ECCI's insistence that a compromise be found. In the situation of despair and bitterness that gripped the party in 1924 a left current made itself more and more powerfully felt. The left demanded that the party concentrate on the final goal of proletarian dictatorship. The immediate task was to 'organise the real revolution, lead the proletariat to victory in the armed uprising and set up a dictatorship of the proletariat'.[20] 'The task of the party is to organise the revolution', wrote Maslow in April 1924, 'the situation continues to be objectively revolutionary.'[21] The centre group, on the other hand, combined an insistence on further work within the trade unions with a demand for 'Bolshevisation' of the party, which meant above all its reconstruction on the basis of factory cells.[22]

In the period of illegality (the ban on the KPD was not lifted until 1 March 1924) the left carried all before it in party discussions at the base, among the ordinary workers. At this stage in the party's history it was still possible for grass-roots opinion to make an impact. There were of course regional differences in the strength of this trend. The District Party Conference for Erzgebirge–Vogtland was dominated by the centre, and it nominated Paul Böttcher as KPD candidate for the *Reichstag*, even though he was regarded by the left as partly responsible for the Saxon coalition policy of 1923.[23] The Berlin–Brandenburg District Conference on 23 March was needless to say a triumph for the left – all 101 delegates were adherents of Fischer and Maslow. A member of the centre group was allowed to speak, but his views were unanimously rejected.[24] The Ruhr District went over to the left, as did most other organisations. The overall picture in the party discussion was of a very strong swing to the left, expressed in the passionate debates at the district party conferences, at which a groundswell of disgust with the united front and the Social Democrats among ordinary members came to meet and confirm the agitation of the leftists in the party leadership. Nineteen of the district party conferences gave a majority to the left, seven to the centre (they were East Saxony, Erzgebirge, Bremen, Halle, Westphalia, South Bavaria and East

Prussia), and none at all to the 'Brandlerites'. The total number
of delegates to district party conferences who favoured the left was
910; they faced a strong centre minority of 350 and an
insignificant number faithful to Brandler (11).[25] At the Ninth
Party Congress, which met illegally in Frankfurt and Offenbach
between 7 and 10 April 1924, the left had 92 delegates with voting
rights, the centre 35, and the Brandlerites none.[26]

These developments were not entirely welcome to Zinoviev.
Some of the KPD leftists, such as Arthur Rosenberg and Werner
Scholem, were in favour of ignoring the Free Trade Unions and
abandoning any kind of united front policy: they wanted to return
to the ultra-leftism condemned by Lenin in 1920. Zinoviev
therefore sent two open letters to the Ninth Congress, one
appealing for trade union unity, the other for the continued
application of the united front policy ('from below' this time).[27]
He also sent two separate private letters. One went to Maslow
and Fischer, the other, signed by Bukharin as well, to Thälmann
and Paul Schlecht,[28] saying in both cases that the ultra-left had
been tolerated for too long and there was a danger of the KPD's
turning into a 'KAPD'. Why were two groups within the KPD
leadership picked out in this way? One possible explanation is
that Zinoviev hoped to split the left, with the aim of placing the
less independent-minded but more 'proletarian' Thälmann in
control.

At this stage there was no sign of a split in the top leadership of
the KPD, and it was in no mood to take heed of Zinoviev's
warnings. The left could afford not to listen to him, since, unlike
the centre group, they were not dependent on the ECCI's favour
for their position. Maslow and Fischer rejected a request that they
visit Moscow, and Zinoviev could do nothing but hope that the
'healthy proletarian elements' like Thälmann would gain the
upper hand over the 'intellectuals' (though denying any such
preference in his letters). Looking back two years later, he
explained:

> The party was in a condition of complete despair. The com-
> munist workers of Hamburg, Berlin and the Ruhr did not have
> the slightest confidence in the old Brandler *Zentrale*; but they
> could not imagine a new [one] without its being led by the
> Fischer–Maslow group . . . This group thus gained control,
> although the ECCI was not particularly delighted with them.[29]

With the left setting the tone at Frankfurt, the resolutions of the Ninth Congress were couched in tones of inappropriate revolutionary optimism.

> Despite the defeat of the German proletariat, which is more severe than in 1919, 1920 or 1921, the objective crisis of German capitalism has not thereby been resolved. It persists as strongly as before . . . Class antagonisms are getting sharper and compelling the proletariat to enter new struggles, thus bringing it behind the leadership of the KPD.[30]

> A real stabilisation of the German currency and healing of German capitalism would only be possible if the existing international contradictions were to be abolished by revision of the imperialist robbers' treaties and [granting of] international credits . . . [combined with] such an amelioration of the social crisis as to prevent revolutionary class confrontations. Both these things are impossible.[31]

The conclusion was obvious: 'The party will have to bring its members to a state of readiness for decisive struggles in the most immediate future.'[32]

Kleine-Guralski, speaking for the centre group, was just as optimistic about the prospects for revolution:

> Even now, stabilisation is extremely precarious . . . we must attune the party to meet the rising wave of revolution. The strength of the Bolsheviks was that they attuned themselves to the rising wave after defeats and before victories. Certainly, one must evaluate matters soberly. But when one sees that there is no evidence for a collapse of the revolution, that on the contrary all the factors point to a sharpening of the situation, the party must respond clearly to this.[33]

Zinoviev too, in his official letter to the Congress, had said that 'the present breathing-space gained by the German bourgeoisie will hardly last any longer than one to two years'.[34]

The task of the KPD, therefore, continued to be 'to organise the revolution'. This required a complete break with the whole ideology of the preceding period, when the incorrect application of united front tactics filled the party with a sense of weakness . . . Not only must its ideology be changed, so that all remnants and traditions inherited from Social Democracy disappear, but also organisationally a genuine, rapid, solid reconstruction on the basis of factory cells is necessary, as well as a full readiness to go over to illegality. The party can only endure illegality if it is based in the *factories*.[35]

This was the real meaning of the decisions of the Ninth Congress: the KPD was turning in on itself, concentrating on *internal* faction fighting (hence the reference to the liquidation of 'remnants of Social Democracy': Brandler and the right), ideological Bolshevisation and the erection of an impenetrable barrier cutting it off from outside influences. The last-named function was fulfilled by the identification of Social Democracy with Fascism, first suggested in the despairing aftermath of October, repeated by the ECCI Presidium in January 1924, and now enshrined in a resolution on tactics:

The SPD . . . let fall the mask of democracy . . . helped to set up the undisguised White dictatorship . . . [and] literally went over to Fascism. Social Democracy has been so thoroughly exposed that even a temporary cooperation of the KPD with Social Democratic leaders is out of the question. It is a vital matter for the development of the revolution that this most dangerous counter-revolutionary party be annihilated.[36]

Despite the KPD's apparent optimism about the revolution, there was very little discussion at this congress of the way revolution might occur, or be furthered if it looked like happening. Apart from the endless quarrel about the responsibility for the October defeat, which led the ECCI to appeal in vain 'Look forward, not back! Use all the party's worthwhile cadres, whatever wing they belonged to previously',[37] there were two main issues: the role of factions in the party, and the party's attitude to the trade unions. Everyone was agreed that the Brandler faction could not be tolerated, but Ruth Fischer also described the centre group as lacking in justification,[38] to which Kleine replied that it was needed as a counterweight to leftist tendencies to undermine the authority of the Comintern.

THE FLIGHT FROM THE TRADE UNIONS

Active involvement in the Free Trade Unions was always a hallmark of the KPD right's approach. In 1923, under Brandler, the communist opposition within the ADGB had achieved considerable influence. Heckert later claimed that the proportion of communist-influenced trade unionists in summer 1923 was 30 per cent to 35 per cent.[39] At the election of delegates to the annual conference of the Metalworkers' Union in July 1923 the opposition (KPD and USPD together) won a majority of votes and a third of the seats.[40] The number of communist trade union fractions rose between July and October from 4000 to 6000.[41]

After October 1923 all the trade unions went into decline. In 1923 there were over seven million people in the Free Trade Unions; the corresponding figure for 1924 is four and a half million.[42] The KPD initially advanced the slogan 'save the trade unions' (Brandler was still in control) and some progress was made in this direction. One hundred and eighty committees of the ADGB were persuaded to attend a secret conference in Erfurt, the so-called 'Weimar Conference' of 25 November 1923. It was made up of 175 KPD delegates, 63 SPD, 5 USPD and 18 without party affiliation. There was little opposition at the Weimar Conference to the idea of staying in the Free Trade Unions. A resolution in favour of sending a delegation to the ADGB executive to ask for an emergency congress was passed unanimously. Karl Jannack, the main speaker, said it was the aim of the opposition trade unionists to fight against the tendency to abandon the unions. 'We must uphold the organisations . . . and not engage in experiments like withholding membership dues or creating new unions. This conference should not be the starting-point of a new organisation but the strongest lever to alter the presently existing conditions.'[43]

With the fall of Brandler, the Comintern and the KPD began to change the line on trade unions. The slogan 'save the trade unions' was now said to be wrong, and unorganised workers were encouraged to stay out of the unions and join the Factory Councils instead. But workers already organised in trade unions were to stay where they were.[44] Many communists went further than this: in the months after November 1923 there was a mass abandonment of the trade unions, partly enforced by repressive measures by the social democratic trade union leaders, but partly voluntary. On 27 January 1924 the Berlin District Conference of the ADGB (dominated by the SPD) voted to expel all organisations which refused to sign a document binding them to obey the Federal Executive's instructions.[45] In March 1924 about 60 delegates were expelled by the Textile Workers at their annual congress. The Salaried Employees' Union (*Zentralverband der Angestellten*) expelled 117 communist delegates at its Berlin General Meeting. Many communists were provoked by measures of this kind into founding their own independent unions, or joining independent unions where they existed. The strongest surviving left radical trade union was the *Union der Hand und Kopfarbeiter* (Union of Workers by Hand and Brain), which had emerged in 1921 from a merger of three earlier unions, including the *Freie Arbeiter Union, Gelsenkirchen*, a mining union which had preferred to affiliate to the KPD rather than stay with the Syndicalists. The other two unions were in fact Syndicalist in inclination. Seventy per cent of the 'Hand and Brainworkers' were coalminers, most of them working on the Ruhr. At the beginning of 1924 the union had 55 000 members.[46] Communists expelled from the Free Trade Unions found a congenial home in it. If they were building workers they could join the *Verband der Ausgeschlossenen Bauarbeiter* (Union of Expelled Building Workers), with 22 000 members in 1924, if they were sailors they could join the *Schiffahrtsbund* (16 000 members), while many chemical workers favoured the *Industrieverband der Chemischen Arbeiter*, founded in December 1922 after a long unofficial strike at a Ludwigshafen aniline factory.[47] In fact the unemployed formed an even larger group than any of these by 1924 (1 400 000 in January, 500 000 in July), and particularly within the KPD. An estimated 70 per cent of party members were unemployed at the beginning of 1924, and many of these were unaffected by the improvement in the situation consequent on the Dawes Plan. The Central Rhine District reported 50 per cent unemployment in 1925, and many other districts (e.g. East Prussia, Hamburg, Lower Rhine) reported up to 90 per cent unemployment among party members.[48] This situation naturally lessened inhibitions against an anti-Free Trade Union line.

The flight from the Free Trade Unions was not encouraged by the trade union department of the KPD, which reported to the Ninth Congress in a tone of resignation: 'We did all we could to continue our well-tried trade union tactics.' A conference of trade union secretaries met at the beginning of December 1923, with a representative of the RILU present, and decided to bring the communist workers back into the existing trade unions, since this was 'the sole possible way forward'. Nothing was achieved on these lines, because the party leadership ignored trade union work for months on end, the trade union department claimed.[49] A number of employees of the trade union department sent a letter of complaint to the Ninth Congress, demanding 'rejection of all organizational experiments, such as the funding of separate unions, and a sharp struggle against all who propagate withdrawal from the trade unions'.[50] This was directed against Wilhelm Schumacher, who had split the Berlin Clothing Workers' union and created his own independent union out of the minority. Under the pressure of members of the centre group (August Enderle and Kleine) and the Comintern, Schumacher's policy of splitting the unions was rejected.[51] This did not prevent the proportion of trade union members in the Berlin branch of the KPD from falling from 70 per cent in 1923 to 20–30 per cent in 1924.[52]

The Fischer–Maslow group was divided on this issue. Some members wished to split the unions, others to conquer them from within. A resolution brought in by the left at Frankfurt combined both ideas: work should continue in the old trade unions, but unorganised workers should be organised separately, industry-wide unions should be set up, and a Workers' Congress should be called.[53] Salomon Lozovsky, on behalf of the RILU, strongly objected to this, but the Workers' Congress was not cancelled, simply postponed until June 1924. When it met it was prohibited, surrounded by the police, and all the participants were arrested.[54] At the Frankfurt Congress the left's resolution on trade unions was withdrawn, and Lozovsky's views were taken into account in a compromise formulation: 'A party member may not of his own volition and without the permission of the party leadership leave a trade union . . . To abandon a reformist trade union without a struggle . . . is desertion on the field of battle.' Unorganised workers were to be 'gathered together', but the resolution did not specify that they had to enter the Free Trade Unions.[55] Many party members interpreted this to mean that they could carry on with their own trade union experiments. Only in August 1924 did the Fischer leadership decide to issue the call: 'All into the Free Trade Unions!'[56] Soon afterwards the leaders of the independent trade unions were expelled from the party together with hundreds of their supporters (Wilhelm Schumacher, Paul Weyer of the *Deutscher Industrieverband*, and Paul Kaiser of the *Verband der ausgeschlossenen Bauarbeiter*).[57] The KPD went further: it told its members they must all join the relevant Free Trade Union by 1 February 1925.[58]

ULTRA-LEFT POLITICS AND FRICTION WITH THE COMINTERN

The left regarded the Frankfurt Congress as an opportunity to purge their opponents, both right and centre. Hence they insisted on making up a list of *Reichstag* election candidates which was almost exclusively composed of leftists, rejected the ECCI's advice to include Clara Zetkin in the new *Zentrale*, and elected instead eleven members of their faction and only four from the centre group.[59] The right were of course entirely excluded from the *Zentrale*.

These changes set the stage for a thorough purge and renewal of leading party cadres. The aims of the Congress were summed up by the Fischer leadership in the following words: 'It has to change the political plan, declare all the vital political decisions of the past year in error, overturn the decisions of the previous Congress, and change the leadership of the party.'[60] The purge of the centre group started at the top, and went down through the party to the lesser functionaries in the regions. In the course of 1924 between 60 per cent and 70 per cent of the party functionaries were removed from office.[61] By July the process of purging had been completed. The ZA session of 19–20 July 1924 adopted all its resolutions unanimously, including a vow 'never again to work in alliance with counter-revolutionary Social Democracy'.[62] As Rosenberg commented, somewhat optimistically in view of later developments; 'It can be asserted with complete certainty that there are no longer any groupings and factions in the German party.'[63]

A great change also took place in the KPD's relationship with the Comintern. The years 1924 and 1925 saw a greater degree of independent action by the German communists than at any time since 1921. It was a paradox indeed that those who had entered party activity as opponents of Levi now reverted to his habit of treating the ECCI representatives as equals, or even, in Marxist theoretical understanding, inferiors. The cautious and modest trade unionist Brandler was thus replaced by the self-confident and ambitious intellectuals Fischer and Maslow, surrounded by a group of intellectual ultra-leftists, whose later evolution shows that they were by no means mere camp-followers: Korsch, Rosenberg, Scholem and Katz. Having just failed miserably to make a revolution, the KPD (admittedly under a different leadership) now purported to give lessons to the Comintern, under cover of a defence of the heritage of Lenin.

There were three main areas where the leftists thought the ECCI was 'deviating from Leninism' in 1924: the trade union question, the united front and the workers' government. The head of the RILU, Lozovsky, was betraying red trade unionism, according to the Berlin branch of the KPD, by advocating negotiations with the non-communist Amsterdam trade union international (IFTU).[64] The ZA of the KPD passed a resolution in July 1924 expressing 'serious reservations' about the campaign for international trade union unity mounted by Lozovsky and the RILU.[65] The Comunist Youth Movement in Germany rejected the Communist Youth International's resolution in favour of a united front (11 May 1924); and the party journal, *Die Internationale*, was edited by Karl Korsch, who attacked the whole united front policy, and claimed that a workers' government, in the sense of a coalition with non-communists, was an impossibility in Germany.[66]

This could not go on. The main body of the KPD left was well aware that the ECCI had helped it into power in January 1924, and at the Fifth World Congress of the Comintern it became clear that a division had developed in the KPD between the left and the ultra-left. Zinoviev's attacks on the Italian leftist Amadeo Bordiga and the Germans Karl Korsch and Boris Roninger were approved by the KPD leadership.[67] Korsch was given some 'friendly advice' by Zinoviev: before intervening in his journal on theoretical questions 'he should first study Marxism and Leninism'! Zinoviev also suggested that Korsch be removed from the position of editor of *Die Internationale*, although the party did not take this step until February 1925. The Fifth Comintern Congress marked a decision by the Fischer leadership to abandon the more extreme manifestations of its independence in order to stay in power. The ultra-leftists (apart from Schumacher, whose position on the trade unions placed him entirely beyond the pale) were willing to accept this because the basic line of the Fifth Congress was entirely in accordance with their wishes. They had no objection to 'Bolshevisation', if it meant a purge of rightists. Nor could they disagree with the Congress resolution equating Social Democracy with Fascism. ('As bourgeois society decays, all bourgeois parties, particularly social democracy, take on a more or less Fascist character . . . Fascism and social democracy are two sides of the same instrument of big capitalist dictatorship.')[68] Nor could they object to the assertion that 'the workers' and peasants' government is the slogan of the proletarian dictatorship translated into popular language', or that 'the tactics of the united front *from below* are necessary always and everywhere'. They simply had to put up with the clause allowing 'negotiations with leaders . . . in countries where Social Democracy is still a significant force'.[69]

Having made the verbal concessions required of them, the KPD leaders returned to Germany to continue their policy of independent leftism. In practice this meant trying to make capital out of the state's persecution of communists, which was at its height in 1924 and early 1925. Between January 1924 and August 1925, 6349 workers were sentenced to a total of 4572 years' imprisonment.[70] Whether this justified the party in issuing the curious slogan 'Down with the Rape of the KPD' as its main vote-catcher for the December 1924 *Reichstag* elections is more than doubtful, especially in view of the complete freedom the party enjoyed to conduct its election campaign. The workers were attracted neither by this nor by the fight against the Dawes Plan. The December 1924 elections were not a success: the party's share of votes fell as compared with May from 12.6 per cent to 9 per cent, its number of deputies from 62 to 45. This failure reduced the prestige of the KPD left in Comintern eyes still further. In the meantime there were internal party tasks to be accomplished, possible rivals to be eliminated. The 'rightists' were pursued with vindictive ferocity. On 11 February 1925 Ruth Fischer and her comrades called on the Russian Central Committee to censure Brandler, Thalheimer and Radek and expel them from the Russian Communist Party. Maslow accused the Comintern of temporising with the right and interfering in the internal affairs of the German party. Stalin replied, somewhat hypocritically, 'I am emphatically opposed to the policy of kicking out all dissenting comrades . . . because it gives rise to a regime of intimidation in the party.'[71] In fact the Soviet Politburo was in no hurry to resolve the Brandler issue.[72] Apart from this, there were several issues within Germany on which the Fischer leadership still did not see eye to eye with the Comintern. Cooperation with the SPD against the 'Monarchist danger' thought to arise from the participation of the German Nationalists in the Luther cabinet of January 1925 was hindered by the KPD's announcement that it was 'in every sense the sole workers' party in Germany'.[73]

However, the changing climate of opinion in Moscow led Maslow to switch over and propose a bloc with the SPD and the centre for defence against the monarchists.[74] This initiated a rightward move by the leadership of the KPD, carried out against strong opposition from Scholem and Rosenberg. The initially united left was now split into a moderate and an ultra-left camp. The divisions and the great difficulty experienced by Maslow and Fischer in making their views prevail were revealed by the confusion over the presidential election of March and April 1925. For the first round (29 March) Maslow advocated the withdrawal of Thälmann and support for the SPD's Otto Braun. He was outvoted, and Thälmann duly stood, receiving a miserable 7 per cent of the votes. For the second round the bourgeois parties were able to agree on Field Marshal Hindenburg as their sole candidate, and there was thus a very real danger that a monarchist would be elected president of the Weimar Republic. Only a joint republican candidate could prevent this. At the Fifth Enlarged ECCI, which was meeting just then in Moscow, Zinoviev stated that the choice facing Germany was bourgeois republic or monarchy 'and for the working class there is a real difference between the two'; the KPD should support the former against the latter.[75]

In a last gesture of defiance the Central Committee rejected Zinoviev's advice and stood Thälmann a second time. Thälmann's own *amour-propre* may have induced him to take the side of the ultra-leftists on this occasion.[76] The second round resulted in a victory for Hindenburg, with 48.3 per cent of the votes; if Thälmann's 6.4 per cent had swung behind the 45.3 per cent of the Republican candidate Wilhelm Marx, Hindenburg would have lost.

STEERING A COURSE TO THE RIGHT

After the Thälmann candidature the course to the right was begun in earnest with the offer of 29 April 1925 by the KPD fraction in the Prussian Diet to tolerate the Braun government (SPD) if it carried out certain minimum working-class demands, such as a political amnesty, the eight-hour day in state-owned enterprises, demilitarisation of the police and confiscation of the German princes' property.[77] There was strong opposition to this from the ultra-left, but the leadership won the decisive vote by 58 to 31.[78]

The theoretical groundwork for this tactical turn had been laid by the Fifth Enlarged ECCI, which adopted theses on the partial stabilisation of capitalism and demanded an alteration in the KPD's approach to the Social Democrats.[79] At the same time the policy of Bolshevisation was continued. Zinoviev expounded this at the ECCI session, linking it with the admission that a 'directly revolutionary situation' was absent. 'In some countries, e.g. Germany, no directly revolutionary situation exists for the moment.' He endeavoured to combine together the twin catchwords of the time, 'stabilisation' and 'Bolshevisation', narrowly avoiding the ludicrous with the phrase 'Let us stabilise ourselves and Bolshevise our parties.' 'What advice would Lenin have given?' asked Zinoviev. 'Beat the Rights without making any political concessions to the ultra-lefts.'[80] According to the Fifth Plenum's 'Theses on Bolshevisation', 'the slogan of Bolshevisation arose in the struggle against the right danger' – it was under this slogan that the Fischer leadership had purged the right in 1924 – 'but Bolshevisation is impossible without a simultaneous struggle against ultra-left tendencies.'[81] The current Soviet view was that there was a 'temporary stabilisation of capitalism', but this was counterbalanced by the stabilisation of the Soviet order. 'Thus we have two stabilisations', said Stalin in May.[82]

If there was no immediate prospect of a revolutionary offensive, what were the tasks of the KPD? Here we must regard Stalin's contemporary enumeration of the five tasks of a communist party as authoritative. The two most relevant to the KPD were no. 1, 'to utilise contradictions in the bourgeois camp' – which implied that the party should emerge from its political isolation of 1924 – and no. 5, defence of the Soviet Union, perhaps the most important in Stalin's mind: 'The fifth task of a foreign communist party is to support the Soviet regime and frustrate the interventionist machinations of imperialism against the Soviet Union.'[83]

For Germany this question was not acute in the mid-1920s: the absence of any prospect of overthrowing the bourgeois German government, combined with the friendly diplomatic and military relationship between the Soviet Union and Germany, meant that the KPD was hardly required to undertake any serious action in defence of the Soviet Union. When it did, it tended to find itself on the same side as the nationalists and Nazis, since what the Russians feared above all was a *rapprochement* between Germany and the West. Thus a campaign against the Dawes Plan meant that the KPD and the DNVP (German Nationalists) constituted the main opposition when the *Reichstag* voted on this in August 1924; in electoral terms it was a failure, leading to the loss of 17 seats in December 1924. In 1925 there was the Locarno Treaty to oppose. It was greeted with indignation in Russia, and the KPD spent much time agitating against it. Thälmann told the *Reichstag* in November that Locarno was 'an attempt by English imperialism to organise Europe as an English front against the Soviet Union . . . Germany by accepting it thereby passes over into the ranks of the enemies of Soviet Russia.'[84]

The communist attitude to foreign policy was unaffected by the decisions of the Fifth ECCI Plenum. But in other respects there was a definite rightward move. This was spelled out in a resolution on 'Bolshevisation in Germany'. Among its ten points were: (1) 'the liquidation of left errors in the trade union question'; (2) 'no vacillations on the question of the admissibility of partial demands' (i.e. they were definitely admissible); (3) 'the application of united front tactics'; (7) 'propagation of the slogan of a workers' and peasants' government'; (9) 'the fight against new deviations to be conducted . . . via a broad . . . campaign of enlightenment . . . The best forces should be drawn into the work even from previous oppositional elements'; and (10) 'party members are to be convinced of the correctness of the line adopted by the party by discussion'.[85] The Fischer leadership now had the task of implementing the Fifth Plenum resolutions in Germany. It did so without hesitation. The only really principled leftists were the so-called ultra-left around Scholem, Rosenberg and Korsch, and Fischer hoped to save her own position at the head of the party by abandoning them. 'Our party lacks not democracy but discipline', she said.[86] The ZA session of 10 May 1925 marked a clear example of the way the 'right turn' was applied in the German context. The *Volksblock* (People's Bloc), that combination of republican and democratic parties which had been originally set up to stop Hindenburg, was now to be supported by the KPD both in the *Reichstag* and the Prussian Diet against the *Reichsblock* group of nationalists and monarchists. The ultra-leftists in the ZA fought strongly against the idea, and received support from the fraternal Polish delegate, Henryk Domski, but they lost by 35 votes to 15. Rosenberg said that the *Volksblock* and the *Reichsblock* both represented the interests of big business: to support one against the other would be to abandon the party's revolutionary character.[87] The *Zentrale* replied to these arguments by saying that the *Volksblock* was a 'combination of petty bourgeois and proletarians against finance capital in the interests of as yet untrustified industry. If the KPD does not organise this petty-bourgeois opposition, it will be left behind when the *Volksblock* springs into life again in opposition to Hindenburg.'[88] The majority resolution accepted negotiations at the summit with the SPD, describing resistance to this as 'inverted opportunism'.[89] A campaign was now mounted, following the example already set by the open letter of April 1925 to the SPD.[90] The ultra-leftists promised to abide by 'Bolshevik discipline' and implement these resolutions loyally, but this did not help them. They were removed from all posts of authority in the party. (Scholem was taken off the organisational directorate, Korsch had already been replaced by Ernst Schneller as editor of *Die Internationale* in March 1925, Theodor Neubauer was replaced again by his predecessor Wilhelm Schwan as political director of the Ruhr District.[91]) These measures were not encouraged by Manuilsky, the ECCI representative in Germany. He, and the ECCI Presidium, preferred the use of 'open discussion and argument against the Katz–Scholem–Rosenberg group'.[92] By a judicious combination of 'open discussion' and organisational measures the Fischer leadership was able to enforce the turn to the right on all oppositional districts during the next two months, with the sole exception of the Palatinate, Hans Weber's stronghold.[93] Scholem tried to win over the Berlin communists with the argument that the situation had not changed since Frankfurt, hence the party's tactics should remain the same. But he was defeated and removed along with Rosenberg from the Berlin BL.[94] The ultra-leftists were now presented in the party press as opponents of Bolshevisation to whom it was a matter of indifference whether Germany was a monarchy or a republic. Scholem, Rosenberg and Katz wrote a joint reply on the monarchist danger, saying 'the present conflicts are over the most effective way the KPD can combat the monarchist danger . . . The KPD can only fight monarchism effectively by confronting the bourgeoisie, as the vehicle of monarchism, with the red class front.' [95]

THE TENTH PARTY CONGRESS

The issue was fought out at the Tenth Party Congress, held in Berlin between 12 and 17 July 1925. Out of the 170 delegates only twelve were supporters of the ultra-left: three *Zentrale* members (Katz, Rosenberg and Scholem), three from the Palatinate, and a sprinkling of delegates from other districts. A letter from Zinoviev was read out to the Congress. He invited the German party 'to recognise openly the fact of a temporary stabilisation of capitalism in Germany', without however 'abandoning the basis of preparations for the second revolution'. (It was never wise to rule out the prospect of revolution entirely if you were head of the Comintern.)[96] The SPD remained a Fascist party, he said, but 'this does not absolve us from the need to examine the reasons for its continuing survival. . . . It rather increases our obligation to try to understand why this . . . wing of Fascism is still able to lead beneath its banner such a great mass of the proletariat.' Only the new tactics of manoeuvre and compromise could overcome such a stubborn opponent. These tactics required that the party 'free itself of its feverish condition of ultra-leftism'. The nucleus of the *Zentrale* was itself healthy, and continued to deserve the party's confidence. But Rosenberg and Scholem were specifically accused of 'falsifying communism', Korsch had 'nothing in common with Bolshevism' and the unspoken implication of Zinoviev's remarks was that the healthy elements should get rid of such people. He also hinted at possible replacements: 'The new *Zentrale* should have no fear of drawing into the work the best comrades from earlier groups not belonging to the left; on the contrary, it should do this.'[97] This statement did not refer to Brandler, who was condemned by name in Zinoviev's letter: it meant the centre group, which had itself sent a letter to this Congress, signed by Ernst Meyer, Paul Frölich and Karl Becker, advising a turn to the right, more unambiguously than Zinoviev had done: 'The conquest of the majority of the proletariat stands once again in the forefront of our goals. We must anchor ourselves in the middle strata. This can only be achieved by a deliberate, flexible and powerful employment of united front tactics. . . . To do this we must draw up a programme of action which corresponds to the tasks of the moment.'[98]

At the Tenth Party Congress the Fischer group was more concerned to ward off the attack from the ultra-left than to move in the direction suggested by Zinoviev and Meyer. However, measured by Comintern standards Ruth Fischer's polemics against the ultra-left were curiously halfhearted. She warned them not to form their own faction, or else the severest measures would be taken; she warned the rest of the comrades: 'we shall very soon have difficulties with this group, despite the small size of its representation at this Congress'.[99] To warn of measures in the future was hardly to impose iron Bolshevik discipline in the present, and in fact at a secret session of the Congress she made a deal with Scholem and Rosenberg whereby they would be re-elected to the Central Committee, along with Hans Weber, provided they supported her against the ECCI. The new Central Committee, including these three ultra-leftists, was then elected unanimously.[100] Rosenberg, who thus kept his place on the supreme policy-making body of the KPD, had condemned the Comintern at the Tenth Congress for 'abandoning the correct left standpoint adopted at the Fifth World Congress on the decisive question of united front tactics, on the Marxist theory of the state, and on the question of leadership . . . The ECCI's letter stated clearly enough that you must include the Right and the Centre in the leadership. I hope the Congress will have enough backbone to refuse.'[101] The continued inclusion of Rosenberg in the Central Committee was bad enough; the refusal to include anyone from the centre group was worse. This had been directly demanded by Manuilsky in a closed session of the Congress. He mentioned Clara Zetkin, Georg Schumann and Walter Ulbricht as suitable candidates for inclusion. The suggestion was almost unanimously rejected and Manuilsky was called to order by the chairman for speaking out of turn. In the emotion-laden atmosphere one delegate called to Manuilsky 'Go back to Moscow.' The loyal Bolshevik Ruth Fischer is said to have laughed aloud at this witticism.[102]

Another piece of defiance by the Fischer group was the refusal even to mention the Comintern's demand for the setting up of a large trade union section, twenty strong, to demonstrate the importance of trade union work in Germany.

Manuilsky, deeply hurt, returned to Moscow to report on the dangerous spirit abroad in the KPD. But these were largely questions of personality. How far did the actual policy adopted by the KPD in 1925 reflect the ECCI's half-turn to the right? The temporary stabilisation of capitalism was conceded by the KPD; the Russian Bolsheviks were congratulated for their successful policy of constructing socialism in one country. 'The main task of the party in the present epoch' was still 'to break the influence of the social democratic counter-revolutionaries on the masses'.[103] The KPD remained 'the sole party of the working class', but in order to gain the leadership of the proletariat it must 'Bolshevise itself' yet again. In practical terms, the Congress adopted an Action Programme of 'proletarian demands', which were moderate enough to form a basis for cooperation with the Social Democrats (eight hour day, minimum wage, factory legislation, abolition of industrial and agricultural tariffs, removal of all taxes which bear disproportionately on the masses, confiscation of entailed estates, political amnesty, removal of reactionary officials, bursting the shackles of the Versailles Treaty, merger between Austria and Germany, removal of particularism, separation of church and state). Mixed in with these, without any clear distinction between the two, were specifically communist demands, which the SPD would never accept (control of production by factory councils, dissolution of the army and the security police, the setting up of revolutionary cells in all war-related industries, anti-militarist propaganda). The party affirmed that it was ready to cooperate with the SPD in the fight against the League of Nations (an institution of which the SPD were the strongest German supporters!), the Versailles Treaty and world imperialism 'provided it at least clearly commits itself to the unity of the trade unions, and the elementary minimum demands of the working class in the economic and political spheres, and condemns the anti-Bolshevik agitation and the preparations for a reactionary war'.[104]

The 'proletarian demands' of the 1925 Action Programme were not very different from those adopted at the previous Congress, when the leftists were firmly in control.[105] But whereas the 1924 programme had culminated in a call to revolutionary struggle, against both capitalists and reformists (i.e. the SPD), and had simply counterposed the future dictatorship of the proletariat to the present dictatorship of the bourgeoisie, the 1925 programme stressed the foreign policy objectives of the party, and held out the prospect of a joint effort by both SPD and KPD to attain them. This was an acceptable transposition to German conditions of the ECCI's more moderate and more foreign-policy oriented line of 1925. The same could be said of the resolution on the trade unions, introduced by Thälmann: every member of the KPD had to enter and be active in the relevant Free Trade Union, communist fractions should be set up as quickly as possible in every local trade union organisation, the most important task was 'the struggle for trade union unity . . . promoted by a campaign for the closest links between the German trade unions and the revolutionary proletariat of Soviet Russia . . . and the formation of unity committees consisting of workers from as many different trade unions and party tendencies as possible'.[106]

THE FALL OF RUTH FISCHER

Were these resolutions implemented by the Fischer leadership? The leading figures in the Comintern claimed later that they were not. Here it is hard to disentangle personal motives from genuine political differences. Manuilsky's *amour-propre* no doubt played a part. Zinoviev may have wanted to put absolutely reliable leaders in charge of the German party, so as to secure a power base in preparation for his forthcoming attempt to unseat Stalin and Bukharin at home. He may, on the contrary, have been pushed into the whole thing by Stalin himself.[107] Zinoviev's position was ambiguous. He was advocating a move to the left in Russia, and simultaneously a move to the right in the KPD.

One thing is certain: Fischer and Maslow lacked the kind of veneration for the Bolshevik Party expected by Moscow. Maslow had just written a book entitled *The Two Revolutions of 1917* in which he openly criticised Lenin for making a mistake in 1921 in launching the united front tactic for the Comintern. He was speaking no more than the truth when he wrote 'the Levites saw themselves as the victors at the Third Congress'.[108] And he explicitly stated that the idea of the united front was 'Lenin's sole mistake'. For the Russian Politburo this was tantamount to opposing Leninism, and Heinz Neumann, an ambitious young communist with strong Russian connections, was commissioned to write an immediate counterblast, entitled *Maslow's Offensive against Leninism.*[109]

The claim that the KPD failed to apply the resolutions of the Tenth Party Congress was advanced almost immediately: the German Commission of the ECCI called on the German party to send a delegation to Moscow 'to clarify the German question' a mere ten days after the end of the Congress (29 July 1925). The spirit of defiance was still strong in the KPD leadership. By four votes (Fischer, Geschke, Schneller, Scholem) to three (Thälmann, Philip Dengel, Hermann Remmele) the KPD Politburo refused to send anyone.[110] Only after the Comintern had threatened a complete break did the Germans decide to comply. When the delegation arrived in Moscow it was subjected to a series of complaints from Zinoviev and Bukharin. The latter retailed the scandalous events at the Tenth Congress, which according to him breathed 'an absolutely rotten spirit of Social Democratic orientation'; he accused Ruth Fischer of pursuing a system of 'double book-keeping' towards the Comintern; and reproached the KPD with refusing to accept control either from above (the ECCI) or below (the party membership), adding that it had become entirely divorced from the masses.[111] The ECCI had always had its doubts about Fischer and Maslow, said Zinoviev, but had not intervened earlier because of Thälmann's silence. 'Now, when Dengel and Thälmann have spoken out, we can act.' The good proletarian elements had been won over, and the intellectual group could be sent packing.[112] Zinoviev left Ruth Fischer and Maslow a bolt-hole: he described them as 'an unknown quantity at the moment, one cannot tell what will happen'. Ruth Fischer hastened to take advantage of this and signed the resolution which condemned her conduct of the party's affairs. When the open letter came before the public, therefore, it was a unanimous statement by the German delegation and the ECCI. 'I was driven to sign my own political death warrant and to confess my sins in public', she commented later.[113]

The publication of the open letter, on 1 September 1925, marked another turning-point in the KPD's relationship to the Comintern. In effect it meant the end of the German party's attempt to pursue a semi-independent policy. The Fischer group's defiance was at an end. The real leader of the KPD was now Thälmann. The open letter underlined the personal character of the changes required by noting that 'it is not the left in the KPD which is bankrupt, but certain leaders of the left, and the left will assert itself [henceforth] along different lines'.[114]

Apart from this, the open letter enumerated a series of party tasks, including a drive for trade union unity, the formation of cells in all proletarian mass organisations with the aim of building up a left wing in the German working-class movement on the English model (which was regarded as very promising at the time) and the strengthening of the working-class resistance to the increasing tendency of the German bourgeoisie to side with the Entente imperialists. *Pravda* put these points more succinctly: 'Nearer to the Social Democratic workers! Real application of united front tactics, not in words but in deeds! Energetic strengthening of trade union unity!'[115]

The degree to which Ruth Fischer's position had been dependent on the confidence of the Comintern rather than of KPD members was now demonstrated: opposition to the open letter within the party was minimal, even though it was immediately recognised as marking the end of the Fischer leadership[116] and though Fischer spoke repeatedly against it. At a conference of all district political directors and editors of local KPD newspapers on 1 September 1925 the voting was 42 to 7, the opposition coming from ultra-leftists. This did not mean a recovery by the centre group: Ernst Meyer's amendments to the open letter were rejected by 53 to 3 votes.[117] The subsequent local discussions of the open letter showed that the only resistance came from ultra-left influenced districts (West Saxony; Rhine–Saar; Hesse–Kassel), from Pomerania, where the followers of Meyer and Frölich thought the open letter still too far to the left, and from Berlin–Brandenburg, where Ruth Fischer's supporters joined forces with the ultra-left to reject the open letter by 13 to 4.[118]

The Berliners also sent a telegram of solidarity to Maslow (who was in prison, having secured a fairly light sentence from a German court by playing on his physical absence from the scene at the time of the October rising). In view of his condemnation by the ECCI for un-Bolshevik conduct before a bourgeois court this was defiance.[119] Even so, the Berlin communists were not immune to appeals to their 'Bolshevik loyalty'. Kuusinen was sent to Berlin as a special emissary, and he managed to win over

Theodor Koegler and Ernst Torgler, leading figures in the Berlin KPD. The central executive of the Berlin–Brandenburg district finally voted by 28 to 1 with 24 abstentions to accept the open letter.[120]

The discussion was in practice closed by the First Party Conference, held on 31 October and 1 November in Berlin, and attended by 253 delegates, 33 of whom supported the opposition (ultra-left rather than Fischerite). The task of this conference was to remove Fischer and Maslow from the leadership, although this was something of a formality since Thälmann and Dengel had been in control since 20 August.[121] Thälmann gave the main speech, and took care to preserve an equal distance from the 'ultra-left' (meaning both Scholem and Fischer) and the 'right' (meaning Meyer) although he offered Meyer and Frölich a way back from their isolation 'if they were prepared to conduct a serious struggle against the Brandler people'.[122] Meyer was stung by this into retorting: 'There is no Brandler faction, there is only a faction that has been characterised as ''right'' because of its year and a half of struggle against the ultra-left course of the party.'[123]

It fell to Philip Dengel to spell out the political decisions of the First Conference. They were to improve trade union work; to direct work in parliament increasingly towards positive steps in the interests of the proletariat, with the slogan 'Down with the Luther government, set up a workers' and peasants' government'; to campaign against intervention with the slogan 'Hands off Soviet Russia!'; finally to reconstruct the party on a factory cell basis.[124]

After the conference the Thälmann–Dengel leadership proceeded with disciplinary measures against the left and ultra-left. The paper of the Berlin KPD, *Der Funke*, was closed down for six months; leading Berlin supporters of Fischer were rendered harmless by being sent to other districts safely in the hands of Thälmann's followers. The KPD CC joined the ECCI in declaring Maslow guilty of unworthy conduct at his trial (8 January 1926). Countermeasures by the opposition were distinctly hampered by the new factory cell organisation. Dahlem underlined the importance of the change to a factory cell basis: 'It guaranteed the implementation of the Comintern line. Without it the victory over the Fischer opposition in Berlin would have been much more difficult.'[125] One immediate casualty was the Katz

4   Ernst Thälmann in RFB uniform

group, expelled in January. Katz immediately set up an organisation outside the party, entitled Left Opposition (LO). In May 1926 he was followed out of the KPD by Karl Korsch and Ernst Schwarz, who assembled their followers in a group called the Intransigent Left (*Entschiedene Linke*). Once outside the party, these groups subdivided further, on the basis of differing analyses of the situation both in Germany and the Soviet Union. This resulted in the formation of a number of minute splinter groups, whose history, though interesting, does not belong here.[126]

THE PARTY UNDER ERNST THÄLMANN

While clearing its opponents out of leading positions, the Thälmann leadership simultaneously implemented the turn to the right implied by the open letter. In one sphere it registered a remarkable success. On 2 December 1925 the party suggested to the SPD, ADGB and other organisations a joint campaign against the Luther cabinet's plan to compensate the former German princely houses for the property they had lost in the revolution of 1918. The KPD called for a national referendum on the issue.[127] The SPD initially rejected the idea, but many rank and file Social Democrats were in favour, and on 16 January the party executive was forced to reverse its attitude. The workers responded enthusiastically. Between 9 and 17 March 1926 twelve and a half million voters put their names down in support of a referendum. The referendum itself took place on 20 June, and fourteen and a half million votes were cast in favour of expropriating the German princes, four million more than the KPD and SPD together achieved in the elections of December 1924. Even so, it was not in fact enough, since alterations in the Weimar Constitution required the support of at least 50 per cent of those eligible to vote. Although not expropriated, the princes were also not compensated, since the SPD voted against this (2 July 1926).

The KPD tried to develop a broad movement out of this campaign against the princes by setting up Unity Committees to link all the current issues together: prevention of compensation for the princes appeared alongside the fight against unemployment and capitalist rationalisation, the control of production by Factory Councils, state participation in enterprises where state credits were to be granted, and the nationalisation of all enterprises which went out of business.[128] The officials of the SPD and the trade unions were unwilling to take part in these committees, but a number of members of the SPD (137), the USP (31) and some Christian trade unionists were prepared to attend a Congress of Working People in December 1926, and listen to Fritz Heckert expounding the danger of war and the impact of rationalisation. A call for a workers' and peasants' government was adopted overwhelmingly (1953 to 3). Most of the delegates were of course members of the KPD. One feature of this assembly was the attempt to forge an 'alliance with the working peasantry and other working middle strata'. It was estimated at the time that ten million people were represented at the Congress; but Dengel later admitted that this was an 'enormous exaggeration'. The fact was that the KPD remained 'on the periphery and not at the heart of the German working class', as Rosenberg told the Eleventh Congress.[129]

The trade union work of the KPD went somewhat better in 1925–6 than before, partly because of a minor economic crisis in the autumn of 1925 (unemployment soared from 5.8 per cent in October to 19.4 per cent in December 1925), partly because of the determined efforts made by the Thälmann leadership to dissolve the independent communist-led unions and reintegrate their members into the Free Trade Unions. By the end of 1925 the membership of the communist unions had fallen from 120 000 (1922) to 36 000.[130] In the November 1925 elections in the Union of Mineworkers (*Bergarbeiterverband*, or BAV), the communist opposition gained control of 35 per cent of the local trade union branches.[131] This was a reflection of the re-entry of the communist miners into the BAV after the dissolution of the *Union*. The most effective form of trade union united front at this time was propaganda for the Soviet Union: delegations of workers went to Russia in 1925 and returned with positive impressions, which even reached the columns of *Vorwärts*.[132]

The continuing high level of unemployment throughout 1926 (annual average of 18.2 per cent) and the tendency of members of the KPD to become unemployed, mainly through victimisation (one in every three members of the party was unemployed in 1925)[133] led the party to stress this aspect of its work. A national conference of unemployed was held in December 1926, and attended by 33 Social Democrats and 114 non-party workers. It set up a central committee and local committees for the unemployed.[134]

However, this practical activity did not constitute the main preoccupation of the KPD in these years. The main concern, both of the German party and of the ECCI, was the factional struggle between the 'left', the 'pro-Comintern left', and the 'centre', or 'conciliators'. This was admitted (and regretted) by all sides at the time. The Seventh ECCI Plenum's resolution on the KPD stated: 'The unrelenting factional struggle of the ultra-left leaders [i.e. everyone from Scholem to Fischer] compelled the KPD in the last year to concentrate a great part of its attention on the internal struggle.'[135] And at the Eleventh Party Congress Dengel declared in the name of the CC: 'For long months we had to concentrate three-quarters or four-fifths of our work on the isolation of such elements as Katz and Korsch, Ruth Fischer and Scholem . . . It was a hellish job.'[136]

The Sixth Enlarged ECCI Plenum started this process, in February 1926. Intercepted letters from Ruth Fischer to Maslow were read out in the German Commission of the Plenum. She had written 'we are condemned to death, since terror reigns in Leningrad. Of the Fifth Congress [of the Comintern] only fragments remain', and 'the Comintern is in process of dissolution'.[137] This was clearly in contradiction with her public statement that she signed the open letter 'because it spells out what we have been fighting for for the last two years' and that 'there are no serious disagreements on the tasks of the party'.[138] No wonder the final resolution described the Ruth Fischer group as 'the most vacillating, most unstable element in the KPD', and condemned 'its habit of saying one thing and doing another, its double book-keeping in policy, and its lack of principle'.[139]

The ultra-leftists were also condemned, of course, and the 'right' did not escape criticism either. 'The struggle against the Brandler group' was to continue. The present course of the KPD did not signify a return to the tactics of pre-October 1923. Ernst Meyer intervened in the German Commission on behalf of the centre group to praise the Thälmann group for carrying out his own policies: 'Why should we not support the policy of the Central Committee? This is the policy we ourselves proposed long ago.'[140] Meyer picked out one point for improvement: a better relationship with the Social Democratic workers must be found. The Social Democrats should no longer be equated with Fascists, and there should be no more street brawls between the communist RFB and the mainly Social Democratic *Reichsbanner*. There was nothing controversial about all this.

But, as Zinoviev said, Meyer had implied in making these points that 'the mountain had come to Mohammed'.[141] The ECCI leaders did not like to be told they had made mistakes. Meyer's views were therefore condemned in the final resolution, and he was kept out of the party leadership for another few months, until he 'unreservedly and unconditionally submitted' and agreed to fight 'the political errors of Brandler and Thalheimer'.[142] Like Levi in 1921, Meyer had anticipated the Comintern's change of line; unlike Levi he was prepared to forget that he had been right in advance of the International. He gained nothing by his submission, as the next two years were to show.

THE EXPULSION OF THE KPD LEFT

The Sixth ECCI Plenum demonstrated that the Thälmann leadership enjoyed the full support of the Comintern against groups to the right and left of it. The right was never a particular threat to Thälmann, since Fischer had already cleared the Brandlerites out of all leading positions. The main battle was against the so-called 'ultra-left'. Once the Intransigent Left around Korsch and Schwarz had been expelled the only ultra-left faction still in the KPD was the Wedding Opposition. But the Sixth ECCI Plenum extended the 'ultra-left' to include the Fischer–Urbahns group, who should more properly be designated the 'left opposition', since unlike Korsch and Schwarz they had accepted the turn to the right demanded by the open letter of September 1925. Hugo Urbahns rapidly became the driving force behind this group, owing to his retention of a place in the CC of the KPD. Like Hans Weber he had not yet provided Thälmann with an excuse to remove him from that body. Urbahns and Fischer were not in dispute with the Thälmann leadership over issues of German internal politics. Their agitation was concerned rather with preserving freedom of discussion within the party, and, above all, assisting Zinoviev and Trotsky's campaign in the Soviet Union. They rejected Stalin's theory of 'Socialism in One Country' and condemned Thälmann as an instrument of the 'right-wing' Soviet leadership which 'rested on the kulaks'.[143]

The German left opposition had no control of the levers of power in the KPD, but it still retained a position in certain local districts. Even in March 1926 the Berlin–Brandenburg District

Directorate (BL) registered a strong minority (8 against 26) against the resolutions of the Sixth ECCI Plenum.[144] Among the ordinary members, 4352 supported the official line, 677 were with Urbahns, 671 with Weber (Wedding Opposition) and 154 with Korsch.[145] The subsequent District Congress (3–4 July 1926) demonstrated that the CC was firmly in control even in Berlin, with 123 delegates in favour. But there was still a substantial minority from the various factions of the opposition: 11 Left Oppositionists (i.e. Urbahns and Fischer supporters), 12 from the Wedding Opposition, and 2 Intransigent Leftists.

In Berlin the left was at its strongest. Elsewhere it was by now completely insignificant. The re-emergence of Maslow (released from prison on 10 July) and Ruth Fischer (who disobeyed Comintern instructions by returning from Moscow in the same month) stiffened the attitude of the left but did little to strengthen it. Maslow was in any case discredited by his behaviour in court in 1925. Fischer and Maslow negotiated with other left groups, including the Intransigents, to arrive at a joint platform of opposition to the theory of 'Socialism in One Country' and support for Zinoviev (who had just been dismissed as chairman of the ECCI). Their cooperation with Korsch was used as the occasion for their expulsion from the KPD (19 August). They were accused of having put forward the slogan 'Against Moscow!' and having thereby become identified with 'the warlike plans of the imperialists'.[146]

Maslow and Fischer were expelled as individuals; lesser members of the Left Opposition remained within the party, four of them actually in the CC, and they were able to collect 700 signatures from party functionaries to an open letter which demanded a 'return to Leninism' and expressed 'complete solidarity with the Leningrad Opposition'.[147] The CC took disciplinary action against the 700, using the weapon of a loyalty declaration. Most of the left refused to sign this and they were therefore expelled on 5 November.[148] Although they could agree on their refusal to submit unconditionally to the Thälmann leadership, the opposition factions could agree on little else. As the CC of the KPD commented: 'there are now six ultra-left factions inside and outside the KPD, around Katz, Schwarz, Korsch, Maslow–Fischer–Urbahns, Weber and Kötter.[149] Our tactics are to increase the differentiation within the ranks of the ultra-leftists in order to separate the working-class element from the leaders of each group.'[150]

THE PSEUDO-CONCENTRATION OF FORCES

With the removal, or submission, of the surviving leftists in the KPD the way was open for the return of Ernst Meyer to the leadership. After his formal submission to the CC he was granted the right 'to exercise criticism within the leading bodies of the party'.[151] A new course of 'Concentration of Forces' was now announced by the ECCI. This meant in practice that Thälmann was obliged to cooperate with the Meyer group, i.e. the so-called Conciliators. Brandler and Thalheimer, however, were still beyond the pale.[152] The new course of the KPD was really a continuation of the old course with a slight change of personnel. Meyer's presence, bought by his subservient declaration of December, was no guarantee of a genuine return to the united front policy he had operated in 1921 and 1922. On the contrary, the CC was very concerned to emphasise the 'left tradition', thereby retaining the option of a move back to the left if necessary at some future date. In fact Meyer had simply been absorbed, and his former comrades Walcher, Böttcher, Frölich and Enderle all drew the conclusion that they must break with him.[153] Böttcher said later, 'A concentration of forces was only possible if the left errors of the past were corrected.'[154] The limits of the turn to the right were clearly indicated in the attitude taken to the SPD at the Eleventh Congress. The Left SPD was described by Thälmann as 'an obstacle to the leftward development of the social democratic workers'.[155] The CC's report to the Congress particularly stressed 'the necessity of fighting the "left" leaders as the main enemy within the SPD'.[156] This argument clearly ruled out any appeal to the left wing within Social Democracy, and it followed the line laid down by the ECCI resolution of December 1926, which had accused the left-wing SPD leaders of 'covering over their counter-revolutionary essence with left phrases'.[157]

The Eleventh Party Congress made it clear that the supreme task of the KPD was no longer to win over the masses, whether in collaboration with the Left Social Democrats or in sharp conflict with them, but simply to defend the Soviet Union. 'We know that the most wonderful thing that exists in the world, which we have to defend, is the Soviet Union', said Dengel.[158] The Soviet Union, it was thought, was threatened from various directions. A new imperialism had arisen in Germany, which was 'preparing a predatory attack on Russia in alliance with English imperialism'.

'One of the main props of the foreign policy of the imperialist German bourgeoisie is undoubtedly the SPD'.[159] The Second International was also involved in these machinations: 'it protests hypocritically against war [but] is in reality conducting an energetic campaign to prepare for intervention against the Soviet Union.'[160] It was therefore clear that the KPD's defence of every aspect of Soviet foreign policy would sour relations between it and the SPD and thus render the partial return to united front tactics somewhat nugatory.

The scandal of the *Reichswehr's* collaboration with the Red Army on technical military matters was one indication of the difficulty of pursuing a policy of defence of the Soviet Union. The *Reichswehr* used its contacts with the Red Army to get round the disarmament clauses of the Versailles Treaty. Arms were shipped from Russia to Germany; German engineers built factories in Russia for the production of aeroplanes, shells and poison gas. These facts were first revealed in the *Manchester Guardian*, then taken up by *Vorwärts* on 5 December 1926 in an editorial enquiring pointedly whether the communist workers who rose in revolt in 1921 and 1923 were shot down with Russian-made ammunition. The ensuing controversy was a clear case of conflict between the KPD's basic aim of defending the Soviet Union and subsidiary objectives like cooperation with other left-wingers to destroy German militarism. The KPD attack on militarism dropped entirely out of sight. The *Reichstag* debate of 16–17 December 1926 revealed a 'united front from Thälmann to Hindenburg', as the expelled ultra-leftist Schwarz put it.[161] The KPD was stung to fury by this 'shameless shell campaign', and replied by bringing up Ebert and Noske's 1919 collaboration with the *Reichswehr*, which successfully clouded the issue.

After the Eleventh Congress the KPD leadership consisted of two groups: the pro-Comintern left under Thälmann and Dengel, and the 'centre' group or 'Conciliators' (as they preferred not to be known) around Meyer. The real power, and the direct line to Stalin, was in Thälmann's hands. He had an overwhelming majority in the CC, and the Politburo, and the only possible danger lay in Moscow. However, for the moment Moscow did not speak with a single voice. Stalin was still in alliance with Bukharin in 1927; they were still battling with the 'leftist' Joint Opposition of Trotsky and Zinoviev, and therefore a course 'to the right' was appropriate internationally. Bukharin certainly favoured Meyer, and he was now the chairman of the ECCI. There is no direct evidence of ECCI intervention in favour of Meyer, but the KPD CC's resolution of 16 July 1927 can hardly be explained otherwise. Meyer's views, put forward as a minority position at the Eleventh Congress, were now adopted by the party leadership. The SPD should not be condemned in its entirety, 'the difference between Right SPD, Left SPD and revolutionary workers' opposition . . . and between the Left SPD leaders and their class-conscious proletarian supporters should be more strongly taken into account'.[162] Another significant statement was the call for 'the overthrow of the *Bürgerblock* government by a common struggle of all working people in town and country'.[163]

The removal from the German scene of Besso Lominadze, the Comintern representative, who was sent by Stalin in July 1927 to carry out a coup in the Chinese party against Chen Tu-hsiu,[164] strengthened Meyer's position, as Lominadze had been strongly opposed to any concessions to the Left SPD, conducting a running battle with the Conciliator Walcher over the issue in the pages of *Die Internationale*.[165] The CC resolution of September 1927 calling on August Thalheimer to return to Germany to take up party journalism again was an indication that Thälmann was no longer in complete control.[166] A few more months, so it seemed, and Meyer would justify his submission by regaining the leadership of the party.

7 The Left Route to Catastrophe

STALIN INTERVENES DECISIVELY

The moderate policy reached its culmination in the offer of 9 October 1927 to tolerate an SPD government in the city of Hamburg. Elections to the local council had proved successful for both left-wing parties. The SPD and KPD together had a majority of 20 over the others. It followed that, if not a coalition government, at least a KPD-tolerated SPD government could be set up. Nothing came of this as the SPD refused the offer.[1] A similar experiment was tried in Brunswick in December. But the 'course to the right' was not to last long, and as long as Thälmann rather than Meyer was in control of the party there was reason to doubt the genuineness of the KPD's conversion to collaboration with the SPD for positive work in a regional framework. The first signs of a change, not just in the KPD but in the whole of the Comintern, emerged in December 1927 at the Fifteenth Congress of the Soviet Communist Party. Bukharin, in his capacity of chairman of the ECCI, was forced by Stalin to deliver a report calling for a 'shift of the accent in united front and trade union policy'. Lominadze and Shatskin called for 'a fight against the right' on the same occasion.[2] Stalin himself provided the theoretical justification for this change in strategy by proclaiming the end of the era of capitalist stabilisation: 'We are living on the eve of a new revolutionary upsurge.'[3] The ECCI underlined this conclusion in January 1928 by referring to 'a most important turning-point in historical development' and 'the first signs of a new rise of the revolutionary wave in the West'.[4] There was no evidence of any kind for these assertions. The year 1928 was a turning-point, not for the capitalist world, but for the Soviet Union. In the USA and Western Europe it was a year of high prosperity. Unemployment in Germany at 8.6 per cent (annual average) was low by Weimar standards; the level of industrial production was higher than at any time since the war, and it would not be exceeded until 1936. In fact, 1928 was the culminating year of the boom of the mid-1920s. There was no sign of the approach of the slump. It would be absurd to claim that Stalin foresaw the crash of 1929 and the subsequent world depression simply because he asserted that it would occur in 1928. The same can be said of the forecasts of Eugen Varga, the Comintern's pet economic analyst. Every year he prophesied a capitalist crisis; he had to be right sooner or later. For the year 1928, Stalin and Varga were wrong. Varga might have found this embarrassing; for Stalin it did not matter. The economic analysis was advanced to justify the elimination of the right and the sharp move to the left in international communist strategy. If the political turn was obediently and smoothly executed the economic analysis would thereby find its justification.

In the first few months after December 1927 the new policy was only hinted at. Thälmann and Dengel knew what was afoot, and they had had a majority in the party's supreme policy-making body, the four-member Political Secretariat, since Meyer fell ill late in 1927. Ewert, the fourth member, was thus the only Conciliator left, and he was often out of the country on Comintern missions to the USA and Britain.[5] However, the new line could only be effectively implemented with public support from the top, i.e. the Comintern, since the Conciliators were entrenched in the trade union section, and what was now proposed was a change in trade union policy, in the one sphere where a genuine and consistent turn to the right had occurred over the previous two years. Hence Thälmann made fierce attacks on 'right deviations' in the trade union section, criticising August Enderle in particular.[6]

The Ninth ECCI Plenum, which met in Moscow in February 1928, defined the new course of the Comintern in both political and personal terms. Politically, it resolved to sharpen the struggle against the Second International and Amsterdam. The Social Democrats in general were enemies, but 'the most dangerous enemies of communism, of the Comintern and the Soviet Union' were 'the so-called left leaders of opportunism, who try to disguise their fight against the Soviet Union with lying phrases of sympathy and ''conditional'' support'.[7] The personal aspect was the renewed attack on 'right deviations'. This expression did not occur in a formal resolution, but in a secret agreement signed on 29 February 1928 by the Conciliators, by which they gave their consent to the suppression of the right. The method was the same as that of the 1925 open letter, which Ruth Fischer had signed despite its attacks on her. The Conciliators ditched Brandler and Thalheimer in the hope of retaining influence in the party. The right deviation was branded as the main danger, and the fight against it the most important party task. 'Indulgence towards those who represented the right danger in the party' was ruled out, a direct hit at Meyer and Ewert. The agreement carried the signatures of Thälmann and his supporters, of the Conciliators Ewert and Gerhart Eisler (Meyer was too ill to attend), and of several top Soviet leaders, including Stalin and Bukharin.[8] It was never published in full, but a summary of the results of the Ninth ECCI Plenum in *Die Internationale* made the change of line apparent to the party's functionaries.[9] At its session of 14 March 1928 the CC of the KPD unanimously confirmed that 'the main danger' was 'the right danger'.[10] Thalheimer, still held in Moscow, was aware of what had happened, and why. In March 1928 he wrote: 'The period which began with the Open Letter [of 1925] is over. An out-and-out course to the left is now beginning, organisationally and politically.' He identified the reason as 'the new conflicts and constellations which are being formed in the CPSU'.[11]

The Conciliators were in a weak position. It became clearer as the year went on that the turn to the left was genuine and lasting. The Fourth Congress of the RILU met in Moscow on 17 March 1928 and proclaimed the 'united front from below'. This was justified in theoretical terms by Lozovsky. He referred to 'the growing together in recent years of the trade unions and the capitalist state' as making necessary 'new forms of class struggle'.[12] The supporters of the RILU were everywhere 'to lead strikes without the permission and against the wishes of the reformist leaders'.[13] Fritz Heckert objected to Lozovsky's 'left deviations' and insisted that the German trade unionists 'would not be diverted from the idea of the unity of the trade union organisations'.[14] He was right to suspect the danger of a splitting policy, although the Fourth RILU Congress did not go as far as to call on communists to split the trade unions. That was to come later.

The KPD went into the May 1928 elections to the *Reichstag* with an address attacking the bourgeoisie and the Social Democrats, the latter as lackeys of the former. The party gained an extra 500 000 votes, and 9 more seats, bringing the total to 54. Simultaneous elections to the Prussian Diet brought an increase from 44 to 56 seats.[15] Other statistics were less impressive. Membership stagnated at around 125 000 (April 1924: 121 000; April 1927: 125 000).[16] When the KPD ventured into the field in isolation, against the SPD government's policy of building an armoured cruiser for the navy (*Panzerkreuzer A*), the voters deserted the party in large numbers. By 16 October only 1 216 500 voters had signed in support of a referendum on the issue, a catastrophic result in comparison with the 3 263 000 communist votes cast in May.[17]

The Sixth World Congress of the Comintern brought demonstrative proof that the Russian leadership was solidly behind the turn to the left. Bukharin, still nominally president of the Comintern, though now no longer able to formulate its policies, delivered the main report. He had previously presented his own draft theses on the international situation to a commission of the ECCI. They were subsequently altered to meet Stalin's criticisms. Bukharin had 'exaggerated the degree of capitalist stabilisation'; 'failed to attack the Conciliators'; not stressed the need for 'iron discipline in communist parties'; and 'failed to recommend a struggle against the left of Social Democracy'.[18] He obediently altered his theses, and the final document emphasised 'an exceedingly rapid development of capitalism's internal contradictions' during the Third Period of postwar history, which had according to this just started. The First Period had been that of revolution, up to 1923. The Second Period, between 1924 and 1928, had been one of 'gradual and partial stabilisation of capitalism'. Now the Third Period would 'further develop the contradictions of capitalist stabilisation, increasingly shake [its] stability, and lead inevitably to the most severe intensification of the general capitalist crisis'. Hence 'the fight against bourgeois labour parties must be intensified' thus shifting 'the emphasis decisively to the united front from below'.[19] 'An orientation totally antagonistic to the Social Democrats' was required.[20]

This was unambiguous, although it did not go far enough for Thälmann, who said: 'the general assessment of the situation could be sharpened' and 'the role of the left wing of Social Democracy' should be picked out, thus taking up again his theme at the Eleventh Party Congress. 'A new period of revolutionary upsurge is ripening', he concluded.[21]

Arthur Ewert then took the floor to defend Bukharin's theses and the position of the Conciliators in the German party. He did not attack the Comintern's left turn, but called for an end to organisational measures against those who 'tended towards indulgence to the Right'. If this were persisted in 'it would lead to the monopoly of a group in the leadership, to a group ideology in the party . . . A majority can degenerate into a group. We have had that happen already in various parties.'[22]

No one else supported this call for a conciliatory approach to the party right. After a series of attacks from Lozovsky (who condemned various KPD trade unionists as right-wingers for opposing the new trade union course), Ulbricht (who attacked Ewert for right-wing factional activity and exaggerating the strength of the Social Democrats and of capitalism) and Lominadze (who said the KPD leadership had taken far too few measures against the right),[23] Bukharin summed up the debate. He offered his personal protection to Ewert: 'The delegation of the CPSU has authorised me to declare that we are against attempts to push Comrade Ewert out of the party leadership.' But Ewert's attempt to alter the political course of the KPD was firmly rejected: the resolution finally adopted called for 'a consistent struggle against Right deviations' and 'the complete overthrow of the Conciliationist trend towards such deviations'.[24] And the Thälmann leadership received full backing: 'the ECCI fully and wholly supports the historically arisen nucleus of the Politburo of the CC with Thälmann at its head.'[25]

After the Sixth Comintern Congress there seemed nothing the Conciliators could do to halt Thälmann. In the long run this was true. But for a short period in 1928 it appeared as if an entirely unexpected turn of events might unseat him: the Wittorf Affair. John Wittorf was a close friend and drinking companion whom Thälmann had appointed in March 1927 to replace Rudolf Lindau as political director of the Hamburg District party organisation. He turned out to be a gambler, who recouped his losses by embezzling the party's funds. A fairly small sum was involved, 1850 marks, and Thälmann attempted a cover-up. But the left communist newspaper *Volkswille* got hold of the story, and this gave the Conciliators their opportunity. Eberlein, the party's financial expert since 1919, visited Hamburg, issued a report describing the place as 'financially a pigsty', and had Wittorf sacked along with three of his friends (23 September 1928). The KPD Politburo met on 25 September; it recommended that the CC suspend Thälmann from all his party functions, leaving the ECCI to decide on his future employment. The next day the CC plenum unanimously condemned 'as sharply as possible Thälmann's concealment of the Hamburg events from the leading organs of the party', which was 'a political error seriously damaging to the party'. The Politburo's recommendations were approved by the CC.[26] Only Lenz-Winternitz and Leo Flieg defended Thälmann. Ulbricht was lucky enough to be away in Moscow at the time. Eberlein insisted that the verdict be published in the party press, and called on Thälmann, in words strangely reminiscent of those Levi had used about Eberlein himself in 1921, to 'do the working-class movement a favour and disappear from it!' The ECCI hurriedly despatched an emissary, Dr Petrovsky-Bennett, to prevent Thälmann from being deposed. He arrived too late. Then Stalin called the German Politburo to Moscow and made it unmistakably clear to them that the Soviet leadership wished Thälmann to remain in charge of the KPD. On 2 October 1928 the Politburo voted by ten votes to nothing with three abstentions (Eberlein, Ewert and Süsskind) that Thälmann 'should remain in the party leadership despite his grave political error'.[27] Soon afterwards the CC came back into line, and the ECCI Presidium rehabilitated Thälmann, while rebuking him for failing to notify the KPD CC immediately of the Wittorf case.[28] With that, the Conciliators' attempted 'palace revolution' was at an end. Their attempt to use the Wittorf Affair to unseat Thälmann immediately rebounded on them. The Thälmann faction had, it is true, deserted him in his hour of need, but only because it seemed he could not be kept afloat. Now they all swung back. The CC meeting of 19 October annulled its resolution of 26 September by 25 votes to 6. Erich Hausen, a candidate member of the CC, declared defiantly: 'The new course [i.e. the left course] represents a new and worsened edition of the policy of Maslow and Ruth Fischer . . . and goes hand in hand with the transformation of the party apparatus into a corrupt bureaucracy.'[29] He was immediately relieved of his functions. Eberlein was thrown out of the Politburo. Meyer and Ewert survived. Neumann at last replaced Süsskind as editor of RF. The Conciliators were also cleared out of the provincial party press. The only district where they retained any influence was Halle–Merseburg.[30]

THE OPEN LETTER AGAINST THE RIGHT

At the end of November the Political Secretariat of the ECCI discussed the German question. Ernst Meyer spoke for the Conciliators, supported strongly by Humbert-Droz. He pointed out that Hans Weber of the Wedding Opposition had been expelled for saying exactly what Heinz Neumann was now asserting with official approval (i.e. that there was no capitalist stabilisation). These were 'Ruth Fischer tendencies', he said, and 'a distortion of the decisions of the Sixth World Congress'. The ECCI should send another open letter to the German party, against the left. Humbert-Droz added that Neumann should be removed from Germany.[31]

Meyer was opposed by Gusev and Kuusinen (for the Comintern); and by Ulbricht and Heinz Neumann (for the KPD). No definite decision was reached, and the Conciliators were allowed to return to Berlin and submit yet another protest against the policy of expelling the right, as well as a long statement attacking 'dangerous "Left" vacillations in the CC majority'. 'Comrades like Brandler, Thalheimer (etc.), co-founders of the Spartacus League . . . should not be equated with traitors like Levi and Friesland or petty bourgeois like Maslow and Ruth Fischer.' The right should be defeated 'in ideological struggle, not by organisational measures'.[32]

An open letter was indeed sent, but not in the form desired by Meyer: it was directed, not against the left but against the right and the Conciliators. It rehearsed the history of Brandler's 'fractional activities' from 1923 onwards. Brandler and Thalheimer had 'proved themselves politically incorrigible'. 'There is no longer any place for conciliationism in the KPD . . . The KPD must demand of the Conciliators a complete break with the Right as well as a consistent struggle against it.'[33]

The sending of the open letter against the right was preceded by a last effort by conciliatory forces within the ECCI Presidium. Humbert-Droz, Tasca and Bukharin all worked to prevent the expulsion of the right. Clara Zetkin advocated a free discussion within the party on the issues and the removal of Heinz Neumann, whom she described as 'an agent provocateur of expulsions and splits'.[34] However, Stalin himself weighed in powerfully with the argument that the right in the KPD 'had broken with Marxism-Leninism and were waging a desperate struggle against the Comintern'. The business of communists was not just to work within the unions, he said, interpreting the decisions of the Fourth RILU Congress, but to organise the unorganised workers 'who were more revolutionary'. This implied the creation of independent red trade unions, but Stalin avoided this conclusion, saying only that 'the creation of parallel mass associations of the working class might be necessary'.[35]

It remained to draw the necessary conclusions from the ECCI's renewed intervention in German affairs. The KPD Politburo welcomed the open letter, with the obvious exception of Ernst Meyer, and expelled eight leading rightists after solemnly putting the question to each of them as to whether they abjured their fractional activity and accepted the decisions of the party.[36] Brandler and Thalheimer could not be expelled from the KPD as they were members of the CPSU, but the Soviet party naturally followed the KPD's example.[37] On 29 December 1928 the right held a national conference, at which 74 delegates were present, most of them still within the party. The meeting decided to set up 'not a new party . . . but an organised communist tendency', with the title KPDO (Communist Party of Germany (Opposition)).[38]

The removal of the leaders of the right was accompanied by a district-by-district purge of the lower ranks of the party. Thuringia was a stronghold of the right, and the Diet deputies were almost unanimously of that inclination. Even there, though, the CC succeeded on 26 January 1929 in winning a vote by 76 to 16 to set up a new, loyal district leadership. By March 1929 there were no rightists left in the party. One estimate gives a figure of 6000 members expelled.[39] Despite this pool of possible supporters, the KPDO remained a sect. It secured 1.5 per cent of the votes in the Thuringian elections of December 1929, but even this level of support could not be maintained. The KPDO had many able leaders, but few followers.

The Conciliators were not purged, but removed in indirect ways from the apparatus. Ewert and Eisler were called to Moscow for employment by the Comintern; only Meyer remained in the Politburo. In any case, they were determined, unlike the right, to avoid a breach with the party, by submitting if necessary. Meyer continued to plead for the maintenance of united front tactics and an active presence in the Free Trade Unions.[40] At a CC session of 15 March 1929 Meyer and Karl Becker called vainly for a break with the majority's 'vacillating and ambiguous attitude on the trade union question'.[41]

These 'vacillations' over the trade unions stemmed from the attitude of Stalin, whose speech of 19 December 1928 could be interpreted in several ways. Lozovsky was firmly convinced that the centre of gravity in trade union work should be transferred to the unorganised workers, and that new, revolutionary trade unions should be set up. Mikhail Tomsky, the leader of the Soviet trade union movement, was able to resist Lozovsky's extremism until he was eliminated from the leadership in December 1928. Early in 1929, the vacillations came to an end. RF issued an appeal in February for the election of separate Red Factory Councils, and separate 'Red Lists' of candidates were put forward in opposition to the trade union lists. In April Thälmann proclaimed that 'the organisation of the RGO [Revolutionary Trade Union Opposition] is the central point of our work'.[42]

THE BARRICADES OF MAY AND THE TWELFTH PARTY CONGRESS

Although it was ultimately decided in Moscow, the ultra-left course was made more acceptable to the ordinary members of the KPD after 1929 by events in Germany. On 1 May 1929 the Berlin police, a force for which the SPD Police Chief, Karl Zörgiebel, was responsible, shot down unarmed communist demonstrators, 25 of whom were killed and 160 wounded. The traditional May Day demonstration had passed off peacefully the previous year, but in 1929 a ban on street demonstrations was in force, and Zörgiebel refused to relax it. This affected both social democratic and communist preparations for May Day, but the KPD alone decided to defy the ban. It called for 'revolutionary mass demonstrations in defiance of all prohibitions'. The SPD was picked out as 'the enemy of the working class' and denounced for its 'Social Fascist regime of terror'.[43]

Whatever the motives behind the provocative approach of the KPD leaders on this occasion (did they want to display their revolutionary enthusiasm to the men in Moscow, as Rosenberg suggests?),[44] it was bound to worsen relations between KPD and SPD, and therefore came at a convenient moment for the advocates of the left course. It seemed to confirm that the SPD was a 'Social Fascist' party; conversely it strengthened the SPD's hostility to communism. The RFB was banned (6 May), and remained illegal for the rest of the Weimar period, and RF was prevented from coming out for three weeks. Albert Grzesinski, the Prussian Minister of the Interior, wanted to ban the KPD itself, but was overruled by his party colleague Karl Severing, the *Reich* Minister of the Interior.[45] An attempt to call a general strike in protest against these acts of repression met with very little response. Walter Rist writes of a strike 'on half a dozen building sites and in a sweet factory'.[46] The failure was blamed on the party's right, and the result was to make the Conciliators very unpopular. As for the Social Democrats, they had clearly shown their Fascist face, and the Twelfth Party Congress (16 to 19 June 1929) was a forum for practically unanimous denunciations of SPD Social Fascism.

It was deliberately held in Wedding, where most of the battles of 1 May had taken place (it had originally been planned for Dresden). The atmosphere was one of blanket uniformity. Thälmann received a long ovation in the appropriate style of the Stalin epoch. The one dissident member elected to the Congress, a worker called Lüttich, from Halle, was forced to abandon his speech owing to constant interruptions.[47] Ewert, Meyer and Eberlein, present *ex officio* as members of the CC, were heard more respectfully. The main political report was delivered by Thälmann, who started from the apparently rational premise that 'the Fascist danger was never so great in the whole world as it is now', and noted 'the active appearance of the National Socialists in all parts of Germany'. But these people were merely the outliers of Fascism, he said. The central role was clearly played by Social Democracy. The German coalition government under Hermann Müller (SPD) and the Labour government in Great Britain were examples of 'an especially dangerous form of Fascist development, the form of Social Fascism . . . Social Fascism consists in paving the way for Fascist dictatorship under the cloak of so-called "pure democracy".'[48]

Apart from the events of 1 May and the general line of the Comintern at the time, there were according to Thälmann sociological reasons for this identification of Social Democracy with Social Fascism. The growth of capitalist rationalisation in the 1920s had produced a new labour aristocracy, which was the social basis for the labour bureaucracy. This stratum dominated the SPD and the trade unions and had penetrated into the state apparatus, leading to a close intertwining of party, trade unions and state.[49] There was nothing new in this analysis of the SPD. It was wheeled out to justify a decision reached on other grounds.

Soviet foreign policy was a far more material factor in the rise of the theory of Social Fascism. The 'danger of imperialist war' was repeatedly stressed at the Twelfth Congress. It was clear to Remmele that the spearhead of any attack on the USSR would be Social Democratic Germany. Germany would serve 'as an example for all the imperialist Great Powers' in this attack.[50] This hysteria derived in fact from the success of Stresemann's policy of fulfilment, involving a settlement of the reparations problem by the Young Plan and the SPD's association with it. According to Thälmann, the Young Plan signified 'the complete insertion of the German bourgeoisie and the German government into the anti-Soviet front'. The Rapallo Treaty, signed in 1922 between Germany and Russia, had become 'a scrap of paper'. Social Democracy no longer played a passive role, as in 1927, but was 'the most active champion of German imperialism and its war policy towards the Soviet Union'.[51] The platform of Social Democracy was now 'the implementation of war policy and of Social Fascism'.[52]

Thälmann presented an optimistic picture of the German situation in order to justify the left course. The masses were becoming 'radicalised and revolutionised', they were 'turning away from treacherous Social Democracy' which was a 'transitional stage of development on the road to the communist party'. The SPD's social basis 'was slowly becoming weaker' while the KPD was 'constantly on the advance'. All the KPD needed to do was 'to bring its ideas to the masses more energetically' and then they would come over to the party in droves.[53] It would have been a sobering experience to confront these claims with the KPD membership figures for the period: end of 1928, 130 000; first half of 1929, 118 157; second half of 1929, 112 511.

There were it is true a number of strikes in the first half of the year (though the number of days lost in 1929 through strikes was only 4 000 000 compared with 20 000 000 the previous year). Thälmann hastened to claim an offensive character for them.[54] They were 'confrontation struggles' which 'already had the form of breakthrough struggles in a certain manner'.[55] This unclear language reflected an attempt to distort reality while not getting too far away from it. The barricades of May 1929 were celebrated as a turning-point in historical development, the first since 1923.[56]

The party's tasks were to fight reformism, 'to put into effect revolutionary united front tactics from below, and to realise the hegemony of the proletariat among the broadest masses of working people'.[57] 'The struggle of class against class has begun', said Heckert. 'The bosses and the Social Democrats stand on the other side.'[58] This line meant a fight within the trade unions and ultimately a split.

Independent strike committees are to be set up to confront the triple alliance of the bosses, the bourgeois state power and the reformist bureaucracy. Efforts are to be concentrated on the unorganised masses, the most impoverished and oppressed strata. The KPD and the RGO must independently lead the economic and political struggles of the working class. Now it is no longer the trade unions but the factories which are the arena of struggle between SPD and KPD.[59]

The struggle against reformism required the creation of a new form of organisation – the revolutionary trade union opposition (RGO).[60] This did not mean new trade unions. Paul Merker rejected 'the immediate foundation of new, parallel trade unions'[61] and the final resolution emphasised that this was not on the agenda at present.[62]

The Conciliators intervened where they could to protest against these developments. Ewert declared that capitalist stabilisation, far from being incomplete and uncertain, was 'fixed and strong'. The enemy for the KPD should be not a phantom of Social Fascism but the actually existing rule of capital in Germany, in the form of the bourgeois–democratic republic. The organised, not the unorganised workers were the vital factor in economic struggles. There was no reason to abandon the traditional line of fighting to gain positions within the Free Trade Unions. The stronger the party was in the Free Trade Unions, the better it would be able to organise the unorganised workers. The elections in Saxony (where the KPD lost two seats and the SPD gained two seats on 12 May 1929) had shown that there was no breakthrough into the camp of Social Democracy.[63] Ernst Meyer pointed out that Heckert himself was forced to admit 'the weakening of communist influence in economic struggle, and I say personally, in the trade unions' in the last year. The action of 1 May had been a mistake: an overestimation of the party's strength had led to the belief that a mere call for demonstrations without political preparation would bring success. The strikes had only occurred where the KPD already had firm control of the trade unions (among cigarette factory workers, cobblers and pipelayers).[64]

Although the Conciliators again emphasised their unshakeable loyalty to the KPD, the Comintern and Soviet Russia, the final resolution of the Congress condemned them as 'followers of the Russian Rightists (the Bukharin group)' and they were all dropped from the CC.[65] The ECCI representative at the Congress, Pierre Sémard, also attacked the Conciliators, as 'the founders of a new Right faction'. In order to stay in the party they had to promise to end all activity as a factional grouping and even withdraw their platform. They obeyed.[66] Meyer, who was less inclined to capitulate than the others, died in any case soon afterwards (in February) and Ewert then disavowed his former 'errors' and agreed to fight both rightism and conciliationism.[67]

The leadership of the party continued to be in the hands of the triumvirate of Thälmann, Remmele and Neumann, which had been in control since 1928.[68] But the Political Secretariat was now enlarged by the addition of Dahlem, Flieg, Heckert, Merker and Ulbricht.[69] Remmele announced: 'For the first time in the history of the party, the Congress has created an absolutely homogeneous, united leadership, and made no concessions at all to groupings within the party.'[70] This 'homogeneous leadership', which henceforth operated independently of any control from below, since no further party congress was held, was destined to preside over the great 'leap into the abyss' (Borkenau) by which the KPD marched blindly to its doom in 1933.

'SOCIAL FASCISM' AND GENUINE FASCISM

In the absence of control from below, the only way of changing the left course was by orders from above. These orders did not come. On the contrary, the Comintern repeatedly confirmed the correctness of the KPD's approach and held it up as an example to other parties. The Tenth ECCI Plenum, which met in July 1929, confirmed the line of the Twelfth KPD Congress. Molotov, apart from attacking Bukharin, whose conflict with Stalin was now out in the open, drew attention to the 'Fascist degeneration of Social Democracy'. The events of 1 May had exposed 'the true nature of Social Fascism to its full extent'.[71] If Italy was the classical country of Fascism, it was said, Germany was the classical country of Social Fascism.[72] In the resolution on Manuilsky's report, the Social Democrats, in coalition with the bourgeoisie, were alleged to be 'organising the crushing of the working class by Fascist methods'.[73]

It was hard to see how this verbal inflation could be carried any further. What could be said if the Social Democrats really started behaving like Fascists? This problem did not need to be faced, as the SPD was soon to leave the *Reich* government rather than reduce unemployment benefit as their coalition partners demanded (March 1930).

Within Germany the KPD's main activities in late 1929 consisted in attacking the 'Social Fascists' (according to Molotov at the Tenth Plenum the attack on Social Fascism had ceased to be 'a question of merely academic discussion'), splitting the trade unions, and 'defending the Soviet Union' by agitating against the Young Plan. In August 1929 the masses were called on to boycott the SPD's *Reichsbanner* as it marched through Berlin: 'Not a drop of water, not a crumb of bread for the Social Fascists', proclaimed *Die Rote Fahne*.[74] 'The policy of the SPD is socialism in words, Fascism in deeds . . . The *Reichsbanner* is Social Fascism under arms.'[75] 'We must ruthlessly purge the ranks of the proletariat in factory and trade union of all rotten elements. He who still belongs to the SPD is rotten and has to go – however radical he may pretend to be.'[76] This meant a return to physical attacks on Social Democrats, as in the period 1924–5.

The other prong of the KPD's policy was the 'organisation of the unorganised', the task of leading 'the million-strong army of the unemployed'.[77] The employed workers were a different matter. Were they to be encouraged to leave the ADGB and join the unorganised under communist leadership? The Comintern authorities were still hesitant about this. The Tenth Plenum resolved in July that 'the creation of new trade unions in countries where an independent revolutionary trade union movement has hitherto been absent (e.g. Germany) must be carried out only in particular cases'. Particular cases soon made their appearance. In October 1929 a strike by the Berlin pipelayers led them to break with the ADGB. Soon afterwards the Berlin branch of the Carpenters' Union was expelled.[78] The KPD reacted by setting up its long-promised rival to the ADGB, the RGO, at a congress at the end of November, when 1100 delegates (the vast majority communists) voted both to carry on independent actions and toT work even more intensively within the ADGB-affiliated unions. Paul Merker, head of the RGO, and director of KPD trade union work since the Twelfth Congress, said that the unorganised workers 'were no longer an obstacle but a factor driving the economic struggle forward'.[79]

Finally, there was the Young Plan to be fought. This agreement for a voluntary payment of reparations by Germany was highly unwelcome to the Soviet Union, as it seemed to confirm Germany's Western orientation. However, a campaign against it by the KPD implied a form of 'united front' with Nazis and Nationalists. The party was not yet psychologically prepared for such a manoeuvre. Thälmann's solution was to oppose the Young Plan in the *Reichstag* but not to vote for Hugenberg and Hitler's 'Law Against the Enslavement of the German People' either there (29 November 1929) or at the subsequent referendum (22 December). He was later criticised for this in Comintern circles.[80]

The KPD could no doubt have continued driving itself into isolation and irrelevance without doing much damage to the German body politic if the Stresemann honeymoon had continued. But the German situation was now transformed by two fateful developments which both encouraged the party in its ultra-left course and made such a policy quite disastrous. The first was the rise of Nazism; the second the coming of the world economic crisis. The impact of the economic crisis on Germany helped the Nazis, but it is clear that they were already gaining ground beforehand. The Nazi gains at the Diet elections in Saxony (May 1929), Baden (October 1929) and above all Thuringia (December 1929) are sufficient evidence of this. The KPD, in contrast, lost ground in Saxony and Thuringia, and its membership figures, after declining somewhat in mid-1929 continued to fluctuate around 130 000 (with a considerable turnover) until autumn 1930 when they began a steady increase which continued until 1932.

The KPD leadership now presented an outward face of complete homogeneity and unity, in contrast to the factional struggles of the previous period. After the removal of the remnants of the Conciliators in 1930 there was no further open opposition to the left course. Two significant disputes did come into the open in 1930, however: there was one deviation to the left and one to the right. On the left, Paul Merker, head of the RGO, tried to resist a small step 'to the right' just taken by the KPD leadership in agreement with the ECCI.[81] At its February 1930 meeting, the Enlarged ECCI Presidium had passed a resolution on the economic crisis, in which, alongside the fight against Social Fascism, stress was laid on 'work in the reformist unions . . . on the basis of the tactics of a united front from below'.[82] Merker thereupon accused the KPD of 'concealing the Social Fascist role of the SPD and the trade union bureaucracy'[83] and tried to form an ultra-left faction. This had a majority in the Central District of Berlin for a short period. However, within a few weeks the Merker opposition had been liquidated. He was removed from his party positions, though not expelled, and the KPD continued on its course, which was after all practically indistinguishable from the one advocated by Merker.

The other opposition came from the 'right'. A group of 60 party officials tried to stop the left course. They were expelled in mid-1930 and mainly joined the SPD.[84] Thenceforward the apparatus ruled unchallenged. There was no more faction-building, at most 'conversations between deviators'.[85] Conflicts within the leadership continued, but on a personal basis, behind the scenes, and without the knowledge of ordinary party members.

It would be wrong to suppose that the KPD line between 1929 and 1933 was carried through without any modifications. Certain changes were made from time to time. It is impossible to judge whether these occurred in response to the Comintern view of the German situation, or, as has been argued, simply reflected Soviet internal and external policy moves.[86] The February 1930 session of the Enlarged ECCI Presidium was taken as the signal within the KPD for attacks on 'left sectarianism'. The 'left sectarians' were criticised for neglecting the united front from below and failing to distinguish the 'counter-revolutionary leaders' of Social

Democracy from the ordinary Social Democratic workers. Remmele attacked the 'theory of the little Zörgiebels', i.e. the idea that every Social Democrat was as hateful as Zörgiebel himself.[87] There was also a temporary recognition of the Nazi danger. The Saxon Diet elections of 22 June 1930 were a surprise: while the KPD only increased its number of seats from 12 to 13 the Nazis leapt from 5 to 14 and became the second largest party in this strongly working-class state. A warning was sounded against 'underestimation of National Socialism'.[88] The KPD's reply to the Hitler threat was the 'Programme for the National and Social Liberation of the German People', an extraordinary mish-mash of nationalist and communist demagogy published in August as the platform for the forthcoming elections to the *Reichstag*.[89] In this programme the KPD claimed to be the only party fighting against the Young Plan and the 'robber peace of Versailles', and endeavoured to outbid the Nazis by reproaching them with treachery to the German-speaking inhabitants of South Tyrol (Hitler had stated his readiness to abandon German claims to South Tyrol in return for Mussolini's friendship). All the German-speaking areas of Poland, Italy and Czechoslovakia could be attached to a future Soviet Germany, claimed the programme. National liberation and socialist revolution were an indissoluble unity.

Thus the KPD sought to fight the NSDAP not by damping down nationalist emotions but by going one better. The idea may well have originated with Stalin himself.[90] In any case very few Nazis could be won over by this method: the example of Lieutenant Richard Scheringer (one of the 'martyrs' of National Socialism who was converted by a communist fellow-prisoner, in March 1931) was not widely followed. Yet the KPD continued this absurd attempt to compete with Hitler in national demagogy for two more years. A special journal 'in the spirit of Lieutenant Scheringer', called *Aufbruch*, was issued by the party under the editorship of Beppo Römer, a former Free Corps leader.[91]

The results of the elections of 14 September 1930 were regarded as a success for the party's strategy. It increased its vote from 3 300 000 to 4 600 000 and its number of deputies from 54 to 77. The really significant result, of course, was the rise of almost 6 000 000 in the Nazi vote. This was not interpreted correctly by the KPD leaders. It was decided, for no good reason, that the Nazis had shot their bolt: '14 September was the highpoint of the

National Socialist movement . . . What comes afterwards can only be decline and fall.'[92] 'The only victor in these elections was the KPD', wrote Remmele.[93] Even later, Thälmann warned against *overestimating* the Fascist danger, saying that '14 September was to a certain extent Hitler's best day, and it will not be followed by any better ones'.[94]

After the September elections the German Chancellor, Heinrich Brüning, no longer had a stable majority in the *Reichstag*, and was thus compelled to rely even more than before on governing the country with emergency ordinances issued by the President under Article 48 of the Weimar Constitution. This was the period of 'presidential dictatorship' tolerated by the *Reichstag* thanks to the votes of the SPD, and it paved the way for Hitler. But it was not yet Fascism, a point emphasised alike by Trotsky from his Turkish exile[95] and by the expelled Brandlerites in Germany.[96] The KPD, on the other hand, viewed even the previous regime, the SPD government of Hermann Müller, as Fascist: Thälmann informed the *Reichstag* in February 1930 that 'Fascism is in power in Germany.'[97] Having refused to differentiate between Müller and Brüning, the party now completely ignored the difference between Brüning, with his retention of parliamentary institutions and his toleration of working-class organisations, and Hitler, who repeatedly boasted that he would destroy such things when he came to power. Instead, the party proclaimed, through Heinz Neumann, 'Fascist dictatorship is no longer merely a threat, it is already here.'[98]

The Brüning government was already a Fascist dictatorship, said Neumann, and the task was to overthrow it.[99] Thälmann, who was later presented in party literature as having avoided the ultra-left errors of Neumann, himself proclaimed in January 1931: 'Fascism does not start with the coming of Hitler. It began long ago.'[100] This did not mean that the Nazis should not be fought. The party returned to the slogan 'smite the Fascists wherever you meet them', heard first in 1924.[101] There were battles in the streets between the RFB and the SA. The main thrust of the party's verbal attacks was against Social Democracy, but the physical conflict was with the Fascists.

The Eleventh ECCI Plenum, which met in March and April 1931, brought certain modifications to the party line on Fascism. Manuilsky adopted a pessimistic tone which might have opened the way to a more realistic evaluation of the German situation.

He condemned the 'revolutionary impatience' of Heinz Neumann, who had put forward the theory that Fascism (both Brüning-Fascism and Hitler-Fascism) was preparing the way for revolution. On the contrary, the crisis would not 'inevitably lead to revolution'.[102] The growth of the NSDAP was not a sign of impending revolution. If the NSDAP came to power the communist vanguard would conduct a fighting retreat, thus saving its honour.[103] The Brüning government itself was not yet Fascism, said Thälmann: it was 'the government of the implementation of the Fascist dictatorship': a subtle distinction, but sufficient to allow for the possibility that what came afterwards might be worse.[104] Unfortunately the final resolution of the Eleventh Plenum gave a completely different impression by stating that 'the successful struggle against Fascism . . . requires the correction of errors arising from the liberal idea of a basic difference between Fascism and bourgeois democracy'. Moreover, the SPD, by inventing the idea of such a difference, blunted mass vigilance and was therefore 'the most active factor in the advance of the capitalist state towards Fascism'.[105] Hence any cooperation with the SPD to resist Nazism was ruled out.

The Social Fascists know that for us there can be no cooperation with them. With the Armoured Cruiser party, with the Police Socialists, with those who prepare the way for Fascism, there can only be a fight to the death . . . No one in the KPD has any illusion that Fascism can be smashed in alliance with Social Fascism.[106]

The only possible form of united front was 'from below', 'a red united front . . . against the Hitler party and the social democratic leadership'.[107] As Trotsky wrote, 'this was a united front with itself'.[108]

The people at the top of the SPD were just as little inclined to join hands in a united front with the communists. There was within that party a left opposition, formed around the idea of working-class unity. But that group, which was the part of the SPD most favourable to the united front, was precisely the target of the KPD's most ferocious propagandistic thunderbolts. We have already seen how Thälmann singled out the left of the SPD for attack in 1927. Now the theory that the left (the 'Centrists') were the most dangerous element in the SPD was developed to its full extent. In July 1930 Thälmann demanded 'a heightening of the struggle against Social Fascism, especially "left" Social Fascism'.[109] One of Bukharin's 'errors' according to Stalin in April 1929 had been his failure to mention the fight against Left Social Democracy.[110] In January 1931 the CC of the KPD proclaimed that 'the sharpest struggle must be conducted against the "left" SPD as the most dangerous enemy within Social Democracy'.

The anti-SPD course reached its height in 1931. Calls to fight Fascism as the main enemy disappeared from the party press. The main attack was directed against Social Democracy. It was in Manuilsky's words 'the main social support of the bourgeoisie in the working class and the most active agent in implementing the Fascistisation of the bourgeois state and thereby the main enemy in the camp of the working class'.[111] And three months later: 'All the party's forces must be thrown into the fight against Social Democracy.'[112] In 1931 the KPD actually regarded certain parts of the middle class as more favourable material for a united front than the Social Democratic workers. In January, the slogan of the 'People's Revolution' was issued. This was described confusingly as 'a synonym of the proletarian revolution'[113] but was meant to apply above all to the peasantry. In May Thälmann announced a 'Peasant Aid Programme', in which the party promised to support various measures, such as freedom to distil spirits and extension of the permitted area of sugar beet cultivation, with the aim of driving a wedge between the big landowners and the 'working peasantry'. The peasants were then expected to join the 'struggle of the proletariat'. A struggle against Fascism? No, 'against the Young Plan and for the cessation of reparations payments'.[114]

Having tried to secure a united front with the conservative peasantry, the KPD moved on to what was effectively a united front with the Fascists: the so-called Red Referendum. Early in 1931 the Nazis and Nationalists mounted a campaign for the dissolution of the Prussian Diet, so that new elections could be held as a result of which the SPD government would lose its majority there, and fall from power. At first the KPD refused to take part in this 'swindle', and took up 'a clear offensive position against Fascism'.[115] Most of the party's leaders, including Thälmann, were opposed initially to participating in the Nazi-Nationalist referendum. Only Heinz Neumann was in favour.

Then the Comintern intervened. Manuilsky too was opposed, but he was overruled by Stalin and Molotov, and the ECCI sent instructions to the KPD to reverse its attitude.[116] A political justification for supporting Hitler and Hugenberg against Braun was easily found: the KPD sent Braun an ultimatum, demanding the removal of the ban on the RFB (imposed in 1929 and still in force) as the price for keeping out of the referendum.[117] On the refusal of the Social Democrats to pay this price, the KPD called on its supporters to vote for the Nazi-Nationalist proposal, which it renamed 'The Red Referendum'. On 9 August 1931 37 per cent of the Prussian Diet electorate voted in favour of the dissolution of the Prussian Diet. It was a large proportion, but not enough. Many communists had defied orders and stayed away.

The result of the Red Referendum was to deepen still further the abyss between communist and Social Democratic workers and make the formation of a united front against Fascism even more difficult. Yet it became more and more apparent that the working class was faced with a mortal danger.

In October 1931 the Nazis and Nationalists crowned their joint participation in the campaign to remove the Prussian SPD government by setting up a 'united front' of their own (the so-called 'Harzburg Front'). The demand for a united front of the working-class parties grew considerably stronger. A constant stream of pamphlets was directed against both the constitutionalism of the SPD and the isolationism of the KPD by the many dissident groupings in German socialism (in particular the Brandlerites of the KPDO; the United KPD Opposition around Anton Grylewicz, which had only 500 members but possessed the great advantage of Leon Trotsky's superb literary and polemical talent; and the left-wingers in the SPD, who formed themselves into the Socialist Workers' Party (SAP) in October 1931 on a programme of proletarian unity). It cannot be said that any of these endeavours was successful: neither of the major working-class parties shifted their positions very far. Yet there were some slight changes. In November 1931 Rudolf Breitscheid, one of the leaders of the SPD, offered a united front to the KPD, which was rejected as a 'demagogic manoeuvre'. Thälmann replied with a call for a 'Red United Front'.[118] But he insisted that Fascism could not be defeated without first defeating Social Democracy. This idea was repeated in January 1932: 'The united front led by the KPD will create the conditions necessary for annihilating the mass influence of the SPD.'[119] Under the slogan 'Class against class. For the Red United Front against the entire reaction, from Severing to Hitler' the KPD put forward Thälmann as a candidate in the presidential elections of March and April 1932. In the first round he received 13.2 per cent, in the second round 10.2 per cent. One million communist voters had apparently been seduced into supporting Hindenburg against Hitler by 'the liberal tendency to draw a distinction . . . between bourgeois democracy and Fascist dictatorship'.

'ANTI-FASCIST ACTION' IN THEORY AND PRACTICE

After this a slight change occurred in the communist position on the united front. The ZK issued a declaration on 25 April that the party was ready 'to fight together with any organisation in which workers are assembled together and which genuinely wants to conduct the fight against cuts in pay and unemployment assistance'.[120] The idea of the 'Anti-Fascist Action', launched soon afterwards, looked like a move towards a genuine united front. However, the limits of the change were shown by the CC declaration of 5 June which set it up. It was aimed at the working class; the 'reformist organisations' were specifically excluded. Moreover, Thälmann denied that any change in policy had taken place: what was happening was 'the still sharper implementation of our political line and the party's principled class politics'.[121] After setting up the Anti-Fascist Action the CC received a telegram from Moscow condemning 'excrescences of opportunism' which arose from the united front tactic and rebuking people who neglected the struggle against Social Democracy because they overestimated the danger from Nazism.[122] The KPD was reminded of the continued need to struggle against Social Democracy by the events of 17 July in Altona, where the Prussian police (under Social Democratic control) protected a provocative march by the Nazi storm troops against the local communists. Eighteen lives were lost, and the SPD was held responsible for this 'bloodbath of Altona' by the KPD.

In right-wing circles the SPD was held to have committed the opposite fault: it had failed to protect public order in Altona from the communist threat, and Chancellor von Papen used the events as an excuse to remove the Prussian SPD government from office (20 July 1932). The KPD replied to von Papen's *coup d'état* with a call for a general strike, to be conducted jointly with the reformist organisations. This sudden, and very short-lived, return to the united front (from above) did not meet with success. The SPD and ADGB leaders preferred the path of capitulation, and the turn in the policy of the KPD was so unexpected that most members were unable to readjust to it. The news of the fall of Severing and Braun was greeted with applause in some communist meetings; the party leaders concentrated on 'technical measures to secure the party's transition to illegality instead of trying to mobilise the workers for the struggle'.[123] It was hardly surprising that no resistance took place, since the communist workers were expected to rise up spontaneously in defence of a party they had been taught to regard as essentially in league with Fascism. Moreover, anyone with a taste for direct action was officially discouraged by the Central Committee's condemnation of 'individual terror'.

Within days of the coup of 20 July the party had reverted to its attack on the SPD. The KPD went into the July elections saying that a vote for Severing was a vote for strengthening 'the Hitler–Papen dictatorship'.[124] It increased its vote from 13.1 per cent to 14.3 per cent, and could claim it was the 'sole victor'. As in 1930, however, the really significant result was the vast increase in the NSDAP vote, from 18.3 per cent to 37.3 per cent. The KPD did not allow this to affect its policy. Heinz Neumann's suggestion that the main attack should now be directed against the Nazis was dealt with by his removal from the leadership (24 May, confirmed on 21 August by the ECCI). At the Third Party Conference, in October, Neumann was blamed for 'underestimating Fascism', 'softening the principled struggle against Social Democracy', 'neglecting the anti-Fascist struggle' and 'unprincipled opposition'.[125] This barrage of words barely served to conceal the real decision reached here, which was to continue the anti-Social Democratic line without any attenuation.

The KPD in these final years was caught up in a contradiction between its political line and the instinctively felt requirements of the time. The setting up of the *Antifa* (Anti-Fascist Action) groups corresponded to a real need to defend working-class organisations and areas against the increasingly bold intervention of the Nazi storm troops; but the party's insistence that non-communists could only participate as individuals, under communist leadership, and that there could be no 'return to the Weimar Republic' even in case of a successful defence meant that it turned into a purely communist operation. Similarly, it was clear that the unemployed should be organised, but the Committees of the Unemployed were staffed by members of the RGO or the KPD 'in most cases', as Ulbricht admitted.[126]

Another side of the KPD's activity in these years was the stimulation of strikes wherever possible. The theory behind this was that partial strikes over economic issues could be 'raised to a higher level' and given a political character.[127] This was the main task of the RGO. Unfortunately the number of strikers went down year by year (234 500 in 1929, 224 900 in 1930, 177 600 in 1931) although there was a slight increase in the number of strikes (from 441 to 497). In 1932 the opportunity seemed to have come to organise at last the political mass strike called for by the Twelfth ECCI Plenum. On 3 November the 20 000 workers of the Berlin Transport Company went on strike against a two-pfennig wage reduction. The ADGB refused its support, on the ground that less than 75 per cent of them had voted to strike. The KPD and the RGO stepped in. They led a five-day strike which they hoped would start a wave of strikes over the country with an 'ever clearer political character'. Thälmann later described it as the 'greatest positive revolutionary achievement so far' by the party. Other people could not help noticing that the united front had been achieved not with the Social Democrats but with the Nazis. The NSBO (the Nazi trade union) joined the strike. The KPD was later rebuked by the ECCI for 'involuntarily concealing the strike-breaking character of Fascism'.[128]

In the meantime, fresh elections to the *Reichstag* (6 November) had resulted in a further increase in the communist vote (to 16.9 per cent), which the party interpreted as a great victory and a sign of the inevitability of communism. The slight decline in Nazi support (from 37.3 per cent to 33.1 per cent) was a sign of the 'disintegration of the Fascist mass movement'. The game with the word 'Fascist' continued: the Schleicher government (formed on 2 December) was 'a sharper stage of the Fascist régime'. Meanwhile the real Fascists continued to act simultaneously behind the scenes and on the streets. Against the background of negotiations between von Papen and Hitler, crowned with success by the appointment of the Nazi leader as Chancellor on 30

January, the SA felt strong enough to march on the Bülow-Platz in Berlin, where the communist headquarters was situated (22 January). The party leadership preferred to evade this trial of strength by ordering the members to 'ignore' the provocation, and mounted instead a peaceful counter-demonstration three days later. The effect on rank-and-file Berlin communists was to produce a feeling of powerlessness. The refusal of the party to fight (at least in Berlin) prefigured the débâcle of 30 January, when the KPD called on the SPD, ADGB, Employees' and Christian trade unions to join it and the RGO in a general strike 'against the Fascist dictatorship of Hitler–Hugenberg–Papen'. Only in a very few places (e.g. Lübeck where there was a one-day strike) was the call taken up. The SPD's tactics continued to be based on constitutionalist illusions; but the KPD's supporters failed to react as well. Theodor Neubauer commented that 'only small and medium-sized factories went on strike, while the large factories remained passive'.[129] This situation was a reflection of the KPD's weakness in most large factories. The party's reaction to the failure of the strike was of course to blame the SPD and the trade union bosses. The SPD had committed a 'monstrous crime against the German working class', thereby proving that it was 'the most valuable support for the Hitler–Papen–Hugenberg dictatorship'.[130]

The failure of the general strike call of 30 January meant that the question of armed resistance was hardly likely to be raised either. In any case, the illegal RFB was in no condition for armed action; its weapon supplies and level of training were quite inadequate.[131] Moreover, the party leaders' first thought was to anticipate expected defeat, i.e. to prepare the transition to illegality. These defensive tactics were subsequently approved by Manuilsky at the Thirteenth ECCI Plenum in December 1933. He stated that 'it would have been sheer putschism if the KPD, relying for support on one part of the proletariat . . . and isolated from the peasantry and the urban petty bourgeoisie, having no armed force at its disposal, had gone in for a struggle against the various Fascist bands and the *Reichswehr*.'[132]

Instead the party spent most of its time preparing for the next *Reichstag* elections. The communist leaders seemed to believe that they could enjoy a period of legal activity even under Hitler, so the preparations for illegality were not pushed ahead sufficiently rapidly. On the night of 27 February the *Reichstag* building went

*5   Communist poster of February 1933 for the
last Weimar election*

up in flames, providing a convenient pretext for the government to outlaw the communist party on the ground that it had intended to use the conflagration as a signal for revolt. Göring ordered the immediate arrest of 4000 party officials, prohibited the entire party press, and destroyed all the party's subsidiary organisations. Thälmann himself was arrested on 3 March. The party replied by calling on all anti-Fascists to 'fight the counter-revolution' by voting for List Three (KPD), a rather pointless activity under the circumstances. Even so, the 4 800 000 votes cast for the KPD on 5 March 1933 were a testimony to the loyalty and courage of their supporters in the face of the terror campaign of the Nazis. The elections were in fact a farce since the party was only permitted to contest them because the government hoped thereby to prevent the SPD from picking up extra seats. Any of the 81 KPD deputies who could be found was immediately arrested.

From then onwards, the party was not only illegal, but largely irrelevant as a factor in German politics. By the end of 1933, 130 000 communists had been thrown into concentration camps, and 2500 murdered. The price of being a communist was high; the price of active resistance was even higher. The repressions carried out by the police after 1933 almost entirely broke the continuity of the KPD as a mass movement. When it re-emerged in Germany in 1945 it was under conditions quite different from those discussed here.[134]

8 Some Structural Features of the KPD

It is now necessary to jump off the comforting step-ladder of chronology and seek for possible permanent or semi-permanent characteristics of the party's internal structure and its relationship to the world outside. In some respects this will merely be a matter of bringing out what is already implicit in the account given so far of the party's history under Weimar; in others new ground must be broken. I have selected three important structural aspects which respond well to an analytical approach: the sociology of the membership and electorate of the KPD, the party's organisation and its international connections.

SOCIOLOGY

The KPD regarded itself as a working-class party, indeed, during its periods of ultra-leftism, as the 'only working-class party'. What was meant by this? In part the statement was purely declaratory: the KPD thereby proclaimed that it alone had the interests of the working class at heart. But it would have been paradoxical if, in a country with a large working class, the party representing that class's interests was sociologically non-proletarian. In fact the claim to be working class was meant to extend to sociological reality as well. One way of justifying it was Lenin's theory of the 'labour aristocracy'. In contrast to the SPD, a party of the upper stratum of highly-paid skilled workers, corrupted by imperialist profits, manoeuvred by venal bureaucrats, the KPD contained, it was said, the less well-paid and the oppressed sections of society in general. There was also a further justification: the communist party was, if not the party of the working class, at least the party of its vanguard. But who was the 'vanguard'? The less well-paid?

172

The skilled workers? The workers in the larger factories, as opposed to small workshops?

Some of these claims can be tested, thanks to the Comintern's efforts in the later 1920s to classify and categorise its sections from all possible points of view. A veritable information-seeking mania seized hold of the Moscow offices. Many national parties sent information to Pyatnitsky, but the German party in particular distinguished itself by its thoroughness. The best statistics we have date from 1927, for in that year the KPD carried through a check of its human resources by sending a detailed questionnaire to all its members. The results were analysed by Wienand Kaasch in an article on the social structure of the party which appeared in 1928 in the Comintern's theoretical periodical, *Die Kommunistische Internationale*.[1] It forms a useful starting-point.

First, age structure. 32.7 per cent of the members were between 30 and 40 years old, only 13.6 per cent were over 50. A young party, therefore, in contrast to the SPD, 27 per cent of whose members were over 50, but not a party of the very young. Only 12.3 per cent of KPD members were under 25. This indicated the failure of the German Communist Youth movement to act as a transmission belt to the party. Second, class composition. 68 per cent were workers in industry, with skilled workers outweighing unskilled (39.92 per cent to 28.18 per cent). There were very few country people in the party (2.21 per cent agricultural workers and 0.10 per cent peasants). The complete failure of the party in the countryside was brought out by comparing the proportion of Germany's agricultural proletariat organised in the KPD (0.06 per cent) with the proportion of industrial workers and craftsmen (0.59 per cent). The remainder of the membership fell into the following categories: 10 per cent craftsmen, hence a grand total of 80 per cent could be described as 'workers' of one kind or another; 2.2 per cent *Mittelstand*, including middle-ranking officials, shopkeepers and professional people; 0.7 per cent lesser officials; 1.7 per cent apprentices; 2.6 per cent cooperative and trade union employees; 1.6 per cent party employees; 11.1 per cent others (including housewives).

The third type of statistic relates to factory size. The Russian example, and common sense, suggested that the party would succeed if it could build strategic bastions in the giant factories characteristic of modern capitalism. The results of the enquiry were disappointing from this point of view. Of the 68 per cent

industrial workers, only 53 per cent were employed in factories
(the remainder were unemployed). Of this 53 per cent, 36 per
cent worked in factories with less than 50 workers, 34 per cent in
factories with between 50 and 500 workers, and only 3 per cent in
factories of over 5000 workers. In Berlin itself it was even worse:
only 1.5 per cent of the members worked in factories employing
over 5000 people. Kaasch concludes: 'The big factories are
dominated above all by the SPD, followed by the Centre party or
the Fascists, especially the *Stahlhelm*.' A dismal picture!

Fourthly, the party past of members was enquired into. 28 per
cent had been in the KPD since the Unification. 63 per cent had
been members since 1923. 30 per cent came into the party from
the SPD; 31 per cent from the USPD (these two groups
overlapped substantially, since the 'main route' to KPD
membership was first SPD, then (1919–20) USPD, then VKPD).
Only 9 per cent had entered directly from the Spartacus League,
a reasonable proportion in view of the small size of the KPD(S) in
1920, before the merger (78 000). The party therefore had 'a firm
nucleus of well-tried comrades', as Kaasch concluded. But this
could simultaneously be viewed as a negative factor: the large
number of ex-Social Democrats meant that the party had to be on
its guard against Social Democratic survivals and traditions.

Finally there was the question of influence in mass non-party
organisations. Some 62 per cent of the members were organised
in trade unions; over a quarter (30 per cent) of this group were
metalworkers, followed by building workers (12 per cent). The
remainder were spread over a large number of unions. The best
districts for trade union membership were those with an old-
established working-class movement, dating back to the years
before the First World War: Württemberg (78 per cent), West
Saxony (75 per cent), Berlin (72 per cent). The figures from the
Ruhr were less satisfactory – 50 per cent – but there was a heavy
concentration on two occupational groups. Among miners (BAV)
there was 1 communist to every 30 union members; among
metalworkers (DMV) there was 1 to every 38 in the Ruhr. It was
difficult to dissuade the Catholic workers of the Ruhr from going
to church: 22 per cent of party members there did so.

Other mass organisations where the party had influence were
the cooperative movement (33 per cent communist), and the three
theoretically non-party organisations which were in practice
under communist direction: Red Aid (not to be confused with the

International Workers' Aid), 56 per cent communist; the Red Front Fighters' League (RFB), with its youth section the Red Youth Front (RJF), 22 per cent; and the Union of Proletarian Free Thinkers, 31 per cent.

Detailed comparisons have been made between the 1927 party statistics and the wage scales current at the time for various types of worker.[2] It emerges clearly that the well-paid skilled workers (defined as those groups earning on average more than 50 marks a week in 1928) were by no means hostile to communism. If we are to give any material meaning to the term 'labour aristocracy', then we must admit that large parts of it inclined towards communism. The skilled building workers, at the top of the scale with 62 marks a week, the skilled miners, with 58 marks, and the skilled metalworkers, especially the steel workers of Solingen, formed the industrial backbone of the KPD. Conversely, the textile workers, paper workers and agricultural workers, at the bottom of both the skilled and unskilled scales, tended to support the SPD. The printers were also inclined towards Social Democracy, and with 54 marks a week they were better off than any unskilled worker, and near the top of the scale for skilled workers. The thesis that the 'labour aristocrats' favoured Social Democracy cannot be maintained; neither can the opposite thesis. In the middle years of the Weimar Republic political choices were not determined by sociological location within the working class. It is however true that the SPD was more likely to attract middle-class groups than the KPD. The figures here are 22 per cent (SPD) as against roughly 10 per cent (KPD).[3]

We have no information of comparable depth for the early period of the party's history. However, the results painstakingly arrived at by the late Robert Wheeler in his study of the split of 1920 in the USPD tend to suggest a similar picture. The Central German textile area – North Bavaria, South-West Saxony and Eastern Thuringia – provided over 10 per cent of the vote at Halle against the 21 Conditions. The textile industry was characterised here by a high level of unemployment in 1920 (20.5 per cent), low pay and a largely female labour force (65 per cent of the members of the textile union were women). Conversely, in areas of coal and chemical production the proportion of supporters of the 21 Conditions (in other words, future communists) was much higher than average. Essen voted 7000 to 700, Mansfeld 3000 to 100, Halle 7500 to 1500, Merseburg 5500 to 1000. In the metal industry Remscheid and Solingen were overwhelmingly in favour, Düsseldorf and Hagen equally divided. Leipzig as a centre of the printing and textile trades opposed the Conditions, and in Berlin the predominance of the electrical goods and clothing industries may be a reason for Teltow-Beeskow's equal division.[4] A factor which favoured the KPD was the presence of strong concentrations of workers in particular suburbs. In Berlin the districts of Wedding (57 per cent industrial workers), Friedrichshain (52.1 per cent) and Neukölln (51.4 per cent) were constantly top of the list for communist support from 1924 onwards, and the same was true in Hamburg for St Pauli (60 per cent industrial workers), Neustadt (56 per cent) and Barmbeck (52.6 per cent).[5]

With the coming of the mass unemployment the later years of the Weimar Republic it was natural that the KPD would recruit increasingly among unemployed workers. This phenomenon can be observed from 1924 onwards. In September 1924 25 per cent of the members in the district of Berlin–Brandenburg were unemployed, in April 1925 15 per cent, in March 1927 30 per cent. A figure of 15 per cent over the whole of the German membership can be deduced from Kaasch's 1927 figures. This compares with a national average of only 9 per cent unemployment over that year. When unemployment began to rise sharply, in 1929, the proportion of unemployed members of the KPD followed the trend. In 1930, with national unemployment at 23 per cent, 40 per cent were unemployed, as against 44 per cent employed in factories. The proportion steadily increased, reaching 78–80 per cent in 1931 and possibly 85 per cent at the end of 1932.[6] As Walter Rist wrote in that year, 'The KPD is very much a party of the unemployed.'[7] There were certainly sociological grounds for the readiness of the membership to follow Thälmann on his ultra-left course in these last years: lack of contact with SPD workers in the factories made it easy to regard them as enemies.

Another change in the character of the party's membership which helped to reduce resistance to the theory and practice of 'Social Fascism' from 1929 to 1933 was the increase in turnover of members. Pyatnitsky's 1931 figures showed that while the party had gained 143 000 members during 1930 it had lost roughly 95 000. A similar loss took place the next year. With a total membership of 200 000 or so, this would indicate the entry of a completely fresh set of members in the course of two years. One would assume a lesser degree of fluctuation among functionaries, but even so, 81.6 per cent of the delegates to the Berlin–Brandenburg District Congress of 1931 had been in the party for less than five years.[8] Their ignorance of the party's past made them less likely to listen to the warnings of expelled leaders like Brandler or former luminaries of the Third International and the Russian Revolution like Trotsky. The reason for the fluctuation is not hard to find: the immense burden of party work which even ordinary members had to shoulder meant that they burned themselves out very quickly. Pyatnitsky himself complained about this, but could do nothing: it lay in the situation. He quoted a list of meetings held in six months during 1927 by communist trade union fractions in the Berlin–Brandenburg District. The total came to 600. 'This is no proper Bolshevism any more, when every party member has to attend 30 meetings a month. Every evening the member comes home late; thereby the party erects a Chinese wall between itself and the workers, because they are unwilling to take so many duties on themselves.'[9]

We must now consider what Annie Kriegel has called 'the outer circle' – the communist electorate.[10] There is a mass of material available on those who voted communist, which has by no means been thoroughly analysed. Here we shall draw in part upon Ossip Flechtheim's pioneering investigations of 1948.[11] The election results reveal a geographical rather than a sociological division in the working-class vote during the 1920s. Things changed in the 1930s, when the KPD became the 'party of the unemployed'. But in the 1920s divisions on a regional basis can be traced as far back as the first election in which the KPD put forward candidates, that of 1920. There was a concentration of communist support in certain specific places. In Hesse there was the town of Hanau and the surrounding district, already famous as a centre of revolutionism in 1848 (Hanau Town 24.6 per cent SPD, 7.2 per cent USPD, 25.5 per cent KPD, Hanau Rural District 28.2 per cent SPD, 7 per cent USPD, 24.5 per cent KPD). On the Ruhr there were a number of mining towns where the KPD was stronger than the SPD in 1920 – Mülheim (15.6 per cent KPD, 12.4 per cent SPD), Hamborn (27 per cent KPD, 14.9 per cent SPD), Dinslaken (20.3 per cent KPD, 18.3 per cent SPD). Finally, and above all, in West Saxony the results of the wartime activities of Brandler and Heckert made themselves felt.

In Chemnitz the KPD gained 13.5 per cent of the vote; in the surrounding district 22.5 per cent; in the town of Limbach (an old-established centre of working-class organisation) 36.4 per cent.

The merger with the Left USPD in December 1920 naturally changed the situation, but it was not possible properly to evaluate the changes in electoral terms until the next nationwide election, in May 1924. Then it became clear that the regional character of KPD support had been still further accentuated. There were four regions in which, taking 20 per cent of the valid votes cast as a measure of strength, the KPD was 'strong' in May 1924. They were Berlin (20.6 per cent); Halle–Merseburg (25.7 per cent); Düsseldorf East (24.9 per cent); and Westphalia South (21.9 per cent).[12] In the corresponding KPD districts of Berlin–Brandenburg, Halle–Merseburg and Lower Rhine the proportion of industrial workers was respectively 43 per cent, 70 per cent and 82 per cent. The first proportion is comparatively small because of the concentration of administrative workers in Berlin. Berlin–Brandenburg was 85 per cent Protestant, Halle–Merseburg was 95 per cent Protestant, Lower Rhine was 65 per cent Catholic. No particular conclusions emerge from these data, which is why the results have to be put through a more finely-meshed net.

Where was the KPD strongest at a local level? One may discover 17 administrative districts where the KPD vote was over 16 per cent in 1924. Of these, 10 were subdivisions of the city of Berlin. The rest were in Upper Silesia, the Ruhr, the Erzgebirge (Chemnitz) and Hamburg. There is no common factor uniting all these districts; urbanisation holds for most but not all. A town-by-town analysis suggests the following characteristics: the KPD was strong in coalmining districts, in large towns situated in mining areas (Hindenburg, Beuthen and Ratibor in Upper Silesia, Hamborn, Gelsenkirchen,Bottrop and Essen on the Ruhr), in metal-producing areas – Gleiwitz, Düsseldorf, Hamborn, Essen – and in centres of the chemical industry – Halle, Mansfeld, Ludwigshafen. It was exceptionally weak in the countryside, in general, and in South Germany (Bavaria and Baden), North-West Germany (Lower Saxony) and the Prussian heartland (Pomerania).

It would be unwise to assume that political affiliation can simply be read off from occupational distribution in each area. Many districts went in opposite directions politically, despite having the same spectrum of occupations in their social make-up. For coalmining one need only contrast Hindenburg (Upper Silesia), pro-KPD, with Waldenburg (Lower Silesia), pro-SPD. In the textile industry the workers of Plauen (Saxony, SPD) can be contrasted with those of München-Gladbach (Rhineland, KPD); in the manufacture of iron and steel goods we have Suhl (Thuringia, SPD) to contrast with Solingen (the KPD stronghold in the Rhineland).[13]

Detailed local studies would be required to give a full explanation of these differences, but one part of an explanation is that two different types of historical tradition went to make up the KPD. Two routes were taken by the masses to the party. One was a continuous line, with almost unbroken continuity, perhaps going back as far as 1848 (e.g. Hanau), but usually beginning with the development of a radical left wing within the prewar SPD. The route then followed was through the left of the USPD during the war, and in most cases an immediate transition to communism after it. Remscheid, Solingen, Hanau, Mülheim, Hamborn, Dinslaken and Limbach were already voting for the SPD in 1890. We have seen that the KPD did well in most of these places in 1920, despite being insignificant on a national scale. They then remained faithful to the party throughout the Weimar years, to finish by showing substantial proportions of communist support as late as 1949 under the Federal Republic.[14]

Then there was the other route to communism, via the detour of the postwar USPD. A sudden break from earlier political passivity, at the very end of the war, followed by entry into the USPD in 1918–19, then the break with Centrism in 1920 and acceptance of the 21 Conditions of Admission to the Comintern. The coalminers of Upper Silesia and the chemical workers of Prussian Saxony were only politicised in 1918 with the ending of the First World War. In some cases the industries were entirely new, the results of wartime demand. The massive Leuna works in Mansfeld only started operating in 1916 and employed 23 000 workers by 1921. Even where some industrialisation had taken place before 1914, Social Democratic traditions had not had time to become implanted. Hence there was no psychological obstacle to entry into the KPD in 1920.

Franz Borkenau, the first writer to concern himself with this phenomenon, drew far-reaching, indeed exaggerated conclusions. He emphasised the radical discontinuity between the postwar KPD and the prewar German working-class movement. His view was that politically inexperienced workers formed the mass base of the KPD. Our examination of election statistics does not entirely confirm this view. The KPD drew support both from traditional SPD strongholds and from the newly politicised sections of the working class. Social Democratic traditions were not in fact an obstacle to the formation of a strong communist party. If we compare the elections of 1912 with those of 1924 we find that communist strength in 1924 is closely correlated with SPD strength in 1912 in every district except one (Upper Silesia). Negatively, too, it is interesting to note that the failure of the SPD in 1912 to win a single seat in any of the 132 electoral districts where agriculture was the predominant occupation[15] was paralleled by a similar failure by the KPD in 1924. The Social Democrats themselves, in contrast, had made advances precisely in those agricultural districts. If we take the 53 electoral subdivisions[16] where the KPD secured over 25 per cent of the vote in May 1924 we find that 30 of them were overwhelmingly industrial (less than 5 per cent of the labour force engaged in agriculture), 6 largely industrial (between 5 and 20 per cent engaged in agriculture), and 17 mixed (between 20 and 50 per cent in agriculture). The mixed districts were concentrated in the two areas of Upper Silesia and Merseburg, which were unusual in Germany in displaying a balance of agricultural and industrial occupations (Upper Silesia 30.7 per cent agriculture, 36.5 per cent industry, Merseburg 22.5 per cent agriculture, 46.1 per cent industry). In Upper Silesia overwhelmingly industrial districts such as Beuthen (3.4 per cent/70.9 per cent) stood alongside largely agricultural districts like Rybnik (42.5 per cent/29.9 per cent). This difference had some impact on the KPD vote (Beuthen 51.8 per cent, Rybnik 25.1 per cent), but the case of Tarnowitz, which gave the KPD the highest proportion of votes in the whole of Germany (57 per cent), while 26.5 per cent of its labour force was agricultural, 53 per cent industrial, shows that here at least the KPD had managed to break through into the countryside. Similarly, in Halle–Merseburg, the rural district of Saalkreis, with 25.9 per cent employed in agriculture, gave 41.3 per cent of its votes to the KPD. The case of Tarnowitz could easily be explained by pointing to the 69 per cent of non-Germans who lived there but no such explanation is available for Saalkreis. One can only assume that the overwhelming majority of the industrial workers (46.6 per cent here) voted KPD, leaving the country people to support the SPD. Outside Upper Silesia and Merseburg it is clear that there is a correlation between proletarianisation and KPD support. Those 'proletarians in the countryside', on the other hand, the agricultural workers of East Germany did not show any greater tendency to follow the KPD in 1924 than the small farmers of the south. The town/country contrast in voting patterns (KPD in the town, SPD in the country) noted by Guttsman for East Prussia[17] (one might add Mecklenburg) is reproduced in Württemberg, though here the opponent in the countryside was the Centre Party.

Let us conclude by looking at changes in voting patterns over the Weimar period. If we compare the elections of December 1924 with those of May 1928, we find that the slight increase in KPD support over the country as a whole (from 9 per cent to 10.6 per cent) conceals considerable changes in regional distribution. The city of Berlin, and the whole surrounding area (Potsdam I, Potsdam II) registered considerable increases (Berlin itself added over 10 per cent in four years, the others 5 per cent and 6 per cent respectively). In East Saxony too the KPD probably benefited from the 1926 split in the local SPD, increasing its vote by 4 per cent in both Dresden and Leipzig. Gains in these favoured districts were balanced by losses elsewhere: in Thuringia, Westphalia South, South Hanover–Brunswick and Württemberg.

The Ruhr did not form one of the KPD's electoral strongholds until the post-1929 economic crisis hit Germany; the party's West German heartland was further south, around Düsseldorf. The stability of the party's best districts under pressure was remarkable: in the March 1933 elections four out of the five top districts of May 1924 were still there at the top of the list (Berlin, Chemnitz, Merseburg, Düsseldorf East), and of the twelve top districts in May 1924, eleven were still there in 1933 (although the rank order within this group had changed somewhat). The picture is not startlingly different if one compares the intervening elections (December 1924 eleven out of twelve, 1928 ten out of twelve, 1930 eleven out of twelve, July 1932 eleven out of twelve, November 1932 eleven out of twelve).[18]

If we look now at the other end of the scale, we can say that stony ground in 1924 remained stony for the rest of the period. Only one of the twelve worst districts of May 1924 had improved its performance enough to change its rank order by 1933 –

Dresden-Bautzen. The case is significant, for East Saxony was an area which had long been highly industrialised and had a solidly implanted SPD organisation. In the crisis of the early 1930s there was a tendency for former SPD voters to move over to the KPD. But this tendency did not operate in two other cases: Lower Saxony and Lower Silesia. Neither could be dismissed as agricultural. Their substantial urban working-class populations remained mysteriously faithful to the SPD to the very end.[19] If they did desert, it was to the Nazis.

The overall pattern of KPD support therefore did not undergo any great changes once the Left USPD had been absorbed. And the 'outer circle' of election-time sympathisers was usually at its strongest where the party was most firmly implanted as an organisation. The only exception to this was Upper Silesia, where voting strength (which in any case had a tendency to fall off in 'difficult' periods) had no correlation with party membership. If we take the top six party districts in 1929 (Berlin–Brandenburg, Halle–Merseburg, Wasserkante, Lower Rhine, Erzgebirge–Chemnitz, Ruhr) we find that they accounted for 56 per cent of the party's membership and 56.5 per cent of the party vote in 1928, but contained only 33 per cent of the total German population. This indicates both the concentration of KPD support in certain areas and the normally close correlation between membership and voting. The corresponding figures for 1931 were similar: 60 per cent of the members in the same six districts, and 53.8 per cent of the vote (1930 elections). The only change within the top group (both in electoral and membership terms) was a slight, but not dramatic, increase in the weight of Berlin at the expense of the others. The Berlin–Brandenburg proportion of members rose from 13 per cent in 1921 to 15.8 per cent in 1931. Outside the top group one can discern a tendency towards a more even distribution of members, no doubt a result of the increased sophistication of the party organisation.

Finally it is perhaps hardly necessary to point out that the KPD was, like all others, but even more so, a male-dominated party. In 1922 only 12.2 per cent of the members were women (the SPD proportion was 18.7 per cent).[20] The 1929 figure for the KPD is slightly higher (16.5 per cent).[21] Women were less likely than men to vote communist.[22] Of course this was also true of the SPD, but the gap was not so great.[23] Once a woman had entered the party she had little chance of rising to a top position: between 1919 and

1935 the number of women in the party leadership varied from nought to two, and the 1929 Congress elected three women and thirty-five men to the Central Committee. The Second, Third and Fourth Congresses removed the 'woman question' at the last moment from the agenda so as to have time to discuss 'more urgent' matters. The presence of a few women at the top (Rosa Luxemburg, Clara Zetkin, Ruth Fischer) should not blind us to the fact that the KPD was a party of the male urban working class.[24]

ORGANISATION AND DISCIPLINE IN THE KPD

The attitude and practice of the KPD in questions of organisation went through several stages during the party's history. The Founding Congress of 1919 adopted no formal statutes, but the speech of Hugo Eberlein on organisation is clear evidence of the general attitude at the time. He rejected the 'bureaucratic' organisation of the old SPD, and seemed inclined to favour a thorough-going federalism. The Party Districts (*Bezirke*) were to enjoy autonomy, and even the press was not to be centralised: 'The local organisations should always have the possibility of founding their own newspapers, and issuing their own leaflets and pamphlets.'[25] This view reflected both the weakness of the party organisation and the expectation that the masses would make the revolution themselves, without requiring the leadership of a revolutionary party. The form appropriate to the dictatorship of the proletariat would be the Workers' and Soldiers' Council, not the party. At this early period the example of Soviet Russia worked as much in favour of the former as the latter. As Eberlein told the Second Congress, looking back to the beginning of the year, 'Many people believed that it was unnecessary to bind the comrades together organisationally with an extensive apparatus, since the proletariat would shortly take power and then the political organisation would dissolve in the Council System.'[26]

It was therefore partly the force of events that turned the KPD away from federalism, first the evident decline of the spontaneous council movement in 1919 and second Levi's conflict with the Hamburg opposition in the autumn of that year. The Heidelberg Theses of October 1919 proclaimed the need for the 'most rigid centralisation' in times of revolution. This involved the rejection of 'all federalism'.[27] Even so, the party statute adopted at Heidelberg was far removed from the centralised structure which prevailed in later years in the KPD.[28] The local groups (*Ortsgruppen*), the basic building blocks of the party organisation, were to work 'autonomously within the framework of party principles and party decisions' and to 'draw up their own statutes'. The party press was to be controlled locally not centrally; contributions from the party towards the press were to be administered by local organisations. Paid officials could be recalled at any time by the body which elected them; they had to stand for re-election every year. The *Zentrale*, the small group of people which constituted the nerve-centre of the party and occupied an analogous position to the Bolshevik Central Committee in its early days, is only mentioned in passing. This early statute appears to assign a more important role to the *Zentralausschuss*, or Central Commission (ZA). The supreme party body was of course the annual Party Congress; but the Congress 'entrusts the conduct of the party's business to the ZA, consisting of twenty members . . . thirteen of them to be elected from the local districts (*Bezirke*)'. (The other seven were present *ex officio* as members of the *Zentrale*.) The ZA was meant to be supreme when the Congress was not in session, and its composition ensured that the localities could out-vote the *Zentrale* if they so wished. It was, even in name, a survival of the prewar organisation of the SPD.

At the Fifth Party Congress (November 1920), which was called to prepare for the merger with the Left USPD, there was some difference of opinion over centralisation. Hermann Duncker argued that one of the lessons of the Bolshevik Revolution had been the need for a 'tightly organised revolutionary party'.[29] Since the Second Comintern Congress this had been the official line of the International. But Hans Tittel, from Württemberg, underlined the dangers of excessive centralisation: 'We want democratic, not bureaucratic centralism.'[30] Most of the delegates followed Duncker, and the Congress resolved that 'strict centralisation and iron discipline are unconditionally necessary to strengthen the party's fighting capacity'.[31] Steps had already been taken in this direction by 1920: political commissions had been appointed to ensure close contact between the *Zentrale* and the Districts; the *Zentrale* itself was now subdivided into a Politburo and an Orgburo. These bodies met three times a week in 1922.[32]

A new party statute was adopted by the Sixth (Unificat
Congress in December 1920. It was much closer to the
'democratic centralism' of the Bolshevik Party than the 1919
statute had been.[33] The prerogatives of the *Zentrale* were spelled
out for the first time: 'The *Zentrale* constitutes the political and
organisational direction of the party', and its task is to 'supervise
all organs and functionaries'. The *Zentrale* was in its turn to be
supervised, as before, by the ZA, which was to meet every three
months. The employment of party functionaries was now made
conditional on the approval of the *Zentrale*, though where
differences of opinion came up the ZA had the final decision.
There was no reappearance of the 1919 clause on annual re-
election of functionaries by the membership. The political and
tactical line of the party press was now firmly subordinated to the
Zentrale. Party newspapers had to print everything submitted to
them by the *Zentrale*. The District Directorate (*Bezirksleitung*, or BL)
had the right to expel members (subject to appeal). The local
groups continued to be the basic party organisations at the lowest
level, although members were advised to form factory cells where
possible. The Seventh Party Congress, held in August 1921,
made few changes, but it did add a new paragraph on discipline:
'The KPD is a centralist party organisation, which has to have
regard to strict discipline in its own ranks. The decisions of the
organisations and their leading bodies must be unconditionally
implemented.'[34] Membership qualifications were also tightened
up: from now on party members had to 'take part in day-to-day
party work'.[35] This was a clear move towards the Leninist
conception of an élite party.

The 1921 statute only governed the KPD until 1925, when a
new one was adopted as part of the Comintern's efforts at
systematisation, based on a 'model statute' prescribed for all
communist parties throughout the world. The basic structure of
the party remained the same, but there were a number of
significant changes of detail. Much more emphasis was now laid
on factory cells. All party members had to join the appropriate
factory cell. If they were not actually working in a factory or other
enterprise they were assigned to existing factory cells. Only if this
was impossible were they to join a street cell. The party's supreme
directing body, the *Zentrale*, was now renamed the Central
Committee (*Zentralkomitee*), in line with the Russian
nomenclature, and its power was enhanced by the abolition of the
ZA (*Zentralausschuss*), the quarterly conference of district

representatives which had previously served as a channel of communication and a control organ whereby local party opinion could override the decisions of the *Zentrale*. The ZA was condemned as a 'Social Democratic survival' and replaced by a Party Conference, whose decisions required confirmation by the ZK. The Party Conference was also to meet less frequently than the ZA ('twice a year as a rule').[36] There was considerable opposition at the Tenth Party Congress to the proposal to abolish the ZA. Herbert Müller, of the district of Rhine-Saar, said its control functions should be retained, adding 'the present leadership does not yet possess sufficient authority to appear unconditionally infallible'.[37] However no one carried his opposition so far as to vote against the new statute.

The 1925 Statute governed the organisation of the party for the remainder of the period of legality. Even so, there were several changes in the way the statute was applied. The old *Zentrale* had met frequently in the earlier years (usually once a week). It genuinely acted as the party leadership. The new ZK was a large and unwieldy body, with 19 members in 1925, 35 in 1927, and 38 in 1929. It met much less frequently (once a month in 1925, once every two months in 1929, two or three times a year between 1930 and 1932). The real work and the day-to-day decision-making devolved on the Politburo (nine members in 1927; meeting at least once a week), the Orgburo (until its dissolution in 1926) and the Secretariat (which in 1926 took over the Orgburo's key function of assigning party tasks). As time went on the three- or four-strong Secretariat became the most powerful party institution. In 1929 its powers were further increased by the direct subordination of the previously separate Organisation Section to it.[38]

The Bolshevik Party had passed through an identical development (after victory), with the Politburo substituting itself for the Central Committee, and the Secretariat finally achieving supreme power under Stalin. In Germany, the control functions of the ZA, which were supposed to have been taken over by the Party Conference after 1925, in fact ceased to operate, because the Conference only met three times between 1925 and 1933, notwithstanding the 1925 Statute's provision for biannual conferences. The Congress too became a rare occasion (as in the Soviet Union). Whereas there had been no less than seven Congresses in the first two years of the KPD's existence, there were only three after 1925, and none between 1929 and 1933. Once again, this contradicted the 1925 Statute, which provided for annual Party Congresses.

At the district level the ZK exercised a progressively tighter control of the District Directorates (BLs). The BL had to report on its work to the ZK at least once a month.[39] The contents of the BL's report would not have surprised the ZK, because since 1926 a member of the ZK always sat in on BL sessions. The BL itself underwent the same process as the central body: it was provided with an inner leadership of from seven to ten people, and a secretariat of three or four, but here the work ultimately devolved on one person, the Political Director (*Polleiter*). 'The *Polleiter* directs, supervises and links up the work of all departments and organs.'[40] This trend towards individual leadership was strengthened after 1929 by the growth of a personality cult around Thälmann. If Thälmann was 'Der Führer' it was natural to present the District *Polleiter* as his analogy at the local level. Until 1926 the *Polleiter* and the secretaries were elected by the District Party Conference (*Bezirksparteitag*) directly. After that year, indirect election by the BL was the system.[41] In that narrower body unpleasant surprises were less likely. The KPD's Districts each comprised a number of Subdistricts (*Unterbezirke*). Here too the elective principle previously prevailed, but after 1925 the Subdistrict Secretaries were appointed by the BL.

In 1928 the 'Conciliators' demanded reintroduction of election of functionaries by the membership. The Thälmann leadership replied: 'If all functionaries were elected by the members this would contradict democratic centralism.' Only the party leadership should be subject to election. The elected leadership then had the right to appoint people to the party's technical and organisational departments. This was the meaning of 'democratic centralism'.[42] These appointed, not elected, functionaries formed a homogeneous group, which enforced its decisions in party meetings by the use of disciplinary measures. Their salaries depended on obedience to the party line. But this was not entirely a question of money (the life of a KPD functionary was hardly a bed of roses). According to some statistics compiled in 1930, 31.9 per cent of KPD members exercised some party function.[43] Most were unpaid, given that the 1927 figure of 1.64 per cent of members actually employed by the party itself was unlikely to have changed much.[44]

But what of the grass roots level? It was here, in street and factory, that the party's health and sickess was likely to be determined. Such was the customary (and no doubt correct) view of the Comintern. In the latter half of the 1920s organisation of the members in factory cells instead of residential districts was regarded as the key to this problem. Successive party leaderships went at the task of conversion to a factory basis with vigour and determination. Already in May 1923 the *Zentrale* had set up a special department under the young Walter Ulbricht to organise the factory cells systematically.[45] 'Our power does not lie in public meetings alone . . . It is much more important that we work successfully in the factories and trade unions.'[46]

Conversion to a factory cell basis was an essential part of the process of 'Bolshevisation', which the KPD, like all other communist parties, carried through in 1924 and 1925. The Second Organisation Conference of the CI, held in March 1926, resolved that 'the factory cell is the appropriate basic unit for all parties in capitalist countries' and that members of the party 'must be associated together in factory cells and take an active part in them'.[47]

One might expect that with all this encouragement the factory cells would go from strength to strength. It was not so. The movement towards factory cells was so hesitant, it seemed so difficult to persuade the members to enter them, that the party hid its embarrassment by submitting exaggerated figures to the ECCI. The factory cell statistics are in a state of some confusion, since the ECCI countered by issuing its own, lower, figures.[48]

Even if we take the more optimistic version each time, we are obliged to conclude that the number of factory cells, after rising between 1924 and 1926 in a gratifying way, fell progressively from 1556 in 1928 to 1441 in August 1930. 'One of the weakest points of our party work', said Creutzburg, 'continues to be in the factories . . . In Germany there are 191 211 factories employing between 11 and 5000 people . . . The party had factory cells in August 1930 in a total of 1441 of all factories, i.e. 0.73 per cent.'[49] Pyatnitsky, the man in charge of these matters in Moscow, was able to note a slight improvement after 1930. In the course of 1931 the number of factory cells rose from 1524 to 1802, and by the end of 1932 the party had 2210 factory cells. But this trend was balanced by another one, which had long been of concern: the number of street cells increased much faster, 'like mushrooms after rain' (Pyatnitsky). In 1924 there were 110; in 1926 1928; in 1927 2597.[50] During 1931 the number rose from 3394 to 5888; at the end of 1932 there were 'roughly 6000'.[51]

The factory cells were intended in part to encourage ordinary members to take a more active part in party life: complaints of their failure to participate abound in the literature. In fact, the theory of democratic centralism left a large place for the participation of the mass of party members in political decision-making – or at least in the confirmation of decisions previously arrived at. A Tenth Party Congress resolution even boasted that the party could 'bridge the gap between leadership and masses, between functionaries and members'.[52] There is little evidence that this happened in practice after 1924. The political line was determined at the top, and outside Germany, in its broad outlines. In matters of detail the Politburo of the KPD made the decisions. These were unlikely to be questioned. The ECCI stressed in its 1928 report that 'Communist Parties must be built up as . . . absolutely monolithic organisations.'[53] This statement was directed above all against the creation of inner-party factions, which had been such a pronounced feature of the period between 1921 and 1924. Once the left had come to power in 1924 it did its best to liquidate all opposition factions. As we have seen, it did not succeed immediately. Factions continued to exist both on the right (the Centre group, or 'Conciliators', and the 'Brandlerites') and on the left (the ultra-left). The intervention of the Comintern worsened the factional divisions in the short term. By 1927 there were six factions within the party, although four had already been expelled. The Eleventh Congress sought to improve the situation by setting up 'control commissions'[54] and ordering the 'dissolution of all groups and factions' on pain of expulsion.[55]

By 1929 all the factions were outside the party except Thälmann's 'pro-Comintern left': this *was* the party. At last the KPD was 'monolithic' and 'Bolshevik'. But the cost was high: the end of inner-party democracy and the conversion of the KPD into an obedient instrument in the hands of the apparatus.

THE INTERNATIONAL DIMENSION

For reasons of convenience we have treated the KPD as an independent unit, operating within an independent state. So it was, in a sense. But, like Germany itself, the KPD was tied by a thousand threads to the external world. What happened beyond the frontier was of intimate concern to it. No one felt the international dimension of the KPD's activity more strongly than its first leader, Rosa Luxemburg. For her Spartacus was part of the army of the international proletariat, and the involvement of Germany in the First World War set Spartacus tasks which were first and foremost international in their character.

The Spartacists therefore took an active part in the attempt to resuscitate socialist internationalism known to history as the Zimmerwald Movement. But, as we saw in Chapter 1, the first Zimmerwald Conference showed a clear split between the centre and the left, between the advocates of a peace of reconciliation and the supporters of Lenin, who wanted to 'turn the imperialist war into a civil war'. The *Gruppe Internationale* voted against Lenin and for Ledebour and Hoffmann, who rejected active revolutionary measures against the war or any break with the Social Democrats. The position of the Spartacists had not changed by the time of the second Zimmerwald Conference, held at Kienthal in April 1916. The Zimmerwald Left were supported by Frölich, on behalf of the Bremen Left Radicals, but not by Meyer, the Spartacist, who abstained from voting on Radek's (i.e. Lenin's) theses.[56] In any case, the Spartacists had no very high opinion of the Zimmerwald Movement itself. 'How can the socialist international be recreated?' asked the Spartacus Letter of May 1916.

> Evidently, not by manifestos and resolutions of some bureau or conference . . . The International can only arise again . . . when socialism, the revolutionary class struggle, becomes a reality in all countries and above all in Germany. . . . International Socialism does not consist in conferences, resolutions, manifestos, but in deeds, in struggle, in mass actions.[57]

In this perspective, the revolution which broke out in Russia in 1917 was of far greater significance than anything which emerged from Zimmerwald. It was naturally welcomed by the Spartacists, and by all other German socialists, though for different reasons. For the SPD the overthrow of Tsarism achieved their main war aim, and opened the way to a victorious peace with Russia; for the USPD the Russian Revolution was a step to universal peace; for the Spartacists it was an example to be followed by the German proletariat. The Bolshevik Revolution of November 1917 was also generally greeted, for the same mixture of reasons. Rosa Luxemburg understood from the outset (as early as August 1917) that if the German workers did not follow the example of the Russians immediately the Bolsheviks were doomed. But it was better for the Russian proletariat to go under with honour, she added, than to imitate the shameful passivity of the German working class. The Russian republic was in a tragic impasse. By continuing to fight the German army it acted in the interests of Entente imperialism. But if it made a separate peace with the Entente it would render 'invaluable services to German imperialism'. In fact, even the policy of standing on the defensive pursued in practice by the army of the Russian Revolution in 1917 was of great help to the German High Command. Rosa Luxemburg reached the uncomfortable conclusion that 'there is simply no correct tactic for the Russian proletariat to follow today; whatever it chooses to do will be wrong'.[58] The way out of the impasse chosen by the Bolsheviks was to make peace with Germany, and it was entirely consistent with the Spartacist line of 1917 for both Liebknecht and Luxemburg to criticise Lenin for his readiness to conclude a separate peace, which would inevitably strengthen German imperialism and thereby weaken the resistance of the German proletariat. Liebknecht kept his views to himself, writing on his manuscript 'Not to be published! Not to be discussed! We must beware of anti-Leninism in principle! German criticism of the Russian proletariat must be conducted with the most extreme caution and tact!'[59] His attitude was symptomatic of an unwillingness to criticise the successful Russian Revolution which was ultimately to rebound on the KPD and make it a willing instrument of the Stalin faction. Rosa, on the other hand, allowed her criticism of the Brest-Litovsk negotiations to come to the surface in the Spartacus Letters of January and September 1918. But she was ready to excuse the Bolsheviks because they were in an impossible situation. The international proletariat, the German in particular, was to blame for not rising in revolt. 'There is only one solution to Russia's tragic situation: an uprising in the rear of German imperialism, the rising of the German masses.'[60]

Rosa criticised the policy of the Bolsheviks in 1918 from several different angles. The Treaty of Brest-Litovsk was a capitulation in the face of German imperialism, but also it had failed to produce peace; the dissolution of the Constituent Assembly and the suppression of the non-Bolshevik parties was creating a dictatorship in the bad, bourgeois sense, not a genuine dictatorship of the proletariat; the division of land among the peasants would produce a social stratum even more dangerous to the proletariat than the big landowners had been; finally the 'absurd slogan of national self-determination' led to the abandonment of the non-Russian proletariat to the respective national bourgeoisies. Her pamphlet on the Russian Revolution thus contained attacks on some of the most basic Bolshevik policies, though she also affirmed her solidarity with the revolution. It was this reflex of solidarity which prevented her from publishing her criticisms of Bolshevik internal, as opposed to foreign, policy. In any case, her views were not shared by her fellow-Spartacists. Clara Zetkin, Ernst Meyer and Franz Mehring are all on record in 1918 as accepting the Soviet system as the appropriate form of the dictatorship of the proletariat.[61] It is not known for certain whether Rosa decided later that her criticisms had been exaggerated. There was ample opportunity after November 1918 to publicise her views on these issues and she did not do so. In any case, she certainly insisted that it was too early to found a new, third International, in the absence of a mass communist movement outside Russia. Hence the KPD delegate to the conference called in Moscow to found the Third International, Hugo Eberlein, was mandated to call for a postponement. In the event, Eberlein's objections were overruled owing to the change in mood induced by an enthusiastic speech from the Austrian delegate, Steinhardt. The Moscow Conference turned itself into the First Congress of the Communist International (4 March 1919), and Eberlein abstained from voting so as to give the resolution an air of unanimity.[62]

The KPD was thus bound to the Comintern. This did not itself imply subjection to Soviet foreign policy, but the failure of a socialist revolution to occur anywhere except in Russia had this fateful result. One obvious consequence of the Comintern connection was the establishment of close personal contacts with the Moscow headquarters of world communism. There were several methods: regular presence of KPD delegates at all important Comintern gatherings (six congresses and twelve meetings of the Enlarged ECCI Plenum fall within our period), not to mention attendance at various congresses of subsidiary organisations like the RILU, the Communist Youth International, and the International of Communist Women; and semi-permanent residence in Moscow resulting from election to the Executive Committee of the Communist International (it always contained at least two KPD representatives). Then there was the flow in the opposite direction: the ECCI sent agents and plenipotentiaries to Germany, to give advice, often of an ultimative character. Karl Radek went to and fro repeatedly until he was made a scapegoat for the October débâcle; Brónski (M. J. Braun) was a permanent representative in 1919 and 1920; Guralski (A. Kleine) followed him between 1921 and 1924, and was actually a member of the *Zentrale* in 1923 (although he had a right to sit in on meetings irrespective of this); later Comintern representatives included Dimitry Manuilsky, Karl Kilbom and Besso Lominadze. At a lower level, there were the military experts sent to advise on insurrection in 1923, who stayed on to organise the illegal activities which came to the surface in the so-called 'Cheka trial' of 1925.[63] Finally, there was Jacob Mirov-Abramov, the man who handed out the money from 1921 to 1930 as Berlin representative of the OMS (International Relations Section) of the Comintern.[64] It was therefore impossible to pretend ignorance of the Comintern's wishes. Similarly, it was impossible to keep the ECCI in ignorance of events in the German party. Any attempt at 'double book-keeping', of the kind practised by Fischer and Maslow in 1925, would be found out and punished. And international discipline required obedience. Obedience to a genuinely international organisation was one thing; but the Comintern gradually developed into an instrument of the foreign policy of the first socialist state. For most of the time the theoretical contradiction between the role of a revolutionary party and the foreign policy of the Soviet Union lay beneath the surface. Some writers have alleged that it emerged in 1921, with the March Action, or in 1923, with the 'Schlageter-Course', or, above all, after 1929. It is not easy to decide this question; before we do so we have to answer another. What was a 'communist' foreign policy? Certain abstract principles were fairly clear: (1) communists must fight imperialism at home and abroad; (2) communists must defend oppressed nations; (3) communists must examine foreign policy decisions, like all others, in the light of the interests of the proletariat. Germany had changed from being an imperialist to an oppressed country with the Versailles Treaty. She had to be defended against Entente imperialism. This much was clear to all communists. But to leave it there was to risk falling into 'National Bolshevism'. Laufenberg and Wolffheim had in 1919 followed this rigid logic to its conclusion of an alliance with the German bourgeoisie. Similarly, the 'Schlageter-Course' of 1923 led communists to share public platforms with Nationalists and Nazis. The error of National Bolshevism consisted in ignoring point (3), the interests of the proletariat.

Most acts of foreign policy by bourgeois governments could be treated in two different ways: they could either be used to advance the communist cause, and agitation could be based on the assertion that only the victorious proletarian revolution could solve the national problem, whether on the Ruhr or in Upper Silesia; or they could be analysed as imposing new burdens on the workers, as a capitalist plot. The settlement of the Ruhr conflict and the Dawes Plan were seen in this light. The theme was taken up strongly in 1924 during the KPD's Left course. The argument that the burden of reparations under the Dawes Plan would fall on the 'workers, employees, and *Mittelstand*', who would all be squeezed dry by the alliance of German and Entente capitalists was put forward in August 1924 in the *Reichstag* by Wilhelm Koenen.[65] The election campaign of November to December 1924 was fought largely around this issue. Denunciations of the Dawes Plan did not appear to secure many votes, and the KPD was much less successful in December than it had been in May.

It is possible to discuss the foreign policy of the KPD without even mentioning the interests of the Soviet Union. But it would be artificial to do so. The Russian connection existed, and it did have an effect. Its result was to heighten the distinctiveness of KPD foreign policy within the German context, to give a sharper edge to it. In the case of the Dawes Plan, there were actually three reasons for opposition: it turned Germany into a colony of the Entente (the 'National Bolshevik' argument); it conceded reparations payments which could only be made at the expense of the German workers' standard of living (the orthodox communist argument); and finally it opened the way to a Western orientation for Germany and hence deprived the Treaty of Rapallo of significance (the Soviet foreign policy argument).

The needs of Soviet foreign policy were more and more openly referred to after 1925. The way to confront the 'war danger'

which Stalin thought threatened the USSR in the late 1920s was
to break up any possible alliance between Germany and the
Western Powers. In 1925 the call 'Down with the Locarno Pact'
was combined with 'Hands off Soviet Russia'. Germany's entry
into the League of Nations would turn the country into 'the
assembly point and field of battle for the war against Soviet
Russia'.[66] In 1927 the 'danger' of an English attack on the USSR
was used as an argument for turning on 'the enemy in our own
ranks', 'reformism and social imperialism which is in alliance
with the German bourgeoisie'.[67] Here the foreign policy
requirements of Stalin's Russia had a determining effect on the
KPD's attitude towards Social Democracy. The more dangerous
the Western orientation of Germany appeared to be, the greater
the hostility towards the Social Democrats, the main advocates of
such an orientation. This may well be the key to the abrupt turn
to the left in 1927–8 and the subsequent insistence on the 'Social
Fascist' nature of the SPD. Weingartner has found some
remarkable evidence of how Stalin's concern to prevent a
rapprochement between Germany and the West affected his attitude
to German internal politics. Thus *Pravda* reported the September
1930 elections as a 'vote for social liberation and the casting off of
the yoke of Versailles'.[68] This could be interpreted as suggesting
that the great Nazi success in the elections was itself a favourable
factor, since it destroyed all prospect of cooperation between
France and Germany. Did Stalin actually desire the victory of the
Nazis over the Weimar Republic to improve Russia's diplomatic
position?

If a Machiavellian plan of this kind had existed, the KPD
would have been unable to resist it. For by that time it had lost its
independence as a political party. The increase in its dependence
on the Comintern is another aspect of the international dimension
we must consider. By the end of the 1920s the Comintern was
used as an instrument in settling tactical controversies of Russian
rather than international significance. Thalheimer's comments
are apposite here:

Perhaps this is . . . inadequate Bolshevisation on my part, but
. . . I can well imagine that a 'left' danger in Java or Borneo
. . . might exist at the same time as a 'right' danger in the
Soviet Union, and that in another country there might be a
'dangerous tendency' not even represented in the Russian
factional struggle.[69]

Every time Stalin took a turn to the right or left, the whole Comintern shook with denunciations of his defeated opponents, whether Trotsky, Zinoviev or Bukharin. The KPD naturally approved all steps taken by the CPSU against any of these opponents, from 1924 onwards.

It would be a mistake to ascribe this readiness to fall into line to crude material dependence. A very understandable psychological mechanism pushed communists along the road from respect and admiration for the first workers' state to unconditional acceptance of the decisions of whatever Soviet leadership was in power. But we should not entirely disregard the financial aspect. How was the KPD actually financed? Not just through the contributions of its members, certainly. The point is shrouded in mystery, owing to the unwillingness of KPD members to play into the hands of bourgeois and Social Democratic politicians, who claimed that the communists were paid agents of Moscow. One of the few official references to financial support comes from Hugo Eberlein, the party treasurer, who told the Second Congress in 1919:

> The whole of the press proclaims that we are mercenaries of the Russian government, quite incorrectly. We admit freely that not the Russian government, but the Russian communist party [a fine distinction!] places funds at our disposal, and we use these for our agitation; if the government socialists [i.e. the SPD] raise a hue and cry about this, they are indulging in wretched hypocrisy, for when we were in the old party [i.e. the pre-war SPD] we were proud that our financial situation enabled us to support our foreign comrades.[70]

Even so, Eberlein admitted that all was not as it should be: the party should learn to stand on its own feet financially.

It did not succeed in this. The existence of subventions from Soviet sources is not in doubt, although the exact amount is uncertain. A figure of 150 000 marks a month has been suggested for 1927.[71] This was only half the income received from other sources (300 000 marks a month). To judge by these figures, Comintern funds provided a useful supplementary income, but no more. The main sources of income were within Germany. Contributions from party members came to 4.5 million marks in 1927, and rents received from buildings owned by the party's newspaper holding company, the *PEUVAG*, made up another million. The party could thus have existed comfortably without financial support from Russia. It would not have been impossible to concede this demand, which was advanced by successive opposition groups inside and outside the party. Ernst Friesland in 1921 saw financial self-sufficiency as the key to restoring the party to health, and he reflected the views of the Levi group, the KAG, which demanded 'complete material independence from the Comintern' at its founding conference in November 1921.[72] Heinrich Brandler, on the same evidence, reached the opposite conclusion: the Comintern's material aid was one of the reasons he gave for not founding a rival communist party after 1923: 'On our own we could hardly even pay a dozen functionaries, as opposed to the KPD's two hundred financed by the Comintern.'[73] The ultra-left tended to blame their defeat after 1925 on the mercenary tendencies of the party's officials: 'The KPD, financially and thereby also ideologically dependent on the Russian state, had to go along willy nilly with the changes within that state.'[74] This crude accusation was in fact unjustified. The Thälmann leadership was not obliged to depend on the Soviet Union for material reasons; they preferred it that way, and saw no reason why the monetary connection should be cut off. Material factors no doubt affected the attitudes of lesser functionaries, but they feared to be cut off from the party for the kind of reason which would weigh equally with an SPD official.

We can distinguish two, or possibly three, stages in the extension of Comintern control over the KPD. Until 1923 there were repeated conflicts between ECCI representatives and KPD leaders. In 1920 Levi complained to Radek about reports sent to Moscow by 'Comrade Thomas' behind his back;[75] then he clashed with Rákosi (early 1921); later in 1921 Friesland complained of a 'shadow leadership' in the party animated by the ECCI representatives Felix Wolf and Helena Stassova;[76] in 1922 finally there was the running battle between Meyer and Kleine-Guralski over the latter's support for the Berlin Left. After 1923 the complaints suddenly cease. The party was led first by Brandler, who took advice when it was given, even against his better judgement, until he was brought down by the German October; then by Fischer and Maslow, who resisted Comintern pressure while pretending it did not exist. This was a period of transition. Manuilsky was sending material to Pyatnitsky in Moscow using his own private channels, but the Fischer leadership only complained indirectly.[77] With the rise of Thälmann in 1925 the problem was solved: here was a man so loyal that it was unnecessary to go behind his back, so firmly in control of his party that the construction of rival factions was impossible (this is how Heinz Neumann came to grief), so adept at following the 'general line' that he could not be wrong-footed.[78]

CONCLUSION

Let me now in conclusion try to disentangle some of the underlying themes in the KPD's history. One leitmotiv is given by the relation of party to class. The KPD was constantly brought up against the contradiction between its claim to be the 'only party' of the working class and its minority position within that class. This claim, which was never abandoned, was justified only in an ideological sense. Sociologically it was nonsense. The rival claim of the SPD could be dismissed with the statement that it was a bourgeois party, but its existence was a hard fact which could not be ignored. The question of the relationship with non-communist workers was thus posed ineluctably at every stage of the party's history. United front tactics were intended to solve this problem. We have seen that certain successes were achieved in 1922–3 and 1926–7 by using this method. But what of the rest of the population, the non-proletarians? There were always two views on this subject. The first was that of the leftists: such people should be ignored, and left to the bourgeois parties. The second view, associated with the right (Levi in 1920, Brandler in 1923), was that a determined effort should be made to appeal to strata outside the working class. Paul Levi was one of the earliest people to stress the significance of the *Mittelstand* (the lower middle class) for any real communist advance; the tendency of the inflation in 1923 to throw this group down into the proletariat increased their importance from this point of view. Another non-proletarian group whose material situation might make them accessible to communist ideas was the poor peasantry, and successive appeals were made to them, from the Agrarian Programme of 1920 to the 'Workers' and Peasants' Government' slogan of 1923, ending with the post-1929 agitation directed at the 'working peasant'. The results were not encouraging. The KPD remained, if not the *workers' party*, at least a *party of workers*. Thälmann's changes in terminology ('the People's Revolution') could not alter the fundamental fact of the KPD's exclusive appeal to the urban working class.

The KPD was also the party of *absolute opposition* to the 'system': this was reflected in its conception of parliamentary tactics. Brief periods of united front flirtation with the SPD did not mean any change in the basic attitude of negation. The expelled ultra-leftists of 1927 feared that the party would lose this quality and become integrated into the system. They were wrong. On the contrary, the party persisted in permanent, hopeless opposition. What were its aims? Not revolution, after 1924. The hope of a proletarian revolution was abandoned in that year. Defence of the achievements of 1918? In communist eyes these were non-existent. Even the SPD leaders experienced difficulties in pulling their party into a defence of democracy *tout court*. For the KPD such a policy did not come into question until 1935, and then it was too late. Hence the party's activities tended to appear purposeless or self-justifying (the winning of new members). One must admit two exceptions here, at a local level. It was regarded as permissible for communists to engage in reforming policies in the town councils; here they appeared as a more radical SPD.[79] Also at a local level democracy was defended against the extreme right, by physical force. The KPD devoted much effort to this and the RFB was founded in 1924 for the purpose. The fight for the streets, waged first against the *Stahlhelm* then against the SA, assumed much greater importance after 1930, with the simultaneous growth of Nazism and unemployment, which transferred 'social space' from the factory to the neighbourhood for many workers and made its defence against marauding gangs of Nazis more urgent.[80] When all is said and done, however, this was a negative kind of activity, involving the defence of working-class districts, i.e. the maintenance of positions already won, and did not differ in quality, though it did differ in method, from the proud, but also pathetic slogan of the SPD: 'Berlin stays red'.

We have noted a turning-point, or at least a change of atmosphere, in 1925. This must not be ascribed to one single factor. If it ultimately had its roots in the consolidation of Stalinism in the Soviet Union, that phenomenon in its turn was conditioned by the failure of revolution in Central Europe. The KPD, like the Comintern, only became an instrument of Soviet foreign policy when it began to appear to the leading Russians that it was not much good for anything else. The gigantic campaign the party mounted in the later 1920s against the 'war danger' allegedly threatening the Soviet Union had a certain rationality. If the USSR was really under threat, and if it was a workers' state, it was reasonable for detachments of the international proletarian army to come to its assistance by attacking those who were promoting this threat. But what of the 'Third Period' policy of 1928 onwards? This is much harder to explain. It is impossible to accept Weingartner's view that Stalin was trying to strengthen Nazism so as to nip in the bud the negotiations of the Brüning government with the West, and thus throw Germany back on the Soviet Union for aid and comfort. Nor can we concur with Borkenau when he sees the Comintern line as somehow twitching to the left in a mere reflex of the great post-1928 crisis of collectivisation and industrialisation within Russia. No more convincing is the contemporary communist explanation that the crisis of capitalism, as it deepened, increased polarisation and thus threw wavering elements like the SPD into the camp of Fascism, necessitating a strong line against them by the party. Chronology is against this view, since the world depression set in long after the 'Third Period' phase had started. The fact is that the Comintern's official theorists reinterpreted the conjuncture to suit the needs of the current tactic, rather than deriving the tactic from the conjuncture.

I have tried to argue in this book that the nature of German communism underwent a radical change during the Weimar Republic. Initially the spontaneous product of working-class indignation at the diverting of the November Revolution into constitutional and bourgeois channels, it became first the instrument of an organised revolution against the Weimar system, then a home for the discontented masses who wanted to show their radicalism in the clearest way possible. Finally, without ceasing to be this, it took on its ultimate function of an instrument of Soviet foreign policy, the function it was to retain (notwithstanding the subjective revolutionism of most party members) through the vicissitudes of resistance to Hitler, concentration camp tortures, and the traumatic experience of a victory in which it had played no part, and where its future depended on the decisions of the occupying power. To say this is not to forget or ignore the courage and dedication of the people who fought and often died for their cause in those years; but qualities of this kind, when unallied to independence of judgement and deeply held humanistic values, are as likely to promote as to prevent the tragedies in which history has always abounded.

Appendix 1   The Sources for the Study of German Communism

The official publications of the KPD and the Comintern constitute by far the most important source for this book and for most accounts of the KPD so far written. A useful guide, with special attention to the pamphlet literature, was produced by Enzo Collotti in 1961 (*Die Kommunistische Partei Deutschlands 1918–1933. Ein bibliographischer beitrag*, Milan, 1961). The main official publication was the daily paper ('central organ') *Die Rote Fahne*, which came out from November 1918 to March 1933, with some short intervals and two long ones (in 1919 and 1923–4). It is a mine of information both for the life of the party and the political events. Secondly there is the Comintern's periodical *Inprekorr* (September 1921 to March 1933), covering all the sections of the international, but often heavily concentrated on the German one. The earlier issues are often lively; after 1925 'it can scarcely be approached without an effort'. For the period before September 1921 there is a dearth of publications from the Comintern side. *Die Kommunistische Internationale* (KI) (1919–39) was always a discussion journal and a place for official ECCI proclamations, and little information was provided about the fate of the national sections, for the good reason that Moscow itself was often in the dark about this in the early years. The journal of the French supporters of the Third International, *Bulletin Communiste* (March 1920 to January 1926), is a useful supplement for this period. There are English-language versions of both *Inprekorr* and *KI*, but many articles on German affairs were omitted. Theoretical articles on capitalism and communist strategy are scattered through all Comintern publications, but the KPD prided itself from the first on its theoretical level and was the first party to start a journal specifically devoted to theory, *Die Internationale* (1915, 1919–32). The more specialised party periodicals, though they provide little extra evidence, should at least be mentioned. Trade unionists had *Die Einheit* and *Der Rote Gewerkschafter*; the IAH (*Internationale Arbeiterhilfe*) had *Der Rote Aufbau*, the RFB had *Die Rote Front*, the military specialists had *Vom Bürgerkrieg* (later *Oktober*), and party functionaries had *Der Parteiarbeiter*. The provincial press (36 daily newspapers in 1927) is often important for local events or when *Die Rote Fahne* was banned. Finally the minutes of the twelve party congresses provide evidence both of the clash of opinions and of the way the party was organised.

Then there are the archives. A glimpse of the hidden wealth of documentation can be seen in Hermann Weber's publications of party records which went astray in the 1920s, either by confiscation or by falling into the hands of police informers, and thereby entered, along with much dross, into the archives of federal and local governments under Weimar. (Hermann Weber, *Die Wandlung des deutschen Kommunismus. Die Stalinisierung der KPD in der Weimarer Republik*, Frankfurt, 1969, vol. 1, appendix). It must be stressed, however, that these are chance finds, 'stray documents', and that the only systematic collections are in the East. A further source, sometimes of extreme value for the early history of the KPD, is the *Nachlass Paul Levi*, now housed in Bonn at the Archiv der sozialen Demokratie (Friedrich Ebert Stiftung).

I have preferred not to attempt to itemise the secondary sources for German communism. An annotated bibliography would easily fill a volume by itself. Information on recent publications can be derived from the various specialist journals, above all the *Internationale Wissenschaftliche Korrespondenz zur Geschichte der deutschen Arbeiterbewegung* (Berlin), ed. by H. Skrzypczak. This West German publication can be supplemented by the *Beiträge zur Geschichte der Arbeiterbewegung* (East Berlin). My own debts to various authors are indicated in the footnotes to the present work.

Appendix 2 Statistical Tables

A.1 The membership of the KPD, district by district, in 1921, 1925 and 1929
A.2 Membership figures, 1919 to 1923
A.3 The KPD leadership, 1919 to 1924
A.4 The KPD leadership, 1924 to 1935

TABLE A.1 The membership of the KPD, district by district, in 1921, 1925 and 1929

Party number	District	1921	%	1925	%	1929	%
11	Halle–Merseburg	67 000	14.5	8 000	6.2	10 800	9.0
20	Lower Rhine	55 000	12.2	12 000	9.3	9 360	7.8
1	Berlin–Brandenburg	52 000	11.2	18 710	14.5	18 960	15.8
16	Wasserkante[1]	40 000	8.6	8 000	6.2	10 680	8.9
13	Thuringia	25 000	5.4	7 000	5.4	5 000	4.7
18/19	Ruhr[2]	27 000	5.8	11 000	8.5	8 040	6.7
26	Württemberg	18 000	3.9	5 160	4.0	2 640	2.2
9	Erzgebirge–Vogtland	16 200	3.6	12 500	9.7	9 000	7.5
10	W Saxony (Leipzig)	14 000	3.0	8 509	6.6	7 320	6.1
23	Hesse–Frankfurt	14 000	3.0	4 632	3.6	4 320	3.6
14	Lower Saxony	13 000	2.8	1 000	0.8	1 800	1.5
17	North Bavaria	12 600	2.8	3 500	2.7	2 640	2.2
25	Baden	12 000	2.6	2 400	1.9	2 020	1.8
4	East Prussia	12 000	2.6	2 000	1.6	2 280	1.9
21	Central Rhine	12 000	2.6	3 500	2.7	2 900	2.4
3	Pomerania	8 500	1.8	1 500	1.2	1 560	1.3
28	South Bavaria	8 000	1.7	2 803	2.2	1 440	1.2
12	Magdeburg–Anhalt	8 000	1.7	2 000	1.6	3 000	2.5
15	Mecklenburg	8 000	1.7	1 000	0.8	840	0.7
8	E Saxony (Dresden)	8 000	1.7	3 000	2.3	4 080	3.4
6	Silesia (Lower)	8 000	1.7	1 500	1.2	1 800	1.5
17	Northwest (Bremen)	7 000	1.5	3 260	2.5	2 803	2.3
24	Palatinate	4 000	0.9	3 200	2.5	960	0.8
7	Upper Silesia	3 000	0.6	500	0.4	960	0.8
22	Hesse-Cassel	3 000	0.6	5 000	0.4	720	0.6
2	Lusatia[3]	2 400	0.5	–		–	
5	Danzig	1 600	0.3	500	0.4	960	0.8
24a	Saar	–		1 000	0.8	1 200	1.0
	Total membership	449 700		128 674		118 083	

1. Wasserkante included Hamburg and Schleswig–Holstein
2. The Ruhr was formed after 1921 by amalgamation of the districts of Western Westphalia and Eastern Westphalia
3. Lusatia was merged with Berlin–Brandenburg after 1921
   Sources for this table:
   1921: *Nachlass Paul Levi*, 99/2, 'Bericht über den Stand der Parteiorganisation Anfang Januar 1921', p. 3
   1925 and 1929: H. Weber, *Die Wandlung des deutschen Kommunismus*, Frankfurt, 1971, pp. 367–94

TABLE A.2   Membership figures, 1919 to 1932

Date	Number	Source
October 1919	106 656	*Bericht 2 Parteitag*, p.27
July 1920	66 373	*Bericht 5 Parteitag*, p.4
October 1920	78 715	Ibid.
January 1921	449 700[1]	NPL 99/2, p.3
Summer 1921	359 613 (claimed)	Pieck, in *Inprekorr*, 1922, No. 216, 9 Nov, pp. 1507–8
	157 168 (paid up)	*Inprekorr*, 1922, pp. 1507–8
September 1922	218 195	Böttcher, in *Inprekorr*, 7 Feb 1923, p.71
October 1922	328 017 (claimed)	*Inprekorr*, 1922, No. 216, 9 Nov, pp. 1507–8
	255 863 (paid up)	Ibid.
September 1923	294 230	*Bericht 9 Parteitag*, p. 58
April 1924	121 394	*Komintern vor dem VI Kongress*, p. 122
April 1925	122 755	Pyatnitsky, in *KI*, 17, 1927, p. 2138
April 1926	134 248	*Komintern vor dem VI Kongress*, p.122
April 1927	124 779	Ibid.
End of 1928	130 000	W. Rist, *Neue Blätter für den Sozialismus*, 1931, pp.79–91
1st half 1929	118 957	Creutzburg, *Organisationsarbeit der KPD*, Hamburg, 1931, pp.53–5
2nd half 1929	112 511	Ibid.
April 1930	120 000	Ibid.
August 1930	127 000	Ibid.
October 1930	149 000	Ibid.
December 1930	176 000	Ibid.
1st quarter 1931	195 083	Weber, *Wandlung*, p.364
2nd quarter 1931	190 182	Ibid.
3rd quarter 1931	213 554	Ibid.
4th quarter 1931	246 513	Ibid.
March 1932	287 180	*Die KI vor dem VII Weltkongress*, p.141
End of 1932	252 000	Ibid.
	330 000	S. Bahne, 'Die KPD', p.662

1. According to Pieck in 1922, the figure of 450 000 'advanced at the unification congress, turned out to be far too high'. (*Inprekorr*, 1922, No. 216, 9 Nov, pp.1507–8.) The figures for 1923 onwards are for paid up members.

206 Appendix 2

TABLE A.3   The KPD leadership, 1919 to 1924 (*Zentrale* members and candidates)

	1919	1920	1921	1922	1923	1924
Karl Becker					——	
Paul Böttcher				———	——	
Heinrich Brandler			——————			
Otto Brass			—			
Bertha Braunthal				—		
Ernst Däumig			—			
Hermann Duncker	——					
Käte Duncker	———					
Hugo Eberlein		———		————————		
Arthur Ewert					———	—
Ruth Fischer						—
Ernst Friesland			—— —	——		
Paul Frölich		———	——			—
Otto Gäbel			—			
Ottomar Geschke						—
Kurt Geyer			—			
Arthur Hammer			—			
Fritz Heckert			————	———		
Edwin Hoernle				————		———
Adolf Hoffmann			—			
Leo Jogiches	—					
August Kleine						———
Wilhelm Koenen				——	———	———
Joseph Köring		—				
Artur König						—
Paul Lange	——	——				
Paul Levi	——	——	———			
Karl Liebknecht	—					
Rudolf Lindau						———
Rosa Luxemburg						
Ernst Meyer						
Hans Pfeiffer					——	
Wilhelm Pieck			—————————			
Hermann Remmele				——————		
Felix Schmidt				———————		
Fritz Schnellbacher		——				
Max Sievers		——				
Walter Stoecker		——			————	
Ernst Thälmann						—
August Thalheimer		——————————				
Walter Ulbricht						———
Jakob Walcher			————————			
Paul Wegmann			—			
Rosi Wolfstein				———	——	
Clara Zetkin		———	——————			

     1 2   3 4 5 6   L 7   F   8   T   9

1 = First Party Congress, January 1919
2 = Second Party Congress, October 1919
3 = Third Party Congress, February 1920
4 = Fourth Party Congress, April 1920
5 = Fifth Party Congress, November 1920
6 = Sixth (Unification) Congress, December 1920
L = Resignation of Levi and others, February 1921
7 = Seventh Party Congress, August 1921
F = Expulsion of Ernst Friesland, January 1922
8 = Eighth Party Congress, January 1923
T = Entry of Thälmann and other members of the Left Opposition into the *Zentrale*, May 1923
9 = Ninth Party Congress, April 1924

TABLE A.4 The KPD leadership, 1924 to 1935 (*Polbüro* members and candidates)

	1924	1925	1926	1927	1928	1929	1935
Konrad Blenkle							
Franz Dahlem							
Philipp Dengel							
Hugo Eberlein							
Gerhardt Eisler							
Arthur Ewert							
Ruth Fischer							
Leo Flieg							
Wilhelm Florin							
Ottomar Geschke							
Fritz Heckert							
Wilhelm Hein							
Wilhelm Kasper							
Iwan Katz							
Arkady Maslow							
Paul Merker							
Ernst Meyer							
Heinz Neumann							
Helene Overlach							
Wilhelm Pieck							
Hermann Remmele							
Artur Rosenberg							
Paul Schlecht							
Ernst Schneller							
Werner Scholem							
Max Schütz							
Fritz Schulte							
Wilhelm Schwan							
Heinrich Süsskind							
Ernst Thälmann							
Walter Ulbricht							
Jean Winterich							

| 1 | 2 3 | | 4 | 5 | 6 | 7 |

1 = Ninth Party Congress, April 1924
2 = Tenth Party Congress, July 1925
3 = First Party Conference, October/November 1925
4 = Eleventh Party Congress, March 1927
5 = Second Party Conference, November 1928
6 = Twelfth Party Congress, June 1929
7 = 'Brussels Conference', October 1935

Notes and References

PREFACE

1. A. Kriegel, *The French Communists. Profile of a People*, Chicago, 1972.
2. There are exceptions, e.g. E. Rosenhaft, 'Working-class life and working-class politics: Communists, Nazis and the state in the battle for the streets, Berlin 1928–32', in R. Bessel and E. J. Feuchtwanger, *Social Change and Political Development in Weimar Germany*. London, 1981, pp.207–40.
3. Factional conflict is the central concern of Professor Hermann Weber's book *Die Wandlung des deutschen Kommunismus*, originally issued in 1969 in two volumes, and in a one-volume version in 1971.
4. As in Werner Angress, *Stillborn Revolution 1921–23*, first published in 1963 and since reissued in an expanded German edition.
5. This is one of the virtues of Pierre Broué's *Révolution en Allemagne 1917–1923*, Paris, 1971.

CHAPTER 1   THE PREHISTORY OF GERMAN COMMUNISM

1. F. Engels, 'On the History of the Communist League', in *Marx-Engels Selected Works* (hereinafter *MESW*), Moscow, 1970, vol.3, p.182.
2. Ibid., p.185.
3. F. Engels, 'Karl Marx and the Neue Rheinische Zeitung', *MESW*, vol.3, p.167.
4. K. Marx and F. Engels, 'Address of the Central Committee to the Communist League, March 1850', in K. Marx, *The Revolutions of 1848*, London, 1973, p.329.
5. F. Engels, 'A Critique of the Draft Social Democratic Programme of 1891', *MESW*, vol.3, pp.433–7.
6. *Protokoll über die Verhandlungen des Parteitages der Sozialdemokratischen Partei Deutschlands,* Jena, 1913, pp. 536–45.
7. H. Wohlgemuth, *Die Entstehung der KPD. Überblick*, Berlin, 1978, p.40.
8. P. Frölich, *Rosa Luxemburg*, London, 1972, p.180.
9. C.E. Schorske, *German Social Democracy 1905–1917. The Development of the Great Schism*, New York, 1972, p.277.
10. *Die Neue Zeit*, 30, ii, no. 49, 6 September 1912, pp.847–54.
11. R. Luxemburg, *Gegen den Reformismus*, Berlin, 1925, p.527.
12. W. Keil, *Erlebnisse eines Sozialdemokraten*, Stuttgart, 1947, vol.1, pp.306–17; E. Prager, *Die Geschichte der USPD*, 2nd edn, Berlin, 1922, pp.39–40.

13. Keil, *Erlebnisse*, vol.1, pp.306, 320.
14. The wartime history of the Chemnitz Left is treated in detail in S. Beckert, 'Die Linken in Chemnitz im Kampf gegen den Opportunismus für die Herausbildung einer revolutionären Partei', *Beiträge zur Geschichte der deutschen Arbeiterbewegung* (hereinafter *BzG*), 1967, no.1, pp.109–118.
15. C. Grünberg, 'Die Internationale und der Weltkrieg', in *Archiv für die Geschichte des Sozialismus und der Arbeiterbewegung*, Leipzig, 1916, p.423.
16. *Dokumente und Materialien zur Geschichte der deutschen Arbeiterbewegung* (hereinafter *DuM*), *Reihe II, Bd. 1*, p.35, no.1.
17. See the memoir by Paul Schwenk, 'Lenin, Mehring und das Niederbarnimer Referentenmaterial', *BzG*, 1960, no.1, pp.158–63.
18. Schorske, *German Social Democracy*, p.297.
19. Rosa Luxemburg to Karl Moor, 12 October 1914, quoted in Wohlgemuth, *Entstehung*, p.65.
20. W. Münzenberg, *Die dritte Front*, Berlin, 1930, pp.204–7.
21. H. Ladermacher (ed.), *Die Zimmerwalder Bewegung. Protokolle und Korrespondenzen*, vol.1, The Hague, 1967, p.150.
22. *DuM* II/I, pp.169–85. The text was actually drawn up in Liebknecht's flat, but it was formulated in such a way as to win centrist support.
23. Prager, *USPD*, pp.72–4.
24. D.W. Morgan, *The Socialist Left and the German Revolution*, London, 1975, p.44.
25. *Die Rote Fahne* (hereinafter RF), 15 January, 1929.
26. Wohlgemuth, *Entstehung*, p.130.
27. For a detailed account of Knief and the Bremen Left up to 1917, see G. Engel, *Johann Knief und die Bremer Linken in der Vorgeschichte der KPD*, Fichte–Schriften 5, Berlin, 1968, pp.7–72.
28. Rühle's article of 12 January 1916 in the Berlin *Vorwärts* is reprinted in *DuM* II/I, pp.301–7.
29. H.M. Bock, *Syndikalismus und Linkskommunismus von 1918 bis 1923*, Meisenheim am Glan, 1969, p.74.
30. *Protokoll über die Verhandlungen des Gründungsparteitages der USPD vom 6 bis 8 April 1917 in Gotha. Mit Anhang: Bericht über die Gemeinsame Konferenz der Arbeitsgemeinschaft und der Spartakusgruppe vom 7 Januar 1917 in Berlin*, Berlin, 1921 (hereinafter *Prot. USPD 1917*), p.107.
31. Prager, *USPD*, p.143.
32. H. Weber (ed.), *Der Gründungsparteitag der KPD. Protokoll und Materialien*, Frankfurt am Main, 1969, p.56.
33. *Prot. USPD 1917*, p.49.
34. Beckert, 'Linken in Chemnitz', *BzG*, 1967, p.109.
35. *Arbeiterpolitik* (Bremen), II, no.9, 3 March 1917, p.66.
36. *Arbeiterpolitik*, II, no.30, 28 July 1917, p.225.
37. G. Badia, *Le Spartakisme*, Paris, 1967, p.263.
38. O. Luban, writing in *Internationale Wissenschaftliche Korrespondenz zur Geschichte der Arbeiterbewegung* (Berlin), (hereinafter *IWK*), 1969, no.8, p.105.
39. *DuM*, II/2, p.133, report attributed to Jogiches.
40. R. Müller, *Vom Kaiserreich zur Republik*, vol.1, Berlin, 1924, p.110.
41. *Illustrierte Geschichte der deutschen Revolution*, Berlin, 1929 (hereinafter *Illustrierte Geschichte*), p.177.

42. *Spartakusbriefe*, Berlin, 1958, p.470. There is some doubt about the date of the Spartacus Conference. *Illustrierte Geschichte*, p.177, gives 1 October.
43. K. Radek, 'November. Eine kleine Seite aus meinen Erinnerungen', in *Archiv für Sozialgeschichte*, II, 1962, p.132.
44. *Illustrierte Geschichte*, p.203.
45. J.S. Drabkin, *Die November-Revolution 1918 in Deutschland*, Berlin, 1968, p.104.
46. E. Kolb, *Die Arbeiterräte in der deutschen Innenpolitik 1918–19*, Düsseldorf, 1962, p.65.
47. *Illustrierte Geschichte der deutschen Novemberrevolution*, Berlin, 1968, pp.128–30.
48. *Vorwärts und nicht vergessen. Erinnerungsberichte aktiver Teilnehmer der Novemberrevolution 1918–19*, Berlin, 1958, pp.469–70.
49. Kolb, *Arbeiterräte*, p.77.
50. W. Pieck, *Gesammelte Reden und Schriften*, vol.1, Berlin, 1959, p.422.
51. Spartacus leaflet of 8 November 1918, in *DuM*, II/2, pp.324–5.
52. *DuM*, II/2, p.326.
53. P. Scheidemann, *Memoirs of a Social Democrat*, London, 1930, vol.2, p.567.
54. Pieck, *Reden und Schriften*, vol.1, p.434.
55. This interpretation was first advanced by Artur Rosenberg in his truly remarkable study, *The History of the German Republic*, London, 1936.
56. *DuM*, II/2, p.457.
57. Pieck, *Reden und Schriften*, vol.1, p.435.
58. Pieck, *Reden und Schriften*, vol.1, pp.437–8.
59. For the RSB, see R. Grau, 'Zur Rolle und Bedeutung des Roten Soldatenbundes', *Zeitschrift für Militärgeschichte*, 1968, no.6, pp.718–32.
60. P. Levi, *Unser Weg. Wider den Putschismus*, 2nd ed, Berlin, 1921, p.14.
61. R. Luxemburg, *Gesammelte Werke*, vol.4, Berlin, 1974, p.410.
62. *Die Freiheit* (Berlin), 18 December 1918.
63. Prager, *USPD*, p.185.
64. *Allgemeiner Kongress der Arbeiter- und Soldatenräte Deutschlands vom 16. bis 21. Dezember 1918. Stenographische Berichte*, Glashütten im Taunus, 1972, col.300.
65. *Allgemeiner Kongress, 1918*, col.227.
66. *Die Freiheit*, 24 December 1918.
67. Pieck, *Reden und Schriften*, vol.1, p.457.
68. *Berichte zum zweiten Kongress der Kommunistischen Internationale*, Hamburg, 1921, p.21.
69. H. Weber, introduction to the best text of the minutes of the first KPD Congress, found in the Levi Papers, and published as *Der Gründungsparteitag der KPD*, Frankfurt am Main, 1969, p.37.
70. *Gründungsparteitag*, p.135.
71. *Gründungsparteitag*, pp.88–96.
72. Rosa Luxemburg to Clara Zetkin, 11 January 1919, printed in *Zeitschrift für Geschichtswissenschaft* (hereinafter *ZfG*), 1963, vol.II, no.8, p.1480. The Luxemburg correspondence is scattered around in a number of Polish and German sources at present. A collected edition is badly needed.
73. *Gründungsparteitag*, pp.199–200.
74. *Gründungsparteitag*, p.164.
75. *Gründungsparteitag*, p.248.
76. *Gründungsparteitag*, p.273.

CHAPTER 2 FROM RADICAL SECT TO MASS PARTY, 1919 TO 1920

1. A. J. Ryder, *The German Revolution of 1918*, Cambridge, 1967, pp.192–3.
2. *Vorwärts*, 1 January 1919, editorial.
3. Radek, 'November', *Archiv für Sozialgeschichte* vol.2, 1962, p.137.
4. RF, 5 September 1920, unsigned article, probably by Levi. The attitude of the *Zentrale* is thoroughly examined by E. Waldmann in *The Spartacist Uprising of 1919*, Milwaukee, 1958, pp.161–96.
5. *Illustrierte Geschichte*, p.247.
6. *DuM*, II/3, p.11.
7. *Illustrierte Geschichte*, p.272.
8. Radek, 'November', p.138.
9. P. Levi, *Was ist das Verbrechen? Die Märzaktion oder die Kritik daran?*, Berlin, 1921, p.33.
10. Drabkin, *November–Revolution*, p.496.
11. *DuM*, II/3, p.35, proclamation of 9 January 1919 by the Revolutionary *Obleute*, the Greater Berlin USPD and the KPD *Zentrale*.
12. *DuM*, II/3, pp.64–5.
13. *DuM*, II/3, p.36, resolution of 9 January.
14. Letter of 9 January 1919, quoted in *Illustrierte Geschichte*, p.282.
15. *DuM*, II/3, pp.41–2, letter of 10 January.
16. RF, 8 and 14 January 1919, printed in *DuM*, II/3, pp.23–6, 71–5.
17. *DuM*, II/3, p.75.
18. *DuM*, II/3, p.79.
19. J. P. Nettl, *Rosa Luxemburg*, London, 1966, vol.2, p.773.
20. Pieck, *Reden und Schriften*, vol.1, p.481.
21. *Vorwärts und nicht vergessen*, p.199; P. Kuckuk (ed.), *Revolution und Räterepublik in Bremen*, Frankfurt, 1969, pp.104–6.
22. *DuM*, II/3, p.90, proclamation of 15 January 1919.
23. Tampke, *The Ruhr and Revolution*, London, 1979, p.123.
24. P. von Oertzen, 'Die grossen Streiks der Ruhrbergarbeiterschaft in Frühjahr 1919', *VJFZ*, vol.6 (1958), p.241.
25. Tampke, *Ruhr and Revolution*, p.135.
26. Tampke, *Ruhr and Revolution*, p.139; *Illustrierte Geschichte*, p.326.
27. *Illustrierte Geschichte*, p.373.
28. *DuM*, II/3, pp.198–9, general strike resolution of 23 February.
29. RF, 27 February 1919.
30. *Illustrierte Geschichte*, p.374; R. Müller, *Der Bürgerkrieg in Deutschland*, Berlin, 1925, p.144.
31. G. A. Ritter and S. Miller, *Die deutsche Revolution 1918–19*, 2nd edn, Frankfurt am Main, 1975, p.188.
32. *DuM*, II/3, p.289.
33. *DuM*, II/3, pp.299–300, leaflet issued by the KPD *Zentrale*, early March 1919.
34. G. Noske, *Von Kiel bis Kapp*, Berlin, 1920, pp.105–110; *Illustrierte Geschichte*, p.362.
35. RF, 4 March 1919.
36. Noske, *Von Kiel bis Kapp*, p.120.
37. *Illustrierte Geschichte*, pp.367–9.

38. *Nachlass Paul Levi* (hereinafter *NPL*), Archiv der sozialen Demokratie, Bonn, Carton 50, shorthand record of 29 March 1919 *Reichskonferenz*, p.5. These shorthand notes were largely deciphered by Richard Löwenthal, who left a typescript of his discoveries with the document.
39. *NPL*, 19/5, report from the *Zentrale* on the 29 March conference.
40. Hartstein (Levi) to Lenin, 27 March 1919, printed in P. Levi, *Zwischen Spartakus und Sozialdemokratie*, ed. and introduced by C. Beradt, Frankfurt, 1969, pp.19–20.
41. RF, 11 April 1919.
42. *NPL* 129/7, manuscript on the history of the KPD up to 1920.
43. See e.g. A. Mitchell, *Revolution in Bavaria*, Princeton, 1965; and, with closer attention to the tactics of the Munich KPD, H. Beyer, *Von der Novemberrevolution zur Räterepublik in München*, Berlin, 1957.
44. *DuM*, II/3, p.322.
45. *Illustrierte Geschichte*, p.391.
46. *DuM*, II/3, p.362.
47. R. Leviné-Meyer, *Leviné*, Farnborough, 1973, p.98.
48. *DuM*, II/3, pp.415–16.
49. Mitchell, *Revolution in Bavaria*, pp.330–1; Beyer, *Novemberrevolution*, pp.136–8.
50. F. L. Carsten, *Revolution in Central Europe 1918–19*, London, 1972, p.176.
51. RF, 25 February 1919.
52. *Die Internationale*, I, 2/3, 30 May 1919, pp.9–14 (Thalheimer); *Die Internationale*, I, 5/6, 5 July 1919, pp.6–13 (M. J. Braun); *Bericht über den 4. Parteitag der KPD, am 14. und 15. April 1920* (hereinafter *Bericht. 4. Parteitag*), p.94, Eduard Alexander's speech; *Bericht über den 5. Parteitag der KPD (Sektion der Kommunistischen Internationale, vom 1. bis 3. November 1920 in Berlin)*, Berlin, 1921 (hereinafter *Bericht. 5. Parteitag*), p.142, Heinrich Brandler's speech.
53. *Kommunistische Räte-Korrespondenz* (*KRK*), 7, 7 July 1919.
54. Kolb, *Arbeiterräte*, p.324.
55. This is the periodisation developed by Annie Kriegel for Western Europe as a whole. It seems reasonable to apply it to Germany as well. See her *Aux origines du communisme français*, Paris, 1964, vol.1, pp.339–40.
56. *Vierteljahreshefte zur Konjunkturforschung. Sonderheft 31*, Berlin, 1933, p.24.
57. *NPL*, 129/7, undated manuscript by Levi on the history of the KPD up to 1920.
58. *NPL*, 19/1, circular issued by the Central Secretariat on 11 June 1919.
59. *NPL*, 50/16, circular from the Central Secretariat to all local groups of the KPD(S), 13 June 1919.
60. *NPL*, 50/13, circular from the Central Secretariat, 19 June 1919.
61. *KRK*, 5, 20 June 1919.
62. Radek, 'November', *Archiv für Sozialforschung*, vol.2, 1962, pp.155–7.
63. D. Mitchell, *1919: Red Mirage*, London, 1970.
64. V. I. Lenin, *Collected Works*, translated into English from the fourth edition, Moscow, 1972, vol.29, p.493. (All subsequent references are to this edition.)
65. *Die Kommunistische Internationale (KI)*, no.1, May 1919, p.XII.
66. *Die Internationale*, II, 21, 25 February 1920, pp.56–60, K. Radek, 'Die Lehren der ungarischen Ereignisse'.

214 *Notes and References*

67. *KRK*, 17, 13 September 1919, circular of 28 August issued by the *Zentrale*.
68. *NPL*, 55/9, *Protokoll der Reichskonferenz*, 16–17 August 1919, p.6, resolution of 17 August.
69. Heidelberg, Wachenburg, Mannheim and Dilsberg am Neckar.
70. *Bericht über der 2. Parteitag der KPD(S) vom.20.bis 24. Oktober 1919* (hereinafter *Bericht.2.Parteitag*), p.31.
71. *Bericht.2.Parteitag*, p.30.
72. *Kommunistische Arbeiter-Zeitung* (Hamburg), 31 July 1919.
73. *Bericht.2.Parteitag*, p.26.
74. *Bericht.2.Parteitag*, p.33.
75. *Bericht.2.Parteitag*, p.6.
76. K. Radek, *Die Entwicklung der deutschen Revolution und die Aufgaben der Kommunistischen Partei*, Berlin, 1919. It was also serialised in *KRK*.
77. Radek, 'November', *Archiv für Sozialgeschichte*, vol.2, 1962, p.157.
78. Lenin, *Collected Works*, vol.30, pp.87–8, letter of 28 October 1919.
79. *Kommunistische Arbeiter-Zeitung* (Hamburg), 1919, no.83, undated.
80. Bock, *Syndikalismus*, p.191.
81. Bock, *Syndikalismus*, p.228.
82. Bock, *Syndikalismus*, p.229.
83. There was a relatively strong Syndicalist movement in the Ruhr, based on the *Freie Vereinigung der Bergarbeiter Deutschlands* (Free Union of the Mining Workers of Germany), but it developed separately from the Spartacus League, although the Gelsenkirchen section of the Syndicalist union later split off and applied to join the KPD. Hans-Manfred Bock has shown that the cry of 'Syndicalism' raised against the left opposition by Levi in 1919 had no justification (Bock, *Syndikalismus*, pp.23–34).
84. D. A. Smart, *Pannekoek and Gorter's Marxism*, London, 1978, pp.35–40.
85. *NPL*, 19/2, report of 28 November 1919, signed by Levi with his pseudonym, Hartstein.
86. *Protokoll über die Verhandlungen des ausserordentlichen Parteitages der USPD in Leipzig vom.30 November bis 6.Dezember*, Berlin, n.d., p.388.
87. RF, 29 November 1919.
88. *Die Internationale*, II, 19/20, 2 February 1920, p.25, A. Struthahn, 'Der Parteitag der Unabhängigen'.
89. *NPL*, 126/5, Levi's draft reply of 7 January 1920; *KI*, 10, pp.172–6, West European Secretariat circular, 15 January 1920.
90. *KI*, 9, pp.152–165; English translation in J. Degras (ed.), *The Communist International 1919–1943, Documents*, London, 1971, vol.1, pp.74–80.
91. *Bericht über den 3. Parteitag der KPD am 25. und 26 Februar, 1920*, p.19 (Thalheimer); RF, 14 January 1920.
92. *Freiheit*, 11 February 1920.
93. *Bericht.3.Parteitag*, p.18.
94. *Bericht.3.Parteitag*, pp.13, 8.
95. *Bericht.3.Parteitag*, pp.9 (Meyer), 27 (Zetkin), 34 (Heckert).
96. *Bericht.3.Parteitag*, p.7.
97. *Bericht.3.Parteitag*, p.87.
98. *Bericht.3.Parteitag*, pp.33–4.
99. Lucas, E., *Märzrevolution 1920*, vol.1, 2nd edn, Frankfurt, 1974, p.62.

100. Rosenberg, *German Republic*, pp.137–8; Lucas, E., *Märzrevolution*, vol.2, Frankfurt, 1973, pp.132–75.
101. *NPL*, 129/3, Circular No. 5, undated, but November 1919 from internal evidence.
102. RF, 10 March 1920.
103. RF, 14 March 1920; printed in *DuM*, II/7/1, pp.211–13.
104. *DuM*, II/7/1, pp.215–17.
105. *Bericht.3.Parteitag*, p.36.
106. H. Brandler, *Die Aktion gegen den Kapp Putsch in Westsachsen*, Berlin, 1920, pp.7–8.
107. Brandler, *Die Aktion*, pp.31–4.
108. M. Hölz, *From White Cross to Red Flag*, London, 1930, pp.84–102.
109. *Bericht über den 4.Parteitag der KPD, am 14. und 15. April 1920*, p.20 (Levi). A strong minority at the Fourth Congress did not share the views of the Levi *Zentrale* on the Hölz affair. Paul Frölich accused Levi of 'converting anti-putschism into quietism'. (*Bericht.4.Parteitag*, p.27.)
110. *Bericht.4.Parteitag*, p 39 (Pieck, in favour); p.42 (Meyer, against); p.44 (Walcher, in favour). The problem is examined in H. Naumann and F. Voigtländer, 'Zum Problem einer Arbeiterregierung nach dem Kapp-putsch', *BzG*, 1963, no.3, pp.461–94.
111. RF, 26 March 1920. V. Mujbegović, *Komunistička Partija Nemačke v Periodu posleratne Krize 1918–23*, Belgrade, 1968, p.203, lists the advocates of 'loyal opposition' in the *Zentrale* as Levi, Pieck, Paul Lange, Jakob Walcher and August Thalheimer.
112. W. Koenen, 'Zur Frage der Möglichkeit einer Arbeiterregierung nach dem Kapp-putsch', *BzG*, 1962, 4, pp.347–9.
113. The second Ruhr rising has been treated in detail by Erhard Lucas, in volume 3 of *Märzrevolution 1920*, Frankfurt, 1978.
114. *DuM*, II/7/1, no.124, KPD appeal of 4 April 1920, pp.245–7.
115. Graphically and emotionally described in the party's official history of the years 1918 to 1920, *Illustrierte Geschichte*, pp.505–8; details in Lucas, *Märzrevolution*, vol.3, pp.353–401.
116. *Bericht.4.Parteitag*, pp.28–9.
117. *Bericht.4.Parteitag*, p.35 (Eulert); p.45 (Hörnle); p.37 (Zetkin); p.42 (Meyer).
118. *Bericht.4.Parteitag*, p.34 (Thalheimer); pp.38–40 (Pieck); pp.50–2 (Levi).
119. *Bericht.4.Parteitag*, p.53.
120. *KI*, II, 12, K. Radek, 'Die KPD während der Kapptage – eine kritische Untersuchung', pp.162–75.
121. *Kommunismus* (Vienna) 1920, no.14, p.410.
122. Lenin, *Collected Works*, vol.31, p.109.
123. *Bericht.4.Parteitag*, pp.106–10.
124. *Freiheit*, 7 June 1920.
125. *Bericht.4.Parteitag*, p.42.
126. *Bericht.4.Parteitag*, p.51. No one ventured to go all the way with Levi in this, although Walcher (p.57) and Zetkin (p.58) distinguished between 'the broad masses of USPD workers' and the 'left' leaders, saying that the former did constitute a genuine left wing.
127. *Freiheit*, 26 June 1920.

128. RF, 24 June 1920.
129. RF, 24 June 1920.
130. Extracts in Degras (ed.), *Communist International*, vol.1, pp.93–9; complete text in *KI*, II (1920), 11, pp.192–213.
131. Morgan, *Socialist Left*, p.348.
132. Degras (ed.), *Communist International*, vol.1, p.168.
133. *Der zweite Kongress der Kommunistischen Internationale. Protokoll der Verhandlungen*, Hamburg, 1921, p.689, speech of 7 August 1920.
134. Degras (ed.), *Communist International*, vol.1, p.165.
135. *NPL*, 126/6, Levi's report to the ZA session of 25 August 1920, p.8.
136. Meyer revealed at the Fifth Party Congress that these views were put to him in Moscow in July (*Bericht über den 5.Parteitag der KPD (Sektion der Kommunistischen Internationale) vom.1. bis 3. November 1920 in Berlin*, Berlin, 1921, pp.27–8).
137. The voting pattern was analysed in detail by the late Robert Wheeler, in *USPD und Internationale*, Frankfurt, 1975, pp.246–58.
138. G. Zinoviev, *Zwölf Tage in Deutschland*, Hamburg, 1921, p.5.
139. Morgan, *Socialist Left*, p.278.

CHAPTER 3   FORCING THE PACE OF REVOLUTION

1. *KI*, II, 14, pp.262–72.
2. *KI*, II, 14, pp.273–4; Degras (ed.), *Communist International*, vol.1, pp.198–9.
3. *KI*, II, 15, pp.414–16.
4. *Bericht über den 5.Parteitag der Kommunistischen Partei Deutschlands (Sektion der Kommunistischen Internationale) vom.1. bis 3. November 1920 in Berlin*, Berlin, 1921 (hereinafter *Bericht.5.Parteitag*), pp.85–6.
5. *Bericht.5.Parteitag*, p.42.
6. Ibid., p.44.
7. Ibid., p.76.
8. Ibid., p.95.
9. Ibid., p.97. Däumig was there as a guest from the USPD (Left).
10. *Bericht.5.Parteitag*, p.100.
11. *Bericht.5.Parteitag*, p.197.
12. After the Jena Congress of 1921 the party reverted to its old title of KPD.
13. *Bericht über die Verhandlungen des Vereinigungsparteitags der USPD (Linke) und der KPD (Spartakusbund), abgehalten in Berlin vom.4. bis 7. Dezember 1920*, Berlin, 1921 (hereinafter *Bericht, Vereinigungsparteitag*), p.220.
14. Fischer, *Stalin and German Communism*, pp.146–7.
15. *Bericht, Vereinigungsparteitag*, p.44.
16. Ibid., p.69.
17. Ibid., p.54 (Meyer), p.66 (Weber), p.144 (Rosenberg).
18. Ibid., pp.222–36.
19. RF, 4 December 1920.
20. *Bericht, Vereinigungsparteitag*, p.232.
21. RF, 4 January 1921.
22. Ibid., 8 January 1921

23. K. Radek, *Soll die Vereinigte Kommunistische Partei Deutschlands eine Massenpartei der revolutionären Aktion oder eine zentristische Partei des Wartens sein?* Hamburg, 1921, p.24; M. Drachkovitch and B. Lazitch, *The Comintern: Historical Highlights*, London, 1966, Speech of Comrade Max to the German *Zentrale* on 28 January 1921, p.292. This document is a translation of the original text in *NPL* 50/5. The reference in the open letter of 8 January to 'parties which rest on the proletariat' rather than 'proletarian parties' is a further reason for assuming Radek's authorship.

24. *Die Internationale*, III, no.1, 1921, pp.1–4, no.2, pp.10–16.

25. *NPL*, 159/44, Curt Geyer to the *Zentrale*, 21 April 1921, a report on the Narrower Bureau Session of 21 February 1921 and the Plenary Session of the ECCI, 22–24 February 1921, p.6.

26. Mujbegović, *Komunistička Partija Nemačke*, p.260, n.7, quoting KPD party archives.

27. Set up in December 1919, with a programme drawn up by the veteran Anarchist Rudolf Rocker.

28. RF, 16 January 1921.

29. *Resoconto stenografico del XVII. Congresso Nazionale del PSI*, Milan, 1962, p.16.

30. RF, 23 January 1921.

31. Drachkovitch and Lazitch, *The Comintern*, p.291.

32. Ibid., p.293.

33. *Die Internationale*, II, no.24, 24 June 1920, p.36.

34. *NPL*, 64/3, p.16.

35. Drachkovitch and Lazitch, *The Comintern*, pp.293–4.

36. Radek, *Soll die VKPD*, p.48 gives the text.

37. ZA resolution of 1 February, RF, 2 February 1921.

38. *Protokoll des III. Kongresses der Kommunistischen Internationale*, Hamburg, 1921, p.283 (Zetkin).

39. *Protokoll, III. Kongress*, p.284 (Zetkin).

40. *NPL*, 50a, Rákosi's report of 16 February 1921.

41. *NPL*, 64, Levi's speech of 24 February 1921 to the ZA, p.22.

42. RF, 28 February 1921.

43. Mujbegović, *Komunistička Partija Nemačke*, p.267, n.22.

44. RF, 1 March 1921.

45. R. Löwenthal, 'The Bolshevisation of the Spartacus League', *St. Anthony's Papers*, No.9, London, 1960, International Communism, ed. D. Footman, p.63.

46. *NPL*, 55/4, Levi to Lenin, 27 March 1921.

47. Lenin, *Collected Works*, vol.45, Moscow, 1970, pp.124–5.

48. *NPL*, 55/3, Radek to Brandler and others, 14 March 1921.

49. *NPL*, 55/5, Curt Geyer's report on the ECCI session of 22 February 1921.

50. For a comparative table see Morgan, *Socialist Left*, p.450.

51. RF, 17 March 1921.

52. *NPL*, 113/22, ZA session of 17 March, Brandler's speech, pp.1–10.

53. *NPL*, 113/22, Frölich's speech, p.13.

54. Mujbegović, *Komunisticka Partija Nemacke*, p.271, quoting KPD party archives.

55. RF, 18, 19 March 1921.
56. *NPL*, 113/5, Lemke's report of 8 April 1921; *Vorwärts*, 25 November 1921, morning edition, Bowitzky's report of 12 April 1921.
57. Hölz, *From White Cross to Red Flag*, pp.126–69.
58. *Taktik und Organisation der revolutionären Offensive*, Berlin, 1921, p.37 (Frölich).
59. RF, 24 March 1921.
60. *NPL*, 83/9, p.14.
61. *Protokoll, III. Kongress*, pp.250–1.
62. *Die Märzkämpfe*, Berlin, 1956, p.79.
63. *Protokoll, III. Kongress*, pp.584–5.
64. *NPL*, 113/24, minutes of a meeting of the *Reichsgewerkschaftszentrale*, held at 5.30 p.m. on 30 March 1921, p.18.
65. RF, 4 April 1921.
66. Ibid., 5 April 1921.
67. The KPD issued a pamphlet with this message, entitled *Taktik und Organisation der revolutionären Offensive. Die Lehren der März-Aktion*. In it the 'lessons of March' were analysed with a view to stimulating fresh revolutionary offensives.
68. *KI*, II, 17, p.415; translated in Degras, *Communist International*, vol.1, pp.217–18.
69. The voting was 24 to 14, at the meeting of 8 April.
70. *NPL*, 159/2, Zetkin to Levi, 11 April 1921, enclosing copy of *Unser Weg*, with Zetkin's emendations.
71. *NPL*, 55/4; printed in Levi, *Zwischen Spartakus und Sozialdemokratie*, pp.37–44.
72. Lenin's reply: 'Why not wait? 1st June, Congress here. Why not a private conversation here *before* the Congress?', Lenin, *Collected Works*, vol.45, Moscow, 1970, pp.124–5.
73. P. Levi, *Unser Weg. Wider den Putschismus*, Berlin, 1921, 2nd edn, p.74.
74. Ibid., p.30.
75. Ibid., p.31.
76. Ibid., p.86.
77. G. P. Maximoff, *The Guillotine at Work*, Chicago, 1940, pp.124–6.
78. RF, 15, 16 April 1921.
79. Ibid., 10 May 1921.
80. P. Levi, *Was ist das Verbrechen? Die März-Aktion oder die Kritik daran?*, Berlin, 1921, p.31, quoting Pieck's speech at the ZA session of 4 May.
81. Levi, *Was ist das Verbrechen?*, p.29.
82. As quoted by Levi in *Unser Weg*, p.94.

CHAPTER 4   THE REFLUX OF REVOLUTION

1. *Bulletin Communiste*, no.24, 9 June 1921, 'La Crise du Parti communiste allemand', p.400.
2. L.D. Trotsky, *The Real Situation in Russia*, New York, 1928, p.247.
3. A. Reisberg, 'Ein Neuer Brief W. I. Lenins', *BzG* (1965), no.4, p.687.
4. *Protokoll, III. Kongress*, p.90.

5. Ibid., p.185.
6. Ibid., p.472.
7. Ibid., pp.527–9.
8. Ibid., p.538.
9. Ibid., p.634.
10. Ibid., pp.638–42. The Theses on Tactics are printed in English in Degras, *The Communist International*, vol.1, pp.241–56.
11. *Protokoll, III. Kongress*, p.671.
12. Bock, *Linkskommunismus*, p.262.
13. Lenin, *Collected Works*, vol.45, p.124.
14. Cf. *Unser Weg (Sowjet), Zeitschrift für kommunistische Politik*, nos.8/9, August 1921, pp.236–7, 'Der Parteitag der VKPD'.
15. ' *NPL*, 113/20, Levi to Mathilde Jacob, August 1921.
16. *Bericht über die Verhandlungen des 2. Parteitags der Kommunistischen Partei Deutschlands (Sektion der Kommunistischen Internationale) abgehalten in Jena vom 22. bis 26. August 1921*, Berlin, 1922 (hereinafter *Bericht.II(7) Parteitag*) pp.174–81.
17. RF, 14/15 July 1921.
18. Lenin, *Collected Works*, vol.32, pp.512–23, 'A Letter to the German Communists', 24 August 1921.
19. *Die Tätigkeit der Exekutive und des Präsidiums der Exekutivkomitee der Kommunistischen Internationale vom 13. Juli 1921 bis 1. Februar 1922*, Petrograd, 1922, pp.108–19.
20. *Unser Weg*, no.10, September 1921, pp.265–8.
21. Reisberg, *An den Quellen der Einheitsfrontpolitik*, Berlin, 1971, p.227.
22. *Bericht.II(7) Parteitag*, pp.415–22, Twelve Point Resolution on Tax Struggles.
23. RF, 27 October 1921.
24. At the Jena Congress the *Zentrale* was split up, like the Russian Central Committee, into two sections, a *Polbüro*, to give political direction, and an *Orgbüro*.
25. E. Reuter, *Schriften, Reden*, Berlin, 1972, vol.1, 'Zur Krise unserer Partei', 20 December 1921, p.605.
26. On 25 November 1921 *Vorwärts* started to publish the documents on the March Action seized from Clara Zetkin by the Prussian police. It was impossible for the party to deny their authenticity, and it later published the same material officially, in *Die Enthüllungen zu den Märzkämpfen*, Halle, 1922.
27. *Die Taktik der Kommunistischen Internationale gegen die Offensive des Kapitals: Bericht über die Konferenz der Erweiterten Executive der K.I., 24 Feb-2 März 1922*, Hamburg, 1922, p.19.
28. *Die Tätigkeit der Exekutive 1921–1922*, p.330 (Remmele).
29. *Inprekorr*, 1922, no.51, 21 April, p.411.
30. Lenin, *Collected Works*, vol.32, p.522.
31. R. Leviné-Meyer, *Inside German Communism*, London, 1977, pp.26–7, Ernst Meyer to Rosa Leviné-Meyer, 24 July 1922.
32. *Die Tätigkeit der Exekutive 1921–22*, letter of 10 January 1922 from the ECCI to the ZA of the KPD, p.383.
33. *Inprekorr*, 1922, no.184, 21 September, p.1222 (P. Maslowski); H. J.

Krusch, 'Zur Bewegung der revolutionären Betriebsräte in den Jahren 1922/1923', *ZfG*, vol.11, 1963, no.2, pp.360–73.

34. *Inprekorr*, 1922, no.227, 30 November, p.1650. (J. Walcher.)
35. Mujbegović, *Komunistička Partija Nemačke*, p.345.
36. *Die Internationale*, V, no.1/2, p.8.
37. *Die Internationale*, V, no.3, p.61.
38. Reisberg, 'Um die Einheitsfront nach dem Rathenaumord', *BzG* (1963), no.5/6, p.1001.
39. Reisberg, 'Um die Einheitsfront', p.1007.
40. *Inprekorr*, 1922, no.136, 18 July, p.865.
41. Ibid., no.216, 9 November, p.1506.
42. Reisberg, *An den Quellen*, p.537.
43. *Protokoll des vierten Kongresses der Kommunistischen Internationale. Petrograd-Moskau, vom.5. November bis.5. Dezember 1922*, Hamburg, 1923 (hereinafter *Protokoll, IV. Kongress*), p.198.
44. Reisberg quotes the minutes of this session in *An den Quellen*, p.546; Meyer's own view at the time is available in his letters to Rosa Leviné-Meyer, printed in R. Leviné-Meyer, *Inside German Communism*, pp.23–31.
45. H. Weber, *Die Wandlung des deutschen Kommunismus*, Frankfurt, 1969, vol.1, p.46.
46. *Die Internationale*, IV, 21, 14 May 1922, p.472. (P. Böttcher.)
47. Reisberg, *An den Quellen*, p.239.
48. *Die Internationale*, V, no.12, 15 December 1922, pp.343–4 (Böttcher, with the Ten Demands).
49. *Die Lehren der deutschen Ereignisse*, Hamburg, 1924, p.50 (R. Fischer); pp.64–5 (Zinoviev). Details of the negotiations are in Reisberg, *An den Quellen*, pp.609–10.
50. *Protokoll, IV. Kongress*, pp.317–18 (Radek).
51. *Inprekorr*, 1922, no.229, 5 December, pp.1668–70.
52. *Protokoll, IV. Kongress*, p.67.
53. Ibid., p.76.
54. Ibid., pp.81–2.
55. *Bericht über die Verhandlungen des III(8) Parteitages der KPD, abgehalten in Leipzig vom 28. Januar bis.1. Februar 1923*, Berlin, 1923 (hereinafter *Bericht.8.Parteitag*), p.240.
56. *Bericht.8.Parteitag*, p.247.
57. Ibid., p.382.
58. Ibid., pp.217-18.
59. Ibid., p.249.
60. Ibid., pp.420-2.
61. *Die Lehren der deutschen Ereignisse*, p.51 (Fischer).

CHAPTER 5   THE FAILED OCTOBER

1. RF, 1 April 1923.
2. J.-C. Favez, *Le Reich devant l'occupation franco-belge de la Ruhr en 1923*, Geneva, 1969, p.197.
3. RF, 21 April 1923.

4. *Die Internationale*, VI, 10 (15 May 1923), p.301, Resolution adopted on 18 April by the Berlin Organisation's Executive, 'Zur Politik der Partei'.
5. *Die Internationale*, VI, 4 (15 February 1923), pp.97–102, 'Einige taktische Fragen des Ruhrkrieges'.
6. *Die Internationale*, VI, 5 (1 March 1923), p.132.
7. Ibid., VI, 7 (1 April 1923), pp.207–11.
8. Ibid., VI, 7 (1 April 1923), p.210.
9. RF, 6 March 1923.
10. R. Wagner, 'Der Kampf um die proletarische Einheitsfront und Arbeiterregierung in Sachsen unmittelbar nach dem VIII Parteitag der KPD', *BzG*, 1963, no.4, p.655.
11. *Deutscher Geschichtskalendar*, 1923, vol.1, Inland, p.211.
12. Wagner, 'Einheitsfront', p.656, quoting party archives.
13. RF, 30 March 1923, Resolution of 13 March adopted by the Berlin BL.
14. *Die Internationale*, VI, 8, 18 April 1923, pp.228–234, Declaration of 10 April by Arthur Ewert, Gerhart Eisler, Hans Pfeiffer and Heinz Neumann.
15. *Material zu den Differenzen mit der Opposition*, Berlin, 1923, pp.23–4.
16. *DuM*, VII/2, p.304, Joint Resolution agreed between the ECCI, the KPD *Zentrale* and the Opposition, 'beginning of May'.
17. Bry, *Wages in Germany*, pp.453–4.
18. Unemployment as percentage of members of the Free Trade Unions, March 1923: 5.6; April 1923: 7.0; May 1923: 6.2; June 1923: 4.1; July 1923: 3.5; August 1923: 6.3; September 1923: 9.9; October 1923: 19.1; November 1923: 23.4; December 1923: 28.2. Figures from E.-C. Schöck, *Arbeitslosigkeit und Rationalisierung. Die Lage der Arbeiter und die Kommunistische Gewerkschaftspolitik 1920–1928*, Frankfurt, 1977, p.233.
19. Short-time working in the Free Trade Unions (in %): July 1923: 14.5; August 1923: 26.0; September 1923: 39.7; October 1923: 47.3; November 1923: 47.5; December 1923: 42.0. Figures from Schöck, *Arbeitslosigkeit*, p.235.
20. *Inprekorr*, 1923, no.135, 20 August, p.1178 (Heckert).
21. H. Gast, 'Die proletarischen Hundertschaften', *ZfG*, 1956, no.3, pp.447–8.
22. *Inprekorr* (Wochenausgabe), no.26, 30 June 1923, p.630.
23. *Protokoll der Konferenz der Erweiterten Exekutive der Kommunistischen Internationale (Moskau 12–23 Juni 1923)*, Hamburg, 1923, pp.240–5.
24. RF, 29 July 1923, speech of 25 July.
25. *Inprekorr*, 1923, no.111, 3 July, p.971.
26. RF, 12 July 1923.
27. *Die Lehren*, p.55.
28. E. H. Carr, *The Interregnum 1923–1924*, London, 1969, p.195.
29. G. Hortschansky, *Der nationale Verrat der deutschen Monopolherren, während des Ruhrkampfes 1923*, Berlin, 1960, p.164.
30. *Vorwärts*, 3 August 1923.
31. *Inprekorr*, 1923, no.128, 3 August, p.1117; RF, 2 August 1923.
32. *Bericht über die Verhandlungen des IX. Parteitages der KPD. Abgehalten in Frankfurt a.M. vom 7. bis 10. April 1924*, Berlin, 1924 (hereinafter *Bericht. 9. Parteitag*), pp.64–74.

33. *RF*, 11 August 1923.
34. W. Ersil, *Aktionseinheit stürzt Cuno*, Berlin, 1963, p.357.
35. A. Thalheimer, *1923: Eine verpasste Revolution?*, Berlin, 1931, p.20.
36. *RF*, 19 August 1923.
37. *Inprekorr*, 1923, no.135, 20 August, p.1175; *RF*, 19 August 1923.
38. As quoted by O. Kuusinen, in 'A Misleading Description of the "German October"', *The Errors of Trotskyism. A Symposium*, London, 1925, pp.347–8.
39. G. Zinoviev, speech to the Thirteenth Party Conference of the RCP(B), printed in German in *Inprekorr*, IV, 1924, no.16, 4 February, p.168.
40. B. Bajanov, *Avec Staline dans le Kremlin*, Paris, 1930, p.140. This is the only extant account of the meeting. Bazhanov's revelations cannot entirely be relied on. It is to be regretted that Trotsky never gave any account of his own role in the decision to mount a 'German October', despite his later view that the October disaster was of vital significance for the future of the Soviet Union and Germany.
41. *Inprekorr*, 1923, no.138, 27 August, p.1198.
42. *Inprekorr*, 1923, no.140, 31 August, p.1220. This was a proclamation by the ECCI and the RILU, drafted by Trotsky, and dated 27 August 1923.
43. *RF*, 21 August 1923.
44. Fischer, *Stalin and German Communism*, p.312; G. Bessedovsky, *Revelations of a Soviet Diplomat*, London, 1931, p.62.
45. *Inprekorr*, 1923, no.152, 26 September, pp.1309–10.
46. *Die Lehren*, p.57 (Radek).
47. *Inprekorr*, 1924, no.22, 18 February, p.241.
48. *Bericht.9.Parteitag*, p.24
49. *Z Pola Walki* (Warsaw), I, 4, 1958, p.137.
50. *Bericht.9.Parteitag*, General Alfred Müller was the local military commander.
51. *Die Lehren*, p.41 (Remmele); Heinrich Brandler to Isaac Deutscher, 8 February 1959, *New Left Review*, 105, p.80. Various dates have been given for the start of the preparations. Werner Angress discusses the evidence in *Stillborn Revolution*, New York, 1963, p.416, note 94, and comes down in favour of 1 October.
52. Skoblevsky's precise identity and background are not known for certain. See Angress, *Stillborn Revolution*, p.418.
53. Gast, 'Hundertschaften', pp.452–7; Angress, *Stillborn Revolution*, pp.416–20.
54. There are many dubious 'sources' for the technical preparations for the uprising. Angress (*Stillborn Revolution*, pp.416-7) concludes that 'the reliability of most of these accounts is open to serious doubts, so that any historical treatment . . . must remain in large part conjectural'.
55. Gast, 'Hundertschaften', p.452. According to D. Davidovich there were 800 'Proletarian Hundreds' in Germany in October 1923, a third of them in Saxony, only 15 in Hamburg. ('Gamburgskoye Vosstaniye 1923 Godu', *Voprosy Istorii*,1948, no.11, November, p.6.)
56. *Die Internationale*, VI, 18 (30 November 1923), p.524.
57. W. Zeutschel, *Im Dienst der Kommunistischen Terror-Organisation*, Berlin, 1931, p.13.

58. Brandler to Deutscher, 12 January 1959, *New Left Review*, 105, p.76.
59. H. Habedank, *Zur Geschichte des Hamburger Aufstandes*, Berlin, 1958, pp.68, 82 and 85.
60. *Schulthess' Europäischer Geschichtskalendar*, Munich, 1923, p.190.
61. Brandler to Deutscher, 18 April 1952, *New Left Review*, 105, p.56.
62. Mujbegović, *Komunistička Partija Nemačke*, p.401, n.93.
63. *Schulthess*, 1923, p.192.
64. Ibid., p.193.
65. O. Gessler, *Reichswehrpolitik in der Weimarer Zeit*, Stuttgart, 1958, pp.260–2.
66. *Bericht. 9. Parteitag*, p.20. This is how the Fischer opposition (now the KPD leadership) viewed the issue in retrospect.
67. This account is based on the only contemporary source, *Vorwärts*, 23 October 1923; Brandler afterwards denied that he had insisted on unanimous acceptance.
68. Thalheimer, *1923*, p.26.
69. Brandler to Deutscher, 12 January 1959, *New Left Review*, 105, p.74.
70. *Inprekorr*, 1923, no.164, 22 October, p.1398, F. Müller, 'Der Arbeiterkongress in Chemnitz'.
71. L. Danner, *Ordnungspolizei in Hamburg*, Hamburg, 1958, pp.71–3.
72. Danner, *Ordnungspolizei*, p.114.
73. Kippenberger's report is printed in pp.81–104 of A. Neuberg, *Armed Insurrection*, London, 1970. The police version is in Danner, *Ordnungspolizei*, pp.74–131. Habedank, *Zur Geschichte des Hamburger Aufstandes* provides much supplementary information.
74. L. Reissner, *Hamburg auf den Barrikaden*, Berlin, 1925. W. Ulbricht, *Zur Geschichte der deutschen Arbeiterbewegung*, Berlin, 1953, vol.1, pp.139–48; E. Thälmann, in RF, 23 October 1925.
75. Text of the 25 October Resolution in *Die Lehren*, pp.7–8. Erroneously dated there 26 October.
76. *DuM*, VII/2, pp.469–71, proclamation in *Der Kämpfer* (Chemnitz), 29 October 1923.
77. H. J. Gordon, 'Die Reichswehr und Sachsen 1923', *Wehrwissenschaftliche Rundschau*, no.12, December 1961, p.687.
78. *Jahrbuch für Wirtschaft, Politik und Arbeiterbewegung 1923–1924*, Hamburg, 1925, p.607.
79. *Die Lehren*, p.10.
80. *Clarté* (Paris), no.52, 1 February 1924, p.66.

CHAPTER 6 COMMUNIST DEFEAT AND CAPITALIST STABILISATION

1. *Die Internationale*, VI, 18 (30 November 1923), pp.516–20.
2. G. Zinoviev, *Probleme der deutschen Revolution*, Hamburg, 1923, preface, p.v.
3. Zinoviev, *Probleme*, pp.105–9.
4. *Inprekorr*, 1924, no.16, 4 February, p.169, report of Zinoviev's speech of 19 January 1924 to the Thirteenth Party Conference of the RCP(B). Thalheimer suggested (*1923: Eine verpasste Revolution?*, p.11) that Zinoviev changed his mind after Radek's speech of 13 December 1923 threatening

that the KPD would side with Trotsky if the Russian Central Committee condemned him. This is highly unlikely in view of the fact that Zinoviev had already attacked the 3 November Resolution in a *Pravda* article of 23 November.

5. Trotsky's article of December 1923, 'Tradition and Revolutionary Policy', included in January 1924 in the collection *The New Course*. See L. Trotsky, *The Challenge of the Left Opposition 1923–5*, New York, 1975, p.95.
6. *Die Lehren*, p.23.
7. L. Trotsky to A. Treint, 13 September 1931, published in *The New International*, February 1938, pp.56–8.
8. *Vsesoyuznaya Kommunisticheskaya Partiya (bol'shevikov) v rezolyutsiyakh*, Moscow, 1941, vol.1, p.534.
9. K. H. Tjaden, *Struktur und Funktion der 'KPD-Opposition' (KPO)*, Meisenheim am Glan, 1964, p.39; *Bericht über die Tätigkeit des EKKI vom IV. bis zum V Kongress*, Hamburg, 1924, p.20.
10. *Pravda*, 23 November 1923; *Inprekorr*, 1923, no.182, 20 December, pp.1540–2.
11. Centre theses, *Inprekorr*, 1923, no.185, 28 December, pp.1565–6; Right theses, *Inprekorr*, 1924, no.5, 15 January, p.40; Left theses, *Inprekorr* 1924, no.6, 18 January, pp.51–2.
12. The speeches are printed in *Die Lehren*, pp.24–57.
13. Ibid., pp.95–109, resolution of 21 January 1924.
14. Thalheimer, *1923: Eine verpasste Revolution?*, p.11.
15. *Inprekorr*, 1923, no.72, 7 November, pp.1457–60.
16. *Die Lehren*, p.109.
17. *Inprekorr*, 1924, no.25, 22 February, p.276.
18. Ibid., no.22, 18 February, p.242.
19. *Bericht. 9. Parteitag*, pp.64–75.
20. From an organisational circular issued in April 1924, quoted in Weber, *Wandlung*, p.59.
21. *Inprekorr*, 1924, no.41, 3 April, p.477.
22. *Die Internationale*, Sonderheft 2/3 (1924), p.47.
23. *Der Kämpfer* (Chemnitz), 18 March 1924.
24. RF, 25 March 1924.
25. Ibid., 6 March 1924.
26. *Bericht. 9. Parteitag*, pp.341 and 399.
27. Letters of 24 March and 26 March 1924, *Inprekorr*, 1924, no.48, 24 April, pp.562–8.
28. *VFZG*, vol.16, no.2, April 1968, p.190, letter from G. Zinoviev to A. Maslow and R. Fischer, 31 March 1924; H. Weber, *Wandlung*, vol.1, pp.399–401, letter from G. Zinoviev and N. Bukharin to E. Thälmann and P. Schlecht, 31 March 1924.
29. *Inprekorr*, 1926, no.63, 27 April, p.923.
30. *Bericht. 9. Parteitag*, p.366.
31. Ibid., p.369.
32. Ibid., p.370.
33. Ibid., p.234.
34. Ibid., p.80.
35. Ibid., p.334.

36. Ibid., p.159.
37. *Inprekorr*, 1924, no.48, 24 April, p.562.
38. *Bericht.9.Parteitag*, p.223.
39. *Bericht über die Verhandlungen des elften Parteitages der KPD*, Berlin, 1927 (hereinafter *Bericht.11. Parteitag*), p.358.
40. *Jahrbuch für Wirtschaft, Politik und Arbeiterbewegung*, 1923–4, p.605; *Bericht.9.Parteitag*, p.62.
41. *Bericht.9.Parteitag*, p.63.
42. Schöck, *Arbeitslosigkeit*, p.237.
43. Schöck, ibid., p.48.
44. *Jahrbuch*, 1923–4, p.585; ECCI proclamation of January 1924, published in *Inprekorr*, 1924, no.25, 22 February, p.276.
45. *Bericht.9.Parteitag*, p.64/8–9.
46. Ibid., p.64/13.
47. RF, 11 December 1922; Weber, *Wandlung*, p.68.
48. Schöck, *Arbeitslosigkeit*, p.58.
49. *Bericht.9.Parteitag*, p.64/3.
50. Ibid., p.102.
51. RF, 25 March, 29 March 1924.
52. *Bericht.9.Parteitag*, p.332.
53. *Bericht.9.Parteitag*, p.335.
54. *Bericht über die Verhandlungen des zehnten Parteitages der KPD*, Berlin, 1925 (hereinafter *Bericht.10. Parteitag*), p.60.
55. *Bericht.9.Parteitag*, p.390.
56. Resolution of 17 August 1924, adopted by 400 communist trade unionists at a national conference, printed in *Inprekorr*, 1924, no.111, 22 August, p.1433.
57. RF, September 1924; *Protokoll des erweiterten EKKI, März–April 1925*, Hamburg, 1925, p.65.
58. *Bericht.10.Parteitag*, p.245, ZA resolution of 20 October 1924.
59. The composition of the *Zentrale* was not made public at the time. Weber, *Wandlung*, p.73, gives the full list, from documents confiscated by the police and preserved in the local archives of Bremen and Munich: Ruth Fischer, Arkady Maslow, Werner Scholem, Ivan Katz, Artur Rosenberg, Ernst Thälmann, Paul Schlecht, Wilhelm Florin, Ottomar Geschke, Artur König, Max Schütz (leftists); Hugo Eberlein, Hermann Remmele, Wilhelm Pieck, Ernst Schneller (Centre group). The official East German list, published in *Geschichte der deutschen Arbeiterbewegung. Chronik, Teil II*, Berlin, 1966, p.164, adds Fritz Heckert and omits Schlecht.
60. *Bericht.9.Parteitag*, p.8.
61. Weber, *Wandlung*, p.74, quoting interviews with former party members; Tjaden, *Struktur und Funktion*, p.44.
62. RF, 22, 24 and 25 July 1924.
63. *Inprekorr*, 1924, no.97, 29 July, p.1257.
64. Lozovsky's offending article, *Pravda*, 7 and 8 June 1924; reprinted in RF, 24, 25 and 27 June 1928.
65. *Inprekorr*, 1924, no.94, 23 July, p.1211; RF, 25 July 1924.
66. *Die Internationale*, VII, nos.10/11 (2 June 1924), pp.320–7; no.12 (15 June 1924), pp.395–401.

67. *Protokoll des fünften Kongresses der Kommunistischen Internationale*, Hamburg, 1925, vol.1, p.98.

68. Degras, *Communist International*, vol.2, p.139, July 1924 Resolution on Fascism.

69. Degras, *Communist International*, vol.2, pp.151–2, theses on tactics, July 1924.

70. *Jahrbuch, 1925/6*, p.735 (Frölich); *Bericht.10. Parteitag*, p.106.

71. J. V. Stalin, *Works*, Moscow, 1954, vol.7, pp.42–7, letter to Comrade Me – rt, 28 February 1923; Fischer, *Stalin and German Communism*, pp.435–9.

72. E. H. Carr, *Socialism in One Country 1924–1926*, vol.3, pt.1, London, 1964, p.314.

73. *Die Internationale*, VIII, Ergänzungsheft 1 (January 1925), p.23, ZA theses of 10–11 January 1925.

74. Fischer, *Stalin and German Communism*, p.416.

75. *Protokoll des erweiterten EKKI, März–April 1925*, p.331, session of 2 April.

76. Fischer, *Stalin and German Communism*, p.422.

77. *Bericht.10.Parteitag*, p.98.

78. Ruhr Conference of 6 May, quoted in Weber, *Wandlung*, p.108.

79. *Bericht.10.Parteitag*, pp.27 and 36.

80. *Protokoll des erweiterten EKKI, März–April 1925*, pp.335–6.

81. *Inprekorr*, 1925, no.77, 8 May, p.1018.

82. Stalin, *Works*, vol.7, pp.91 and 95, speech to the Moscow Party Organisation on the work of the Fourteenth Conference, 9 May 1925.

83. Stalin, *Works*, vol.7, pp.57–8.

84. *Verhandlungen des Reichstags. Stenographische Berichte*, vol.388 (1925), pp.4512–13, 4521.

85. *Die Internationale*, VIII, 7 July 1925, Beilage, p.28.

86. *Protokoll des erweiterten EKKI, März–April 1925* (Third Session, 26 March), p.73.

87. Fischer, *Stalin and German Communism*, p.428.

88. *Die Internationale*, VIII, 5a (end of May 1925), p.288.

89. *DuM*, vol.VIII, Berlin, 1975, p.149.

90. *Inprekorr*, 1925, no.82, 15 May, pp.1113–14 and 1122–3; *Die Internationale*, VIII, 5a (end of May 1925), pp.281–4.

91. Weber, *Wandlung*, p.110.

92. *Inprekorr*, 1925, no.94, 16 June, pp.1286–7.

93. Weber, *Wandlung*, p.110.

94. RF, 9 and 10 June 1925.

95. *Neue Zeitung* (Munich), 10 July 1925, quoted in Weber, *Wandlung*, p.111.

96. *Bericht.10.Parteitag*, pp.167–77.

97. Ibid., p.176.

98. Ibid., pp.257–62; *Die Internationale*, VIII, 8 (15 August 1925), pp.505–7.

99. *Bericht.10.Parteitag*, p.514.

100. Ibid., p.658.

101. Ibid., p.549.

102. Sources for this version of events: Fischer, *Stalin and German Communism*, p.443; *Der neue Kurs*, Berlin, 1925, p.6 (Bukharin's speech); RF, 2, 3 October 1925; *Vorwärts*, 9 September 1925; Weber, *Wandlung*, p.117, quoting archive material.

103. Political resolution, adopted unanimously, *Bericht.10. Parteitag*, p.199.

104. Ibid., pp.220–5.
105. Ibid., pp.387–9.
106. Ibid., pp.244–5.
107. This is Ruth Fischer's interpretation (*Stalin and German Communism*, pp.444–50) but in view of the lack of independent evidence one must regard it as a speculation.
108. Maslow's article of July 1925 in *Der Funke* (organ of the Berlin KPD), quoted in the ECCI open letter of September, in H. Weber (ed.), *Der deutsche Kommunismus. Dokumente*, Cologne, 1963, p.229.
109. H. Neumann, *Maslows Offensive gegen den Leninismus*, Hamburg, 1925.
110. *Der neue Kurs*, p.15 (Zinoviev's speech).
111. RF, 1, 2 and 3 October 1925.
112. RF, 26 and 27 September 1925; *Der neue Kurs*, p.35.
113. Fischer, *Stalin and German Communism*, p.451.
114. RF, 1 September 1925; *Inprekorr*, 1925, no.128, 4 September, p.1863.
115. Carr, *Socialism in One Country*, vol.3, pt.1, p.329.
116. E.g. by Wilhelm Pieck, writing in *KI*, VI, 11, November 1925, pp.1196–206.
117. Weber, *Wandlung*, p.126; RF, 2, 3 September 1925.
118. RF, 6 September 1925; W. Ersil and E. Laboor, 'Die Parteidiskussion im September–October 1925 und ihre Bedeutung für die marxistisch–leninistische Entwicklung der KPD', *BzG*, VIII, 4 (1955), p.602.
119. *Protokoll der erweiterten Exekutive, Februar–März 1926*, Hamburg, 1926, p.206.
120. On 23 October 1925. See RF, 25 October 1925; Ersil and Laboor, 'Parteidiskussion', p.616.
121. W. Pieck, *Gesammelte Reden und Schriften*, vol.3, Berlin, 1961, p.152.
122. RF, 3 November 1925, Thälmann's speech.
123. RF, 3 November 1925, Meyer's speech.
124. RF, 4 November 1925.
125. *Inprekorr*, 1926, no.52, 6 April, p.720.
126. Weber, *Wandlung*, p.141; the later history of the Katz Group is treated in S. Bahne, 'Zwischen Luxemburgismus und Stalinismus', *VFZG*, 9 (1961), pp.366–70.
127. RF, 4 December 1925. The referendum campaign has been examined by U. Schüren, *Der Volksentscheid zur Fürstenenteignung 1926*, Düsseldorf, 1978.
128. *Jahrbuch für Wirtschaft, Politik und Arbeiterbewegung, 1925/26*, p.766 (P. Dietrich); *Die Internationale*, IX, 6 (15 March 1926), pp.181–4 (E. Schneller).
129. *Bericht.11.Parteitag*, p.36 (Dengel) and p.202 (Rosenberg); *Die Internationale*, IX, 22 (15 November 1926), p.676 (A. Kunik).
130. *Jahrbuch 1925/26*, p.747 (Enderle).
131. Ibid., p.755 (Enderle).
132. Ibid., p.756 (Enderle); pp.739 and 754 (Dietrich).
133. *KI*, IX, 7/8, 22 February 1928, p.415 (Remmele).
134. *Inprekorr*, 1926, no.150, 7 December, pp.2647–8.
135. *Inprekorr*, 1927, no.16, 5 February, pp.343–4, Resolution of 7 January 1927.

136. *Bericht.11.Parteitag*, p.41.
137. Carr, *Socialism in One Country*, vol.3, pt.1, p.510.
138. *Protokoll der erweiterten Exekutive Feb.–März 1926*, p.163.
139. Resolution of the Sixth Enlarged ECCI Plenum on the German question, 15 March 1926, printed in Degras, *Communist International,* vol.2, pp.289–90.
140. Meyer's speech of 4 March 1926 to the German Commission as preserved in *Nachlass Ernst Meyer*, quoted in Weber, *Wandlung*, pp.146–7.
141. *Protokoll der erweiterten Exekutive, Feb.–März 1926*, p.507.
142. Meyer's declaration of 24 December 1926, printed in Leviné-Meyer, *Inside German Communism*, p.112.
143. RF, 8 May 1926, article by Urbahns.
144. RF, 30 March 1926.
145. Report of 30 July 1926 to the *Reichskommissar für die Überwachung der öffentlichen Ordnung*, ARK R 43/I/2673 Bd.9, Bundesarchiv, Koblenz.
146. RF, 20 August 1926.
147. *Vorwärts*, 13 September 1926.
148. RF, 7, 9 November 1926.
149. Weber and Kötter both belonged to the Wedding Opposition (Weber in the Palatinate, Kötter in Berlin), but Kötter and some of the Berlin oppositionists (from the Kreuzberg District) had refused to sign the Manifesto of the 700, writing a letter to the CC to explain this. It was printed in RF, 18 September 1926. The reason given was their wish to dissociate themselves from the 'vacillating leaders . . . whose past policy shows that they can never genuinely lead the German Left'.
150. *Tätigkeitsbericht des EKKI, Feb.–Nov.1926*, Hamburg, 1926, p.59.
151. Meyer's declaration of 24 December 1926, in Leviné-Meyer, *Inside German Communism*, pp.111–12.
152. *Protokoll, Erweiterte Exekutive der Kommunistischen Internationale, November–Dezember 1926*, Hamburg, 1927, p.87.
153. RF, 16 and 20 January 1927, reporting speeches at a conference of party workers, 13–14 January 1927.
154. *Bericht.11.Parteitag*, p.197.
155. Ibid., pp. 58ff; RF, 4 March 1927.
156. *Bericht.11.Parteitag*, p.iv.
157. *Inprekorr*, 1927, no.16, 5 February, p.344.
158. *Bericht.11.Parteitag*, p.307.
159. *Bericht.11.Parteitag*, pp.51 and 57, Thälmann's speech.
160. Letter from the ECCI to the Eleventh KPD Congress, printed in Degras, *Communist International* vol.2, p.356.
161. *Verhandlungen des Reichstags*, vol.391, cols 8636–9.
162. *Protokoll der Sitzung des EKKI–Präsidiums. November–Dezember 1928.* Ernst Meyer's speech, p.131. In the *Nachlass Ernst Meyer*, quoted in Weber, *Wandlung*, p.187.
163. RF, 29 July 1927.
164. I. Deutscher, *The Prophet Unarmed. Trotsky: 1921–1929*, Oxford, 1959, p.338.
165. *Die Internationale*, X, 7 (1 April 1927), p.208 (Walcher); X, 11 (1 June 1927), p.213 ('Osten' – Lominadze's pseudonym).
166. CC resolution of 9 September, in RF, 14 September 1927; Tjaden, *Struktur und Funktion*, p.67.

CHAPTER 7   THE LEFT ROUTE TO CATASTROPHE

1. *Inprekorr*, 1927, no.99, 11 October, p.2122 (Meyer); *Inprekorr*, 1927, no.105, 28 October, p.2265 (P. R. Dietrich).
2. *Pyatnadtsatyy s'ezd VKP (b), Dekabr' 1927 Goda. Stenograficheskiy Otchët*, Moscow, 1961, vol.1, pp.623–93 (Bukharin's report), 728 (Shatskin) and 730 (Lominadze).
3. *Piatnadtsatyy s'ezd VKP (b)*, vol.I, p.45.
4. *Inprekorr*, 1928, no.9, 27 January, p.165.
5. E. H. Carr, *Foundations of a Planned Economy 1926–9*, vol.3, London, 1976, p.430.
6. *Inprekorr*, 1928, no.26, 10 March, report of Ninth ECCI Plenum.
7. Degras, *Communist International*, vol.2, p.426.
8. The text of the agreement is printed in *VFZG*, vol.16, no.2, April 1968, pp.207–8.
9. *Die Internationale*, XI, 6 (15 March 1928), pp.161–8.
10. RF, 18 March 1928.
11. Letter of 6 March 1928, printed in Tjaden, *Struktur und Funktion*, pp.75–6.
12. *Protokoll über den vierten Kongress der Roten Gewerkschaftsinternationale*, Moscow, 1928, p.44.
13. Ibid., p.527.
14. Ibid., p.123.
15. *Inprekorr*, 1928, no.49, 22 May.
16. *Die Komintern vor dem VI. Weltkongress. Tätigkeitsbericht der Exekutive der Kommunistischen Internationale vom V. zum VI Weltkongress*, Hamburg, 1928, p.122.
17. *Die Internationale*, XI, 21 (1 November 1928), p.705.
18. Stalin, *Works*, vol.12, Speech of April 1929 to the CC Plenum, pp.21–4.
19. Degras, *Communist International*, vol.2, pp.456–7 and 451.
20. *Protokoll. Sechster Weltkongress der Kommunistischen Internationale*, vol.1, Hamburg, 1928, p.37 (Bukharin).
21. *Protokoll. VI. Weltkongress*, vol.1, pp.300–17.
22. Ibid., vol.1, p.353.
23. Ibid., vol.1, pp.409–18.
24. Ibid., vol.4, p.37.
25. Ibid., vol.1, p.551.
26. RF, 27 September 1928.
27. RF, 5 October 1928.
28. RF, 9 October 1928.
29. Tjaden, *Struktur und Funktion*, p.84.
30. RF, 20 October 1928; *Chronik der deutschen Arbeiterbewegung*, vol.2, p.230; Weber, *Wandlung*, p.207.
31. A copy of Ernst Meyer's speech is preserved in the *Nachlass Ernst Meyer*. The passages quoted are on pp.127, 156 and 165. See also Weber, *Wandlung*, p.214; J. Humbert-Droz, *De Lénine à Staline*, Neuchatel, 1971, pp.326–40.
32. Declaration on the Situation in the Party, *Die Internationale*, XII, 3 (1 February 1929), pp.103–12.
33. Open letter of 19 December 1928, in full in *Inprekorr*, 1928, no.142, 21 December, p.2829; extracts in Degras, *Communist Internationale*, vol.2, pp.567–70.
34. *Inprekorr*, 1929, no.17, 22 February, p.359.

35. *Inprekorr*, 1929, no.1, 4 January 1929, pp.1–4; Stalin, *Works*, vol.11, speech of 19 December 1928 to the ECCI Presidium, 'The Right Danger in the German Communist Party', pp.307–24.

36. *Inprekorr*, 1928, no.143, 28 December, p.2864, reporting the expulsions of 21 December. The eight were Jacob Walcher, Albert Schreiner, Max Köhler, Paul Frölich, August Enderle, Hans Tittel, Alfred Schmidt and Karl Rehbein.

37. On 29 January. See *Inprekorr*, 1929, no.9, 29 January, p.163.

38. Tjaden, *Struktur und Funktion*, vol.1, p.112; T. Bergmann, *50 Jahre KPD (Opposition)*, Hanover, 1978, pp.52–5.

39. Tjaden, *Struktur und Funktion*, p.100.

40. 'Platform of the Conciliators', *Die Internationale*, XII, 13 (1 July 1929), pp.431–6.

41. RF, 21 March 1929.

42. RF, 17 April 1929, speech at the Ruhr District Party Conference.

43. RF, 19 April 1929 (Schneller).

44. Rosenberg, *A History of the German Republic*, p.290.

45. Weber, *Wandlung*, p.322, n.10.

46. *Neue Blätter für den Sozialismus*, II, 9, September 1931, p.437.

47. *Protokoll des 12. Parteitages der KPD*, Berlin, 1929, p.209.

48. Ibid., pp.54–5.

49. Ibid., p.72.

50. Ibid., pp.331–2, Remmele's speech.

51. Ibid., pp.65, 72.

52. Ibid., p.6, Heckert's speech.

53. Ibid., pp.60, 74–8.

54. Ibid., p.417.

55. Ibid., p.81.

56. Ibid., p.91.

57. Ibid., p.97.

58. Ibid., p.6.

59. Ibid., pp.83, 96, 418 and 430.

60. Ibid., p.84.

61. Ibid., p.475.

62. *Waffen für den Klassenkampf: Beschlüsse des XII. Parteitags der KPD*, Berlin, 1929, pp.62–81.

63. *Protokoll. 12. Parteitag*, pp.176–88.

64. Ibid., p.221.

65. Weber, *Wandlung*, p.231.

66. *Protokoll. 12. Parteitag*, p.218, Ewert's Declaration.

67. RF, 23 February 1930.

68. *Chronik der deutschen Arbeiterbewegung*, vol.2, p.288.

69. Ibid., vol.2, p.242.

70. Weber, *Wandlung*, p.232.

71. *Protokoll. 10. Plenum des EKKI*, Hamburg, 1929, pp.419–20.

72. *Protokoll. 10. Plenum*, p.39 (Kuusinen); p.160 (Manuilsky); p.420 (Molotov); p.474 (Neumann).

73. *Inprekorr*, 1929, no.46, 4 September, p.973; Degras, *Communist International*, vol.3, p.46.

74. RF, 7, 8 and 9 August 1929.
75. RF, 8 August 1929.
76. RF, 22 February 1930.
77. *Der Parteiarbeiter* (Berlin), no.2, February 1929.
78. RF, 12 October 1929.
79. *Protokoll des 1.Reichskongresses der RGO, 30 Nov.– 1 Dez. 1929*, Berlin, 1930, pp.74, 94 and 99. The RGO phase is treated briefly, with some polemical asperity, in Freya Eisner, *Das Verhältnis der KPD zu den Gewerkschaften in der Weimarer Republik*, Cologne, 1977.
80. *Die Kommunistische Internationale vor dem VII. Weltkongress. Materialien*, Moscow, 1935, p.120.
81. Trotsky's normal political acumen deserted him when analysing this move. He leapt to the conclusion that Stalin was about to order the abandonment of the ultra-left line: 'A rejection of the tactic of the "third period" in favour of the tactic of the "second period"' (L. D. Trotsky, *The Struggle against Fascism in Germany*, London, 1975, p.19). In reality the only change was the dropping of the phrase 'the third period'. The policy remained the same.
82. *Inprekorr*, 1930, no.23, 7 March, p.547.
83. RF, 6 April 1930.
84. Weber, *Wandlung*, p.245.
85. M. Buber-Neumann, *Von Potsdam nach Moskau*, Stuttgart, 1957, p.288.
86. T. Weingartner, *Stalin und der Aufstieg Hitlers*, Berlin, 1970, passim.
87. *Die Internationale*, XIII, 5/6 (1/15 March 1930), p.151.
88. *Inprekorr*, 1930, no.53, 24 June, p.1165 (H. Jakobs).
89. RF, 24 August 1930.
90. Weingartner, *Stalin und der Aufstieg Hitlers*, p.42.
91. See S. Bahne, in *Jahrbuch für die Geschichte Mittel- und Ostdeutschlands*, vol.13/14, Berlin, 1965, p.323.
92. RF, 16 September 1930.
93. *Die Internationale*, XIII, 18, 15 September 1930.
94. Thälmann, *Reden und Aufsätze*, vol.2, p.304; *KI*, XII, 17/18, 7 May 1931, p.799.
95. L. D. Trotsky, 'Germany, the Key to the International Situation', in *The Struggle against Fascism in Germany*, p.90.
96. 'Die politische Lage und die Aufgaben der Kommunisten in Deutschland. Resolutionsentwurf der Reichsleitung fur die Reichskonferenz der KPD-O'. *Gegen den Strom*, III (1930), no.49, reprinted in *Der Faschismus in Deutschland*, Frankfurt, 1973, p.128.
97. *Verhandlungen des deutschen Reichstags*, vol. 426, 11 February 1930, p.3940.
98. RF, 2 December 1930.
99. *Die Internationale*, XV, 5 (May 1932), p.223.
100. RF, 29 January 1931.
101. RF, 15 May 1924.
102. *KI*, 1931, 17/18, 7 May, p.795.
103. *KI*, 1931, 17/18, 7 May, p.782.
104. Thälmann's report to the 11th ECCI Plenum, in *KI*, XII, 17/18, 7 May 1931, p.796.
105. *Inprekorr*, 1931, no.38, 24 April, p.946.

106. RF, 22 March 1931.
107. *Die Internationale*, XIV, 11/12 (November–December 1931), p.490 (Thälmann).
108. Trotsky, 'What Next?', in *The Struggle against Fascism in Germany*, p.144. It should be added that Trotsky's brilliant pamphlets of this period, though aimed at members of the communist party, had no discernible influence on them.
109. RF, 29 July 1930.
110. Stalin, *Works*, vol.12, 'The Right Deviation in the CPSU(B), Speech at the April 1929 CC Plenum', pp.23–4.
111. *Inprekorr*, 1931, no.49, 29 May, p.1154.
112. *KI*, XII, 25/26, 7 July 1931, p.1154.
113. *Die Internationale*, XIV, 2 (February 1931), p.57.
114. RF, 22 May 1931.
115. *Inprekorr*, 1931, no.14, 17 February, p.386.
116. *Geschichte der deutschen Arbeiterbewegung*, vol.4, p.302.
117. The text of the ultimatum of 21 July is in *Inprekorr*, 1931, no.72, 24 July, p.1614.
118. RF, 29 November 1931.
119. RF, 5 January 1932.
120. *Inprekorr*, 1932, no.34, 27 April, p.1040.
121. RF, 24 May 1932.
122. S. Bahne, 'Die Kommunistische Partei Deutschlands', in E. Matthias and R. Morsey (eds), *Das Ende der Parteien, 1933*, Düsseldorf, 1960, p.671.
123. *Die Internationale*, XV, 7/8 (August 1932), p.320 (Thälmann).
124. Bahne, 'Die KPD', p.673.
125. *Inprekorr*, 1932, no.87, 21 October, p.2809.
126. Bahne, 'Die KPD', p.680.
127. *KI*, XIII, 17/18, 15 December 1932, p.1264 (Florin).
128. *Rundschau*, II, 31, 25 August 1933, p.1150, article by L.K.
129. *Inprekorr*, 1933, no.16, 3 February, p.533.
130. Bahne, 'Die KPD', p.685.
131. H. O. Meissner and H. Wilde, *Die Machtergreifung*, Stuttgart, 1958, pp.195–210.
132. *Rundschau*, III, 11, 30 January 1934, p.386.
133. Bahne, 'Die KPD', p.694. The history of German communism in the intervening period forms no part of our theme. Bahne's treatment, in 'Die KPD', goes as far as 1935; the whole period is covered in H. Duhnke's book, *Die KPD von 1933 bis 1945*, Cologne, 1972, which pays due attention to the growing and eventually overwhelming predominance of the group of party leaders in exile in the Soviet Union.

CHAPTER 8   SOME STRUCTURAL FEATURES OF THE KPD

1. *KI*, IX, 1928, 19, 9 May, W. Kaasch, 'Die soziale Struktur der KPD', pp.1050–67.
2. Flechtheim, *Die KPD*, pp.314–15, Weber; *Wandlung*; p.283.

Notes and References

3. W. L. Guttsman, *The German Social Democratic Party 1875–193?*, 1981, p.159.
4. R. Wheeler, *USPD und Internationale*, p.254.
5. R. Wheeler, 'Zur sozialen Struktur der Arbeiterbewegung am Anfai Weimarer Republik', in *Industrielles System und politische Entwicklung i, Weimarer Republik*, ed. by H. Mommsen, D. Petzina and B. Weisbrod, Düsseldorf, 1974, p.188.
6. S. Bahne, 'Die KPD', pp.661–2.
7. 'W. Rist', in *Neue Blätter für den Sozialismus*, III, 3, March 1932, p.138.
8. 'W. Rist', in *Neue Blätter für den Sozialismus*, II, 9, September 1931, p.441.
9. *KI*, VIII, 24 May 1927, 21, pp.1028–9.
10. Kriegel, *The French Communists*, Chicago, 1972, p.1.
11. Flechtheim, *Die KPD*, pp. 318–20.
12. The May 1924 election results are presented in detail in *Statistik des deutschen Reichs*, vol.315.
13. The data on occupational distribution are derived from the *Berufszählung* of 1925, the results of which were published in *Statistik des deutschen Reichs*, vols 403, 404, 406 and 408.
14. The 1949 election results are in *Statistik der Bundesrepublik Deutschland*, vol.10, Wiesbaden, 1952. Here are some examples: Remscheid-Solingen 20.9 per cent; Hanau 13.8 per cent; Gelsenkirchen 15.3 per cent. KPD average for West Germany: 5.7 per cent. Twenty-two Rhine and Ruhr constituencies in all gave over 10 per cent of their votes to the KPD in 1949.
15. G. A. Ritter, *Die Arbeiterbewegung im Wilhelminischen Reich*, Berlin, 1963, p.68.
16. 'Electoral subdivisions' refers not to the *Wahlbezirke* but to the units into which they were subdivided. Distortions arise here from the fact that some of these subdivisions were very small, some very large. The city of Hamburg, for instance, was always treated in the *Reichstag* electoral statistics as a single unit, which obscures the concentration of communist support in suburbs like Barmbeck, whereas obscure Thuringian villages had whole columns of figures to themselves.
17. Guttsman, *German Social Democratic Party*, p.118.
18. In the presidential election of March 1925, at which Thälmann did so badly (7 per cent), the rank order of districts remained the same as it had been in December 1924. Every district simply lost between 2 per cent and 3 per cent of its vote. In the second round the same situation obtained, except that support for Thälmann in the Berlin district fell a further 4 per cent. The data are in *Statistik des deutschen Reichs*, vol.321, Berlin, 1925.
19. Election results from 1924 to 1933 are conveniently summarised in L. A. Milatz, 'Das Ende der Parteien im Spiegel der Wahlen 1930 bis 1933', Matthias and Morsey, *Das Ende der Parteien*, p.778. Underlying data in *Statistik des deutschen Reichs*, vols 315, 372, 382 and 434.
20. KPD figures: *Inprekorr*, 1923, no.24, 5 February, p.184 (Böttcher). SPD figures: *Protokoll des Parteitages der SPD in Görlitz 1921*, Berlin, 1921, p.11.
21. Weber, *Wandlung*, p.282.
22. G. Bremme, *Die politische Rolle der Frau in Deutschland*, Göttingen, 1956, Table IV, pp.243–52. According to this source the female vote for the

KPD was 9 per cent below the total average in nine sample elections. (See Table 24, p.76 of Bremme.) However the average covers considerable variations. In May 1924 some parts of Thuringia displayed a higher female than male KPD vote, and in March 1925 over the whole of Thuringia the gap between the male and female vote was less than 3 per cent (Thälmann received 11.5 per cent of the male vote, 8.9 per cent of the female) and the female vote was only 1.1 per cent below the total average. See also H. L. Boak, 'Women in Weimar Germany', in Bessel and Feuchtwanger, *Social Change*, pp.155–73, with a table covering four cities and five elections, showing a gap of 3 per cent to 9 per cent between the male and female vote for the KPD.

23. The gap narrowed in the SPD's case during the 1920s, and in 1930 there was two cases of a higher female than male vote (Leipzig 34.5 per cent male, 35.3 per cent female; Magdeburg 37.8 per cent male, 38.2 per cent female). See Boak, 'Women in Weimar Germany', p.169.
24. This does not mean that it was not concerned with women's issues. See S. Kontos, *Die Partei kämpft wie ein Mann. Frauenpolitik der KPD in der Weimarer Republik*, Berlin, 1979.
25. *Gründungsparteitag*, p.247.
26. *Bericht.2.Parteitag*, p.26.
27. Ibid., p.62.
28. Ibid., pp.67–8.
29. Ibid., p.38.
30. Ibid., p.40.
31. Ibid., p.11.
32. Mujbegović, *Komunistička Partija Nemačke*, p.306, n.8.
33. *Bericht, Vereinigungsparteitag*, pp.243–7.
34. *Bericht. 2(7) Parteitag*, p.436.
35. Ibid., p.432.
36. *Bericht.10.Parteitag*, pp.232–9.
37. Ibid., p.474.
38. A. Creutzburg, *Die Organisationsarbeit der KPD*, Hamburg, 1931, p.8.
39. *Inprekorr*, 1926, no.65, 29 April, p.982.
40. *Der Parteiarbeiter*, III, 2, 1925, special supplement, p.1.
41. *Der Parteiarbeiter*, IV, 5 May 1926.
42. RF, 2 November 1928.
43. Creutzburg, *Organisationsarbeit*, p.18.
44. *KI*, IX, 1928, 19, 9 May, p.1052 (Kaasch).
45. RF, 17 May 1923; *DuM*, VII/2, pp.329–30.
46. *Der Parteiarbeiter*, I, 8, 1 August 1923, p.77.
47. *Inprekorr*, 1926, no.65, 29 April, p.980.
48. The rival claims are in *Bericht.10.Parteitag*, p.121 (2673 in May 1925); *KI*, IX, 1928, 38, 19 September, p.2349 (1384 in 1925); *KI*, VIII, 1927, 18, 3 May, pp.889 and 879 (1525 in 1926, 1426 in 1927).
49. *Die Internationale*, XIV, 3 March 1931, p.113 (Creutzburg).
50. *KI*, IX, 1928, 38, 19 September, p.2349 (Pyatnitsky).
51. S. Bahne, *Die KPD und das Ende vom Weimar*, Frankfurt, 1976, pp.16–18.
52. *Bericht.10.Parteitag*, p.226.
53. *Die Komintern vor dem VI Weltkongress*, p.13.

54. *Bericht. 11. Parteitag*, p.401.
55. Ibid., p.390.
56. Lademacher, *Zimmerwalder Bewegung*, p.380.
57. *Spartakusbriefe*, pp.178–9.
58. Ibid., pp.354–5.
59. K. Liebknecht, *Politische Aufzeichnungen aus seinem Nachlass*, Berlin, 1921, p.34.
60. *Spartakusbriefe*, p.453.
61. P. Lösche, *Der Bolschewismus im Urteil der deutschen Sozialdemokratie 1903–1920*, Berlin, 1967, p.156.
62. *Inprekorr*, IV, 1924, no.28, 29 February, p.306 (Eberlein); A. Balabanova, *Erinnerungen und Erlebnisse*, Berlin, 1927, pp.225–6.
63. I have deliberately made no mention of these activities, as the evidence for them is too fragmentary and dubious to allow any definite conclusions. It is not necessary to accept the tales told by police informers like Zeutschel or communists who went over to Nazism like Georg Schwarz (G. Schwarz, *Volker höret die Zentrale. KPD bankrott*, Berlin, 1933), but it is certain that one of the tasks of a communist party was to combine illegal with legal work, and that Comintern instructors were present to make sure this was done. Then there were the intelligence-gathering functions, which assumed greater importance as the prospects of revolution receded. The GPU defector Walter Krivitsky claimed to have organised this side of the work, and to have been very successful: 'Out of the ruins of the communist revolution we built in Germany for Soviet Russia a brilliant intelligence service, the envy of every other nation.' (W. Krivitsky, *I was Stalin's Agent*, London, 1939, p.60.)
64. Krivitsky, ibid., pp.71–2.
65. *Verhandlungen des Deutschen Reichstags*, vol.381 (1924), session of 29 August, p.1070.
66. RF, 15 November 1925. The campaign against Locarno is analysed by N. Madloch in *ZfG*, vol.12 (1964), no.2, pp.231ff.
67. RF, 25 February 1927.
68. *Inprekorr*, 1930, no.79, 19 September, p.1959, quoting *Pravda*.
69. A. Thalheimer, *Um was geht es? Zur Krise in the KPD*, Berlin, 1929, p.4.
70. *Bericht. 2. Parteitag*, p.28.
71. Weber, *Wandlung*, p.309.
72. *Die Internationale*, III, 17 (1 December 1921), p.616.
73. Heinrich Brandler to Isaac Deutscher, 12 January 1959, in *New Left Review*, 105, Sept/Oct. 1977, p.77.
74. *Mitteilungsblatt für den Parteiarbeiter* (organ of the Katz group), no.33, 16 November 1926.
75. J. Freymond (ed.), *Contributions à l'histoire du Comintern*, Geneva, 1965, pp.19–20.
76. Brandt and Löwenthal, *Ernst Reuter*, p.187.
77. *Inprekorr*, 1925, no.45, 1 April, p.646, protest of Giwan and Westphal at the first Organisation Conference, March 1925.
78. Thälmann's one 'mistake' was the failure to take part in the Young Plan referendum in 1930, and he managed to avoid being blamed for it.
79. Cf. B. Herlemann, *Die Kommunalpolitik der KPD*, Wuppertal, 1977.

80. Cf. Eve Rosenhaft, 'Working-class life and working-class politics' in Bessel and Feuchtwanger, *Social Change*.

Index

Russian Communist Party
(Bolsheviks) *see* Soviet Communist
Party
Russian Social Democratic Workers'
Party (RSDRP) 3–4

Saxony: elections of 1922 in 85;
left-wing SPD in 93; left-wing
coalition government in
(1923) 103; elections of 1929
in 157, 159; elections of 1930
in 161
Scheringer, Lieutenant Richard
(Nazi who turned
Communist) 161
'Schlageter Line' (1923) 97
Schleicher, Kurt von (General, and
Chancellor of Germany) 168
Schmit, Vasily (Bolshevik trade
unionist) 54–5, 101
Schneller, Ernst (KPD leader,
Leftist) 103, 128
Scholem, Werner (KPD leader,
Leftist) 123, 128
Schumacher, Wilhelm (KPD trade
union leader, ultraleftist) 121–2,
123
Schwarz, Georg (Communist who
went over to Nazism) 235 n63
Secret Agreement of February
1928 147
Serrati, Giacinto (Italian socialist
leader) 59–60
Short-Time Working, increases
(1923) 221 n19
Skoblevsky, P. S. (Russian General
and Comintern military adviser in
Germany) 103
Social Democracy of the Kingdom of
Poland and Lithuania
(SDKPL) 6
Social Democratic Party of Germany
(SPD): Erfurt Congress of
(1891) 3; Jena Congress of
(1913) 6; pre-war left wing
in 4–7; majority support for war
in (1914) 8; split in (1917) 12;
demands socialisation (1919) 29;
and Kapp *putsch* 44–7; left wing in

favours united front with
KPD 93, 95–6; enters German
government (1923) 100–1; calls
off general strike in Saxony 108;
unwilling to cooperate with
KPD 137–8, 145; held
responsible by KPD for shootings
of May 1929 153; social
character of 155; withdraws
from coalition government
(1930) 158; renewed advocacy of
united front by left wingers
in 163
Social Fascism 162–4, 176; first
statement of theory (1924) 114,
118; possible origin of 195; full
development of theory
(1929) 154–5, 158; extended by
KPD to cover left Social
Democrats 164
Socialisation Movement
(1919) 27–8
Socialist Workers' Party (SAP) 165
Socialist Workers' Party of
Germany, Gotha Congress of
(1875) 2
Soviet Communist Party: Fifteenth
Congress of (1927) 145;
Politburo of 100–1, 111
Soviet Foreign Policy: defence of by
KPD 143; determines political
line of KPD 155
Spartacists 9–23; and USPD 12,
19; October 1918 Conference
of 14, 211 n42; attitude to
Zimmerwald Left 190–1; turn
themselves into KPD 21
Stabilisation of German Capitalism:
declared impossible by KPD
(1924) 117; admitted as
temporary phenomenon by Stalin
(1925) 126; used by Zinoviev to
justify tactics of
compromise 129; end of
proclaimed (1927) 145, 148
Stalin, Josef Vissarionovich 126,
140, 145–6, 150, 152
Stresemann, Gustav (German
Chancellor and Foreign